# About the Authors

Vicky Brewis (born 1973) and Caius Simmons (born 1970) were raised in Northumberland and Cornwall respectively. They have degrees in geography, geology and archaeology related subjects. They both work in historic building conservation and live in Cornwall.

# Inca Hoots

## Vicky Brewis & Caius Simmons

First published 2007

This edition published 2009

ISBN 978-0-9556811-0-3

Cover image: Gordon McIntosh, 2007

Published by Blue Feet Management

# Inca Hoots

## Vicky Brewis
## Caius Simmons

# Ecuador

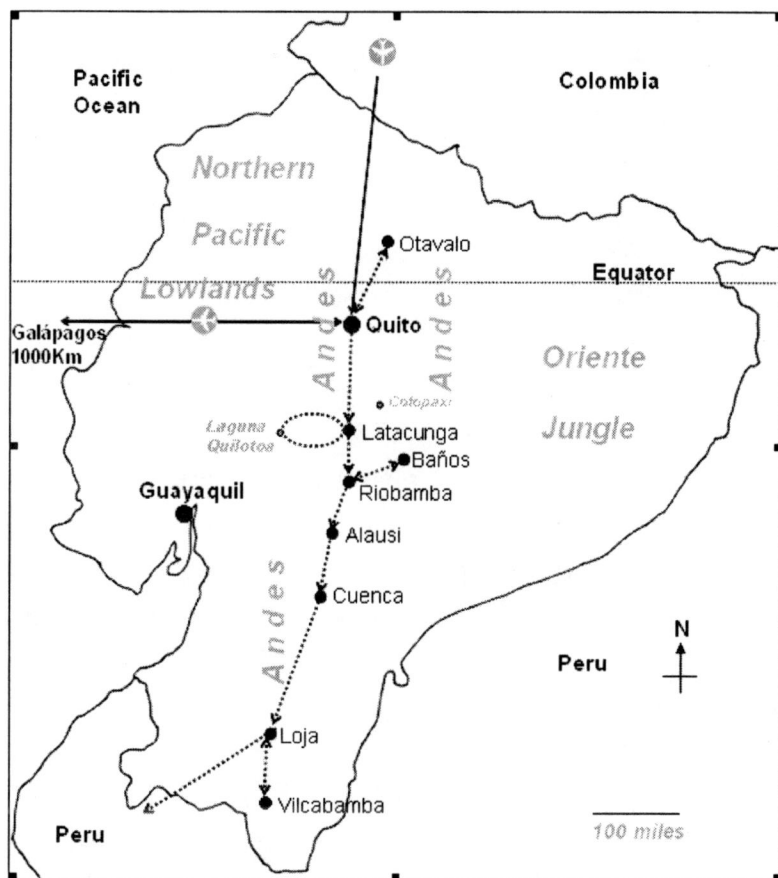

Pacific
Ocean

Colombia

Northern

Pacific

Lowlands

Equator

Galápagos
1000Km

● Otavalo

● Quito

Andes

Andes

Oriente

Jungle

Laguna
Quilotoa

Cotopaxi

● Latacunga

● Baños

Riobamba

Guayaquil

● Alausi

● Cuenca

Andes

N

Peru

● Loja

● Vilcabamba

100 miles

Peru

(not to scale)

# Culture Shock

Arriving in a new country is always such a drama. Every airport has its own different procedures and however much you prepare in your mind how you are going to cope with collecting baggage, passport control and immigration, it never goes according to plan.

We had gone to so much effort to get to this point, packing in our jobs, giving up our house, leaving our regular and stable lives behind us, we half expected an important official, like a mayor, to welcome us warmly to his country, and reassure us that it was all worthwhile. Instead we were greeted by hustle, bustle and total confusion.

Clutching our collection of coloured forms, tickets, passports and mountains of baggage we made our way through the maze of officials, getting various forms stamped before going to the next queue for another stamp. Between queues the relevant forms and passports always seemed to disappear, only to reappear as panic sets in, in a random pocket or money belt. At passport control we were slightly disappointed to receive a computer-generated stamp instead of the usual smudged inkblot.

As we tried to get past the last of the custom officials we were accosted. We managed to squeeze a few desperate words of pigeon Spanish out, explaining that, "we did not want a taxi", lying by saying "we already had one booked, thank you very much". The smartly dressed taxi drivers stepped across and blocked our exit. They persisted by trying to grab our bags, shouting loudly at us. It took us a few confused seconds to realise that they were trying to collect our baggage tags. In an attempt to disguise the fact that we had just stepped off a plane, we had already removed our tags and stuffed them in our pockets. Fortunately we had not deposited the tags in the bin. Collecting back the tags was all part of the security procedure to ensure that we had not pinched someone else's luggage. In hindsight it was probably a good idea, but at 11o'clock at night, arriving in a strange country after nearly 24 hours of travelling, we were not very impressed. The queue of Ecuadorians that were held up behind us didn't seem too amused either.

Before we left home, we thought it a good idea to try and learn some Spanish. We had bought a box of Learning Spanish CDs, which we had not managed to finish. Actually we hadn't even finished the first CD of an eight CD course. Between us, we remembered a small handful of basic phrases and confidently thought we knew enough to get by. We also had a cunning plan for when we arrived, which was to write down where we wanted to go on a piece of paper to give to our taxi driver. Along with the phrases we had been learning on the plane, how could we fail?

Once we had finally got through the last of the customs we were once again bombarded, this time by hundreds of taxi drivers. We had become paranoid about everything (we had just read the chapters called *Arriving at Quito Airport* and *Personal Safety*. Aaaargh! - Don't trust anyone – Everyone is out to rob us!).

Luckily the word for taxi is universal, and we quickly spotted an official looking taxi booth, and agreed it must be run by a legitimate firm. We gave them the nod and we were escorted through the throng to a yellow cab. Giving our driver the piece of paper we blurted the phrase we had been rehearsing on the plane. He looked at us in total confusion. His eyes dropped to the paper we had thrust into his hand, and he suddenly understood what we were trying to say to him. We had no idea what his reply was.

"*Que?*"

He appeared to say the same thing again, possibly a bit quicker, with a hint of annoyance. We think he was trying to make chitchat, but we will never know.

3

We tried another random Spanish phrase, and he looked at us in total disbelief, thinking, "Who are these idiots?"

Having totally failed at our first Spanish conversation was a bit disheartening. To make ourselves feel better we tried convincing ourselves that the reason why we couldn't understand the taxi driver was because he had a speech impediment.

Our fears about being abducted by rogue taxi drivers were soon forgotten as the driver started the engine. Flooring the accelerator, he screamed out of the airport and without looking pulled straight onto a busy dual carriageway, overtaking, undertaking, one hand on the gear the other on the horn, shouting abuse, turning around and talking to us at the same time. We soon realised why hiring a car in South America is not really an option, unless of course you are an experienced rally driver.

The airport is at the far end of a huge valley, so our journey to the other side of the city was a long one. We were thoroughly exhausted by the time our driver pulled up outside our intended destination. We had made it, what a relief. Our euphoria was probably due to the excessive amounts of adrenalin pumping through our body after the taxi ride.

The last hurdle, booking into our room, was relatively simple. Being mega efficient, we had booked a room via e-mail, with the aid of a phrase book, the day before we left home.

"Quiero un reservation ....... by e-mail", was all we could muster up.

The proprietor, Mario, luckily understood and remembered our reservation and showed us to our room. During the whistle stop tour of the hostel, he gabbled the rules and regulations at us. He obviously thought we spoke Spanish, but we just pretended to understand by occasionally saying "Si".

It dawned on us that we did not know the same language they did. We knew how to ask for something (sort of), but that was it. As we stood in the kitchen, making a hot drink, we felt just like new students on the first day of term, not knowing the etiquette and the way things were done, and not understanding what was going on around us.

There was no turning back now; we had to just get on with it. It was going to be a slow process, but we had made it this far, so it gave us some hope. We cheered up slightly when we later learnt that the owner of this hostel was Argentinean and had a particularly unusual accent. Maybe the taxi driver was Argentinean too.

Like most people travelling to South America, one of the first bits of information we wanted to find out was "What diseases or illnesses could we catch?" "How can we avoid catching them?" and "What jabs did we need?" The *Health* section in the guidebooks is not a good place to start for the paranoid traveller, where there are pages and pages of gruesome descriptions about Yellow Fever, Malaria, Rabies, Diarrhoea, Bacillic and Amoebic Dysentery, Hepatitis, Giardia, Dengue Fever, Leishmaniasis, Chagas Disease, the list goes on. After spending over £100 on each arm, we left the doctors feeling confident, and reassured that we were protected against all eventualities.

With the health and safety chapters still in the front of our minds, we searched our rooms for big hairy spiders, snakes, mosquitoes, rats, scorpions and rabid dogs. We slept in our sleeping bag liners (even though the sheets were clean and fresh), we checked under the loo seats, searched our shoes in the middle of the night when we needed to go to the toilet, locked our door, double-checked we had locked it, and put our rucksacks in front of the door just in case someone tried to come in, in the middle of the night. The funny thing was the room was immaculate, and better than many Travel Inns we had stayed in back in the UK.

By the next night we had started to relax a bit, and we didn't bother to put the rucksacks against the door and forgot to check our shoes and under the loo seat. We decided not to get paranoid about everything we had read in the guidebooks, otherwise the three months would be a total nightmare.

# Quito

We are not really city people and we weren't overly impressed with Quito at first. The central area of the city is split into two distinct areas, the Old City and the originally named New City. The Old City, as you could probably guess is the original centre, with interesting colonial churches and historic buildings. These were supposed to be beautiful, but we found it a bit dilapidated, smelly and not wildly exciting. It is true that you could probably say the same about most British city centres. What was different though was that we didn't feel very safe walking around the Old Town, even during daylight. There were a lot of beggars and roguish children who eyed us up, so we kept our heads down and tried not to make eye contact. Scary notices in the hotel telling us which areas to avoid had fuelled our discomfort.

As we relaxed a bit, we began to realise the city wasn't all totally horrible, and we did see some nice colonial bits of architecture and the main plaza was very pleasant. Running along the side of the main square were some arches, each with a shoeshine seat or a small stall. For a small charge (about 20p) Caius got his shoes cleaned for the first time.

In Ecuador, getting your shoes cleaned was a particularly civilised affair and seemed to be part of a daily ritual for many people, like going out to get the daily newspaper or milk. A raised seat is provided for the service. Quite often a newspaper is supplied for you to read while your shoes are cleaned, buffed and polished in no more than a few minutes. They did not use normal hard black shoe polish, but a liquid cleaner that, although made the shoes extra shiny, it also made them sticky so within a day or so they had attracted more dust and required cleaning again. There were also mobile shoe shiners, who traipsed around the streets with their little wooden boxes scanning the pavement for passing dirty shoes. It is a very male dominated profession and the people cleaning the shoes are usually young boys or old men, and throughout the three months away we never saw one girl cleaning shoes. For now it was a novel experience, but as we travelled further south, we realised that wearing black leather Doc Martens was perhaps a mistake.

One of the weirdest things we saw in Quito was a funeral procession while we were taking a stroll around the old district. As we reached the top of the hill leading into the centre, we could hear thumping techno music blasting up the street. At the far end of the road was a slow moving group of people, carrying banners. As we walked forward the music got louder and the procession got closer, but the source of the music was not coming from the procession as we first thought, but from some loud speakers in an arcade that was tuning up for a disco. Just as the procession reached the doorway the shop owner realised what was going on outside and cut the music. An eerie silence followed as the funeral slowly went past. They probably thought we were a bit sick lining up specially to see the funeral procession go by, but from a distance and with the music blaring out we had thought it was some kind of celebratory procession, or demonstration. We certainly weren't as embarrassed as the DJ who was glared at as the convoy passed by.

The easiest way to see most of the city without walking too far was to go to one of the many viewpoints and we opted for the Basílica del Voto Nacional. It is an unfinished, relatively new cathedral with a couple of huge bell towers. Even on the approach road up to the main entrance we had a magnificent view over the city.

Even though Quito is Ecuador's capital, it is only the country's second largest city, after Guayaquil. The population of Ecuador is estimated to be only about 13.5 million, the bulk of whom live within the major cities. Quito alone has a population of 1.5 million, about the same size as Dublin (and according to the Internet – the number of sheep currently resident in the English county of Northumberland). From the top of the Basílica the city appeared a lot bigger, as it sprawled out along the valley below us. Constrained by mountains and a deep gorge the city stretches for 35km along the valley, but it is only about 4km wide and the Basílica del Voto Nacional sits pretty much in the centre. There was a slight pollution haze hanging in the valley, but we could just make out the volcanoes and other mountains that encircled the city.

We still had the towers of the Basilica to conquer, but unfortunately Caius' fear of heights was starting to kick in. Having already managed to squeeze up to the top of one of the bell towers via a series of narrow, steep ladders he thought it better if he did not attempt to climb up the exposed ladder up to one of the steeples. The Health and Safety restrictions in Britain would never have allowed it, which made it even more the reason for Vicky to climb it. Three young girls in front of us had happily clambered up, and Vicky followed a little more cautiously. Even though there was a metal grid in behind the ladder, it still leaned out over the balcony, curling around the outside of one of the towers, with an exposed drop of 30 metres or so to the pavement below. After a few deep breaths, Vicky managed it to the top. The girls had already admired the view and were on their way back down. The floor of the round steeple was made of warped metal, which buckled when she stood on it. The views were magnificent, but it was a huge relief for both us when she reached the bottom of the ladder and stood on something a bit more solid.

A few days before we left home, we had just celebrated the summer solstice and had been enjoying the nice long light evenings. At 6 o'clock it got dark in Quito, not slowly like in England, but like someone had just flicked a switch to turn the lights out. Because we were so close to the equator (only 22km away) the length of the day varies little throughout the year, with 12 hours of daylight between sunrise and sunset and 12 hours of darkness.

This was also Ecuador's dry season, one of the main reasons why we had chosen this time of year to visit. The climate was not dissimilar to an English spring day, generally getting warmer throughout the day (about 13°C-14°C) and then becoming cooler at night. It was a perfect temperature for travelling, not too hot whilst carrying heavy rucksacks, a slim chance of getting wet, and not too cold that we had to wear endless layers of clothing to keep warm.

After a day of sightseeing we were pretty exhausted and realised that being at 2850 metres above sea level (asl) was taking it's toll. At this altitude, the air is thinner, the pressure is lower and there is less oxygen available in the atmosphere. We had noticed that we had been feeling a little bit breathless, and we had being making a conscious effort to drink plenty of water to avoid getting headaches. We didn't feel sick or particularly lethargic like some people do and were pleased we had decided to opt for Quito as our starting point rather than La Paz (in Bolivia) whose altitude is over a kilometre higher. We knew we would have to get used to the lack of oxygen, because the majority of the next three months would be spent at this altitude, or higher.

Most of the tourists hang around the new city, which is crawling with hotels, restaurants, bars, Internet cafes and tour agencies. We were spoilt for choice when it came time to eat. We had had visions of a repeat performance of when we had gone to Spain, a few years previously, where we didn't eat a proper meal for nearly three days. Once again it was our lack of knowledge of the language that had let us down, stupidly asking for la Comidia (comedian), rather than La Comida (food). Luckily the waiters understood the universally known "pointed finger" language. Like most English people, we were particularly fluent in this language.

Quito is supposed to be the language course capital of South America and we met a number of people who had spent a couple of weeks at language school, using the city as a base to visit local towns and villages at the weekends. There was too much of Ecuador to explore, and unfortunately we did not have two weeks spare to spend here.

By the time we left Quito, we had actually grown to quite like its scruffiness, and it turned out to be not nearly as unsafe as we first feared. We had relaxed a bit, but it still felt like we were holding onto the city like a safety blanket, not really wanting to let go and step back into the unknown.

# The Equators

Anyone who has been to Quito will almost certainly have visited La Mitad del Mundo ('the middle of the earth'), the Equator. For the novice traveller to South America, it was an easy day trip from Quito and logical place to begin.

Our guidebook had told us of three different kinds of buses that operated in Quito, light blue, pink and red. We were on the lookout for a pink one as this would take us out of town to Mitad del Mundo. All kinds of buses flew past us as we waited on the side of the road, but not any pink ones. Come to think of it, there weren't any light blue or red ones either. After about 5 minutes we decided that the best thing to do was just get on the first bus that had a sign for Mitad del Mundo displayed on the front, not that we had actually seen any so far. We were right, we boarded the next bus that came trundling along the road, it was green. This catching a bus thing was easy. It was our first bus journey, and just one of many we caught in South America and we both remember it vividly.

After an hour we were still in Quito, crawling along, while the conductor, who was hanging out the bus door, yelled out the destinations. But we had managed to pick up about four more passengers and so the delay had been well worth the effort.

This is one the peculiarities that we got used to in Ecuador. If our guidebook told us it would take two hours to get to our destination, we knew it would be three. We got used to adding on an extra third for 'touting time'. There were bus timetables and, as a rule, the buses usually left on time from the station. It would then crawl along at a snails pace while somebody, usually a young boy touted out of the open door. Occasionally, extra touts would appear and the bus driver would pay them to run alongside drumming up extra business. The bus would stop at the side of the road, or a junction, and then loiter for as long as possible while the tout ran off to get his Grandmother and two sisters out of bed to catch the bus. Traffic police patrolled the junctions, specifically employed, to move these waiting buses on. It could be as long as ten minutes or so for these stops and inevitably the traffic behind would be getting impatient and start honking their horns. If we waited too long, the bus driver would get a fine, and an extra few minutes for more passengers to be found. Sometimes the bus would be jammed by the time we left town, but usually only a handful of passengers got on. We always wondered what these touts had done to persuade these people to suddenly change their travel plans. Maybe Ecuador was full of people who just went where the fancy took them that day and as they stood waiting for a bus to Guayaquil, they would change their minds in an instant just because one for Baños came along first.

In order to fit as many people on the buses as possible, an extra couple of rows of seats had usually been squeezed in. This is not uncommon even in Britain, as anyone travelling on the new Virgin Trains should have noticed. And like the Virgin Trains, the buses are not normally designed for anyone over five foot tall and by the end of the journey you will likely have bruises on your knees, pins and needles in your feet and the feeling (or should we say lack of feeling) in your bum that you will never be able to sit down again. It was not just the leg space that was limited, but also the height of the seats. Most of the seats appeared to be the correct height, but for added comfort, they had been fitted with headrests that consisted of pad at neck level to support your head. Unfortunately, these once again, had been designed for short people and we spent our journey with the pads digging into our shoulders. All the buses were ideal for short journeys, and as many of them were old school buses from the good old US of A, this is what they had been designed for.

The other aspect of the bus journey, that varies from those in Britain, were the vendors. At every main junction a vendor would get on the bus to sell their wares: water, oranges, sweets, biscuits and crisps. It certainly made the journeys mildly entertaining. They would walk up and down the bus trying to sell as much as possible before having to get off again at the next junction. In some cases, the vendor would be allowed to do a sales pitch, but this was usually between longer stops. On the shorter bus journeys, they were usually trying to sell sweets and chocolate, which had a 'special promotion' on. The sales pitch would last for a couple of minutes and as we often sat near to the front of the bus this was usually shouted into our ear, not that we could understand any of it anyway. However, their singing voices, hand gesticulations, waving of chocolate and constant repetition of "special promotion, only 3 bars for a dollar", we soon got the gist of what was going on.

The longer journeys were even more entertaining. The sales person would hover around at the front of the bus until we had reached a point in the journey where it was unlikely anyone would ever get off. This made sure that they had a captive audience - passengers with nothing to do but listen and buy. These sales pitches lasted a lot longer, sometimes as long as half an hour and a "special promotion" was guaranteed, especially if you bought in bulk. Their wares were not usually food. Instead they were things like, special tool kits that contained not only a separate screwdriver, but also one with changeable ends on it. The most common item we saw being sold was herbal medicines of some sort. Miracle cures for backaches, earache, headaches, poor vision and rheumatism. The sales pitch usually accompanied graphic pictures, and one vendor had a jarred tapeworm to illustrate what we probably had in our stomachs that was slowly eating our intestines away. Some of the sales people were not always the best advertisement for the product, like the man selling eyes drops to correct vision, who had an obvious squint, and the girl trying to sell jewellery who hadn't even bothered to wear any of it herself. Once the sales pitch was finished, the item for sale would then be distributed to the passengers, who were given time to look at the product and try and decipher the small print. They were then collected and if you didn't want to buy then you just gave the item back. You could tell the professionals from the amateurs at this, because

12

the professional always started collecting from the back of the bus. By doing it this way the other passengers could not see if the salesperson had managed to sell his goods or not. Usually they left us alone, knowing fine well that tourists were never going to buy anything. The only time that we did buy something was some chocolate that was on 'special promotion', and it was absolutely foul. We were certainly tempted with the cure for tapeworms, but we didn't think we would ever get it through customs.

It was an hour and a half before we arrived La Mitad del Mundo. We had travelled only 23km (15 miles), which by our maths meant that on average we had been travelling at 10 miles per hour all the way. For the bargain price of $0.40 we were not complaining.

A bland monument, topped by a huge brass globe is the centrepiece of the Ciudad Mitad del Mundo complex and this is where all the tourists go to say they have visited the Equator. This is the place to have your photo taken, next to a large sign stating you were at Latitude 0 marked on and a beautifully painted yellow line running across the site. It was worse than visiting Land's End, in Cornwall, on a Bank Holiday August, and it does have the tacky gift shops and extortionate prices to match. Most of the people who visited that day will probably have a photo of two gringos at the bottom of the monument, who looked like they had just wet themselves. They were in fact eating some of the juiciest oranges they had ever tasted and had been dribbling orange juice into huge puddles at their feet.

If GPS technology (Geographical Positioning Systems) had been available to Charles-Marie de la Condamine in 1736 when he first calculated the line of the equator, he would have realised that his measurements were nearly 300m out. The proper line of the equator actually lies in a dusty, eroded valley at the back of a housing estate. It must have been like winning the lottery for the local landowner when they discovered the true line of the equator. Seeing as most of the locals had never even heard of GPS, the museum we visited was pretty quiet.

There are a number of bizarre phenomena that can only be tested at the equator, like balancing an egg on a nail head, or watching water being poured down a plug hole in both the northern and southern hemispheres. Due to the Coriolis effect (a rotating force that deflects water particles to the right in the northern atmosphere and to the left in the southern hemisphere), we should have been able to see the water going down the plughole in a clockwise direction in the northern hemisphere and anticlockwise in the south. We were convinced it was going the same way in both hemispheres, but no one wanted to embarrass the museum guide by telling him. It always seemed to be changing and after many attempts to try and work it out, we got ourselves confused over which way it was supposed to be and gave up. And, of course we just had to take a number of cheesy photos with one leg in the northern hemisphere and the other in the south just to prove we had been there.

As we walked out of the museum we realised it was midday, when the sun was directly overhead, and noticed that our shadows had disappeared.

A short distance from La Mitad del Mundo is an extinct volcanic crater, Pululahua crater, the largest in South America. The views from the rim were supposed to be spectacular. It was an added bonus to learn that our guide was Morgan Freeman, at the very least it was his stunt double. He was an excellent guide and told us all about the fauna on the way to the crater rim. His excellent knowledge on all the medicinal uses for the plants led us to believe he dabbled in shamanism in his spare time. As well as telling us about cures for coughs, period pains, arthritis, to name a few ailments, he also fed us some hallucinogenic berries. Although we would have needed to eat huge quantities for them to have taken any effect at all.

By the time we got to the rim, the crater was full of a mass of swirling low clouds. We could only see about 10 metres in front of us and wished we had eaten a few more of the berries to help us imagine what the view was supposed to be like. Morgan had obviously been before when it was like this, and told us to be patient and watch. After about 20 minutes, we were still being patient and still watching, when suddenly the clouds lifted momentarily and we caught a glimpse of the view below. It was magnificent and the view had been well worth the wait. That is, apart from the fact that we suddenly realised we were standing on the edge of a 150-metre cliff. The micro-climate that exists in the crater, along with the nutrient rich volcanic soil has created a perfect place for growing crops, and a patchwork of fields spread out below us. It was in complete contrast to where we had just come from and within a few minutes of descending from the crater rim we were back in a dusty, hot desert-like environment.

"Buenos Dias" we cheerfully announced as we entered a café and took our seat overlooking the monument.

"Dos menus, por favor", we requested.

"Si, si" said the waiter and off he went.

At least sorting out the most basic things, like ordering food, seemed to be quite straightforward. How wrong we were, when five minutes later, the waiter arrived with two espresso coffees. We eventually managed to get some food by pointing and talking slowly and loudly in English. After eating, we decided it was Vicky's turn to pay, and approaching the bar she asked, "Quiero pagar" (I would like to pay).

"Si, si" replied the waiter, and then proceed to direct her towards the toilet. We laughed as we stepped out into the fresh as it had reminded us of an Irish girl we met at the hostel, who had managed to get a can of Coke when she had asked for a toilet roll.

# Galápagos

When anyone asks us which was the favourite part of our trip, one of our answers is most definitely the Galápagos Islands. Because it stands out so much we have to try and treat it as a separate holiday. How often do you go on a cruise on a luxury boat, looking at wildlife when you go backpacking round developing countries? Not us, the closest we had come to this was a day trip to the Farne Islands in Northumberland to look at Puffins.

By the time we arrived in Quito, the main holiday season was in full swing. Even though it was winter, the season coincides with the Northern Hemisphere summer holidays and it turned out that this was one of the most popular times of the year to visit the Islands.

A trip to the Galápagos was going to seriously hurt our bank account, but having done some research before we left, we were prepared for the shock. If we booked a separate holiday to go specifically to the Galápagos, the majority of the cost is the flight to Ecuador. Seeing as we had already come this far, we were not going to miss out on the opportunity of a lifetime.

All the boats that had been recommended to us were fully booked, even the cheaper tours that our guidebook had said to avoid were also unavailable. We eventually settled for a first class, brand new eco-catamaran, the Archipel. The boat had only been operating for four weeks, no advance reservations had been made for it and they were offering tours at a reduced price in order to get the boat full. It still stung when we passed over £900 ($1400) each for an 8-day trip (but it did include the flight out to the Islands costing nearly $400). No doubt people will tell us they paid a lot less than we had. We congratulated ourselves because we had been expecting to pay this for a lower class boat.

The flight over the Pacific Ocean, from Ecuador, took about 2 hours, which was not surprising as the islands are situated six hundred miles off the mainland. Flying into the Galápagos is a thrilling experience, the aeroplane circles over barren volcanic peaks, surrounded by tropical blue waters. As we descended for landing, all the passengers on the plane started to get excited. It was no point parents telling their kids to be quiet, when it was them that kept dashing from one window to another to try and get a glimpse of the islands for the first time.

The Galápagos consist of 13 major islands, 6 smaller islands, and scores of islets and rocks. The islands are formed as the two Pacific oceanic plates; the Nazca plate and the Cocos plate rub against each other. The pressures created between the two plates result in a chain of underwater volcanoes, the biggest of which poke above the water as islands. We could only really see the island we were flying into, Isla San Cristobal, but it was enough.

The Galápagos Islands were probably first discovered by the Chimu people from the mainland of South America in the 15th century. It is possible the Incas also had some knowledge of them, but the first recorded discovery was by the then bishop of Panama, Fray Tomas de Berlanga, on 10 March 1535. He only discovered them by accident when his ship was becalmed, and drifted onto the islands. The Spanish cleric didn't even bother to give the islands a name, but did make an effort to name the giant tortoises he found roaming over the lands – bestowing them with the name Galápagos, the Spanish word for 'saddle'. From then on, they were referred to as the Islands of the Galápagos.

The popularity of the islands soon grew throughout the 17th and 18th centuries, especially with American and British whalers, sealers and buccaneers seeking a sheltered stopping off point where they could stock up on food and water. The massive tortoises (some weigh up to 250Kg), that had given the islands their name, were a valuable source of fresh meat and the animals would be stacked in the ships holds (alive), for as long as a year until they were required. Unfortunately, persecution of the animal is still an issue. It is estimated that poachers have killed 120 tortoises since 1990.

It wasn't until the 19th century that the islands became famous worldwide, following the scientific voyage of the 'Beagle' by Charles Darwin in 1835. The 26-year-old biologist was inspired to formulate his theory of evolution by natural selection after his visit to the Galápagos. Darwin stated that, "the Natural History of this archipelago is very remarkable: it seems to be a little world within itself". The islands have never been connected to the mainland, but over many thousands of years, animals and plants have managed to find their way there. A combination of the extreme isolation of the islands and lack of natural predators gave animals and plants the opportunity to develop and adapt to their new environment, resulting in some very peculiar and unique wildlife.

Far removed from the image of Darwin and his biologist mates, running around the islands with nets, cages, boxes and bags collecting his newfound species of fauna and flora, is the 20th and 21st century story of the islands. Today, there are more than 65,000 visitors to the Galápagos Islands every year. The only thing they have in common with Darwin is that they too want to experience for themselves the extraordinary wildlife of these mysterious islands.

The Galápagos could be described as a big safari park, where nature enthusiasts, photographers and tourists can walk amongst the unique wildlife. There are only 560 native plant species (not introduced by humans), and of these, almost one third are endemic to the islands, meaning they are found nowhere else on earth. Considering the pioneering plant seeds would have had to cross 1000km of ocean, it is understandable that these plants are quite hardy and explains why there are far fewer species here than in similar environments on the South American mainland.

The Galápagos has become famous, not just for it's plants, but mainly for the wildlife it has to offer. There are many unique animals on the islands, with over 50% of the fauna being endemic. There was a huge list for us to look out for: fourteen sub-species of giant tortoise; reptiles like the marine iguana, land iguanas, lava lizards, geckos and snakes; two species of bat and 13 species of Darwin's finches, that all just happen to be brown and small. In the grand scheme of things these finches appear to be fairly insignificant - admittedly, there are more interesting land birds to look out for, like the hawk, dove, flycatcher, rail or one of four species of mockingbird, but in terms of understanding how evolution occurs they have been very important. They have all adapted to their own separate ways, all feeding on different foods in order to survive and not be out competed by other birds.

Added to this list are the endemic sea birds: flightless cormorant; two species of gull, penguin (the only species to live in tropical waters); plus of course the non-endemic species: blue-footed boobies, red-footed boobies, masked boobies and frigate birds. Not forgetting sea lions and fur seals, dolphins, whales, sea turtles, and over 300 species of fish. Finally, there are also at least 1,600 species of insects, 80 spiders, 300 beetles, 150 mites, 80 land snails, 650 sea shells and other molluscs, 200 starfishes and urchins, 120 crabs, and much more.

Due to the lack of natural predators, the wildlife on the Islands is renowned for being so fearless and approachable. We were spoilt for choice and this was the perfect opportunity for us to pad out our collection of wildlife photos, which up to now consisted of a picture of a black bear and a few birds - both of which could easily be mistaken for specks of dust on the camera lens. If the seemingly, endless list of plants and animals was anything to go by, then we would manage to get to see at least some wildlife.

The Galápagos archipelago was made a National Park in 1959, and is now recognised as the second largest marine reserve in the world, (after The Heard Island and McDonald Islands Marine Reserve - 4,000 kilometres off the south-west coast of Australia) covering 50,000 km2. On our arrival at the airport we had to hand over $100 each to enter the Park. It seemed a lot of money, but when we learnt that at least 90% of it goes to park maintenance we were happy to pay it. In the past the cost was a lot less and the Ecuadorian government took almost all of it to spend on the mainland and failed to reinvest any of it back into the preservation of the Islands. Although the Islands get some external funding, it is an expensive and controversial environment to manage. Ideally there should be no tourists visiting the Islands if the fragile environment is to be preserved. However, in order to do this they need money, which is generated from tourism.

The majority of the other passengers looked at us smugly because the Park fee was all included in their package and they didn't have to queue up to pay it. We smiled inwardly, with the knowledge that all these people were destined for massive cruise liners, and had probably paid more than three times what we had for our tour. And we got a Galápagos stamp in our passports as well and they didn't.

Our guide for the week was George, who looked liked Poncherelo from the 1970's TV cop show 'Chips'. All the boat guides are affiliated to the National Park and are graded depending on their knowledge and experience. George is a Grade III Naturalist Guide, which is regarded as the best, and he deserved it. The guides are employed on every boat to take you onto the Islands, show you around and provide information on the wildlife and generally make sure you get the most out of the trip as possible. George knew everyone and everything; his enthusiasm was contagious, as was his genuine love for the Islands and the wildlife.

We stood on the harbour side on the first day, trying to spot our boat. Because it was so new, they had not even produced a full brochure and we had only seen computer generated images of it. We soon came to recognise it, after all it was the smartest looking boat everywhere it moored. Other tourists would point it out and say, "Wow" and "wish we were on that boat".

We boarded the boat during its fourth week of sailing, by which time the majority of teething problems, apart from the occasional flooded toilet, had been ironed out. It was pristine inside and our cabins led off from a spacious bar and dining area, which was very light and airy. There were only 16 passengers on board and 11-crew who were there to look after us. We were fed three times a day, with plenty of fresh fruit, vegetables and fish. Snacks were also provided, with popcorn and hot chocolate every time we had all been out snorkelling or diving. We were probably spoilt even more because there was a photographer on board who was taking photos for a brochure. Fantastic displays of fresh fruit and cocktails kept appearing on the bar for him to photograph, and of course they had to be eaten at the end of the shoot.

Depending on what the other passengers were like on the boat, the trip could have been a complete headache. Everyone we met on the boat was easy to get along with. Most of the passengers were either keen on diving or interested in the wildlife and the environment. As we had all forked out a small fortune for a once in a lifetime trip, everyone made an effort to get on with each other. Confined to the boat meant we didn't really have much choice but to like each other, or at the very least, tolerate them.

It was interesting to find out how all these people had ended up taking a trip to the Galápagos. No one on the boat had come to the islands specifically, instead combining the trip as part of their other travel plans - American college students studying Spanish in Quito, visiting family, doing voluntary work in Ecuador, but mostly people on round the world trips, or like us, on extended holidays. Charlie and Abbey were reaching the end of their trip and a jaunt to the Galápagos was one of the last things they were doing before going back home to pay for it all. Having spent nine months in Australia and New Zealand working and travelling, they headed for South America. They had done exactly what we planned to do in South America, only they had done it the other way around – starting in Santiago and finishing in Quito. They had been to all the places and seen all the things that we wanted to, and so they wrote us their own personal guide to South America on a scrap of paper. This list of recommendations, places to see, visit, eat and stay, along with the places to avoid was just as good, if not better than any guidebook we had.

A trip to the Galápagos is incomplete without a camera, and plenty of film. Whether it was a small disposable one or a sophisticated SLR digital one, there was always the, "Just one more" photo to be taken, even if you had already taken three rolls of films of seal lions or blue footed boobies. Sherrie and Brett, an American couple, had the mother of all cameras, a Nimbus 2003 or something, along with all the detachable lenses and fancy filters. They even needed a separate rucksack just to carry it all. As gadgets go, it was pretty impressive, but we wouldn't have fancied carrying it around.

Vicky was almost guaranteed to be sea sick, and we hoped the extra stability of being on a catamaran would make the voyage a bit more enjoyable. When we were planning our trip back at home, she opted for homeopathic seasickness tablets, which we both had high hopes for. The other passengers who suffered from seasickness were popping all kinds of drugs, wore copper bracelets and had tiny stickers on pressure points behind their ear. Vicky was determined she was not going to be ill and ate normally, trying to pretend that the boat was completely flat. Every time someone stumbled across the floor, or a glass slid across the table it reminded her that not only was the boat rocking around, but so was her stomach. Trying to move with the motion of the boat helped, but she still had that gross queasy feeling in her stomach, meaning that at any time she might need to rush to the toilet. By day three Vicky was feeling proud and pleased with herself, as she had managed not to be sick, which was a bit of a personal record. It didn't last long and by the third evening she was saying 'hello' to the big white telephone. Anyone who is seasick will know the relief that goes through you once you have vomited. However the thought that we still had another 5 days to endure and that the homeopathic tablets had not lived up to their expectations were a bit worrying. Luckily, half of the passengers were leaving the following day and no longer required their drugs. We were piled with tablets, patches and more tablets. Vicky decided to go with the drugs that someone had got from a pharmacy in Chile. It was a good sign that Jo, who had give Vicky the tablets, had not been ill, even though it had been really rough a few days before we arrived. Maybe it was these drugs, or the fact that Vicky had just got used to the motion, we will never know, but she was fine for the rest of the time on the boat. So much for homeopathic tablets, they were crap.

The sickness did not completely end once we got off the boat. Every time we went to one of the Islands we all felt a bit wobbly and it took us both a few days once we arrived back in Quito to stop swaying around like a couple of drunks.

The tours generally follow a set itinerary, which varied from boat to boat. In this way the National Park authorities can regulate the numbers of tourists visiting an island at any one time. It also ensures that during specific periods, such as certain breeding seasons, or if research is being carried out, visitor numbers can be restricted. Our itinerary was vastly different from all the other tours we had seen, which generally stayed around the main group of Islands, centred around Isla Santa Cruz and with a long voyage out to Genovesa to see the red-footed boobies. The Archipel, was one of the fastest boats available. With a top speed of 16 knots it could easily sail overnight to more distant islands of Isla Fernandina and Isabella. For many of the other boats this was out of their range given the time available and we had the Islands almost to ourselves.

Isla Fernandina and Isla Isabella are the most westerly of the Galápagos archipelago and geologically are the youngest. They are also the most heavily protected of all the Islands. Isla Fernandina does not have any introduced species living there and the park authorities want to keep it that way. Every time we came back onto the boat we had to disinfect our shoes to ensure there was no cross contamination between the islands. The crew were extra scrupulous, scrubbing our shoes and sandals when we went onto Isla Fernandina. By the end of the eight days, our sandals had started to disintegrate, with all the cleaning and rinsing and had to be glued back together.

Our expectations of what the islands were going to be like were completely different to what really exists. The image we had built in our minds was one of lush tropical islands, long sandy beaches and blue crystal clear waters. The beaches and the water lived up to the expectation, but the lush vegetation there was not. A few of the islands, like Santa Cruz and San Cristobal had areas of scrub, woodland and grassland. However most of the plants on these islands are introduced species, spreading uncontrollably and threatening natural habitats.  The remainder of the Islands were dry and pretty barren.

Isla Fernandina, the youngest of all the islands is a black wasteland of sharp volcanic rocks.  This is a harsh environment where only a few cacti have managed to grow amongst the lava fields.  We didn't see any sign of recent volcanic activity, but the La Cumbre volcano is the most active in the archipelago, and has been erupting frequently over the last 200 years.

During high tide, small rock pools fill with water, attracting black and white tipped sharks.  They purposefully strand themselves during low tide, feasting on the small fish that have also been left behind.  Small trees and bushes have established themselves around the older lagoons.  Flamingoes come to feed on the crill within the pools and a variety of finches hopped around the trees branches on the lookout for food.

The shoreline on Isla Fernandina supports a whole host of animals, but they are difficult to spot.  Camouflaged against the dark rocks, flightless cormorants (without the need to fly their wings have adapted and are now stunted and useless), marine iguanas and Galápagos penguins have made their home.

We went specifically to Isla Isabella to see giant tortoises in their natural environment, but they had moved from their usual spot. All we saw were goats, goats, and more goats.  Whalers had introduced the goats in the 18th Century in the southern part of the island.  Unfortunately, when they finally left the island, they also left the goats, who have managed to penetrate a supposedly impenetrable, inhospitable landscape.  Their population reached a peak of about 100,000 by the late 1990s.  We were shown photographs of the changing landscape over the last 30 years - the devastation of the natural vegetation was remarkable.  There has been no improvement despite recent controls and the only hope to curb their destruction is to shoot them from helicopters, a method that has worked with deer in New Zealand.

A result of this degradation to the natural environment is the Galápagos' most famous resident, Lonesome George.  Discovered on Isla Pinta in 1971, he is the world's only surviving Pinta tortoise. Over hunting and the introduction of goats in the 1950s had destroyed the vegetation, wiping out the majority of the tortoises on the island. George, along with all the other old and endangered tortoises, lives at the Charles Darwin Research Station. He looked deeply depressed when we saw him, probably something to do with the fact that he has been spending the last 30 years posing for tourist photos. Scientists have tried to cheer him up by offering him couple of females, but being from a different sub species, he is not interested in them. He is estimated to be about 100 years old and we figured he possibly didn't have the energy to 'perform', especially in front of 50 gawping biologists. Sadly a partner cannot be found for him. When he dies his sub-species will become the fourth sub-species of Galápagos tortoise to become extinct. There is a $10,000 reward for anyone who finds a mate for him, but there is one main condition - it has to be a tortoise.

On each island we followed a set route that had been marked out by the Park Authority. This was to make sure we didn't wander of the path into nesting and breeding areas but it was quite difficult to avoid sometimes as the birds, especially the blue-footed boobies, nest right in the middle of the path. The birds (a seagull with blue webbed feet), would curiously stare back at us as we stepped over them and around them. They all seemed quite happy to pose for the obligatory photograph. The birds were all at different stages of the breeding process – some had old chicks almost as big as themselves, others had new chicks floundering around blindly in the nest, while others had a few eggs or they were still courting.

The courting process of the blue footed booby is highly amusing to watch and the birds didn't seem at all perturbed by the fact that they had 16 people staring and laughing at them. Once the male found a bird he fancied he would approach her with a stick in his beak and place it at the ground at his ladies feet. He would then stretch out his wings, squawk and then perform a bizarre love dance, lifting his bright blue feet slowly up and down. If the lady did not like his stick, or his dance, she would turn her back on him. He would try again, and find another stick, a bigger better one. This ritual can go on for weeks, the male sometimes flying off to other islands to find the right stick. The female didn't even bother to make a nest out of the sticks, just letting them pile up around her. We watched this strange process for a while, and then the female accepted a stick. The lights had changed from red to green and his big moment had arrived. Extremely proud and pleased with himself he jumped on and 10 seconds later the lights were back to red again. This was wildlife pornography at its best.

After many years (thousands probably), without any major interference or threat from humans, the wildlife has absolutely no fear of man, or woman. It was so easy to walk right up to the animals, and they are so tame we probably could have touched them if we had wanted to. The guides were there to ensure that we, the ignorant visitor, didn't touch or wander from the path.

Although we had no option on where we visited, George knew all the best times to see the wildlife. This meant early mornings pretty much every day, but it was worth getting up at 5am, or even earlier. On one occasion we arrived on Española Island before the sun had even risen. Here we spent a relaxing couple of hours, with the entire island to ourselves. That is apart from some sea lions, one of which who had just given birth within the last hour, the steaming afterbirth being devoured by a Galápagos mocking bird. Piles of Marine Iguanas lay huddled together on the rocks, perfectly placed to catch the first rays of sun. These cold-blooded, dinosaur-like creatures need heat, like we needed coffee, to get going in the morning. Just as we were leaving, all the other boats had started to drop their passengers onto the island, by which time the wildlife had started to wake up and leave the island in search of breakfast. The sea lion was still there, trying to shove her young pup closer to the sea, but it was now 3 hours old and there was little evidence left that it had only just been born.

One of the most popular and impressive views in the Galápagos is from the top of Isla Bartolomé. The classic view over Pinnacle Rock is the most photographed feature of the Islands. If you have seen Master and Commander starring Russell Crowe, then you will have seen this view. This island is also known for its lack of wildlife, with only a lizard or two scooting around between the particularly sparse vegetation. Isla Bartolomé is another typical example of a volcanic landscape, with dunes of deep dark volcanic ash sweeping down from rocky outcrops.

There had been a huge cruise boat in the harbour when we were woken up at 5am, but there was no sign of life on the ship. On our return, we sat on deck eating our breakfast, watching endless boats dumping the cruisers passengers onto the island. These huge liners, with several hundred passengers, take hours to disembark and re-embark. As a result they only got to see a fraction of the islands compared to a smaller boat, like the Archipel. With only 16 passengers we could all be ready to leave within a matter of minutes, which meant longer on the islands.

Seeing the wildlife at their best is all to do with being at the right place, at the time, and George knew all of them. We arrived on the southern island of Isla Espanola, at the same time as loads of other groups. We were all heading for Punta Suarez to watch the waved albatross throw themselves of a cliff. The waved albatross breeds solely on Española Island and when we stopped at their nesting site, George was keen for us to hang back and wait until the other groups had passed us. Among the trees, about 20 metres away, were two of these huge birds performing a bizarre dancing display. It was one of the most wonderful and delicate sights, possibly the most beautiful and charming we have ever witnessed. It is quite difficult to describe and has to be seen to fully appreciate it. The two birds were standing opposite each other, and when one made a movement, the other mirrored it. They appeared to be talking to each other during the performance, whereby one of them would make a clacker like noise with its beak, followed by a long pause and then there would be a single snap reply from their partner. There was swaying of heads from side to side and synchronised rising of their feet. The performance lasted almost an hour and we were glued to it, trying our best to capture it on film. The photos will never do it justice, just something to jog our memory of this amazingly beautiful display. We spent that evening watching a video that George had taken. Even though he would probably get to see this almost every week of his life, he never got bored watching the comical display and kept rewinding and watching the footage

27

again and again. One of the great things is that this is not a mating dance, the albatross were already sitting on their eggs, this was just something they enjoyed doing.

After seeing the albatross dance, watching them throw themselves of the cliff was a bit of a let down. Burdened by their huge weight they cannot physically take off from land and the only way they can get airborne is the launch themselves off the cliff edge. They struggle to even walk the short distance from their nests to the ledge. Once they have built up their courage, and energy, they take a couple of steps as fast as they can possibly manage, and they're off. Instantaneously, this clumsy walker becomes a graceful hunter, rising quickly with its huge wings spread wide, circling high above the sea, joining the hoards of boobies and pelicans, who were diving on shoals of unsuspecting fish.

In order to get onto the islands we would have to don life jackets and transfer to smaller powerboats, or pangas as they were called. We also used these small boats to explore mangrove forests where a whole host of wildlife hide themselves away from prying eyes. Deep inside the mangrove we turned off the engines and quietly paddled our way in. This was to make sure we did not disturb the green and rare red backed turtles. Less and less of these return each year and sadly are being hunted into extinction by the Japanese for their aphrodisiac properties. The amount of wildlife we saw on this one panga ride was never ending - pelicans attempting to land on the swaying mangrove trees; a very cute baby sea lion, perched high on a branch having a good old scratch after an afternoon snooze; a swarm of elegant spotted eagle rays, gently gliding under the boat; white tipped sharks and small armies of Galápagos penguins saluted us from the shore.

The Archipel was fully kitted out for diving too. Fellow passengers came back telling stories of shoals of Hammerhead sharks, sea horses and other wonderful beasts of the depths. We were more than satisfied with snorkelling. The water was surprisingly cool, but as soon as our head was underwater, we soon forgot about the temperature. A whole new world opened up with even more wildlife to explore. Huge three metre long manta rays and white tipped sharks rested in the depths below. Closer to the surface there were huge clouds of tropical king angel fish, damsel fish, blunt-head trigger fish, wrasse, parrot fish and many more. Trying to take underwater photographs through our masks turned out to be more difficult than we thought especially when the fish kept moving. Occasionally a green turtle would appear from the depths to join us but the snorkelling highlight had to be swimming with sea lions.

It's not just the cute factor of these mammals that is so exhilarating, but the fact that they are so curious and playful. There were sometimes as many as ten of them swimming and darting around our bodies. By diving down deep into the water, the trails of bubbles would excite their curiosity even more. They would swim up to our faces, stare at us for a second or two and playfully dart away. If we could have worked out what they were saying to us it probably would have been, "Nah, Nah, Nah, Nah, Nah, you can't catch me". When we laid still, arms and legs splayed out, they couldn't resist nibbling or pulling our flippers, and swishing their tailfins against us. George explained that it was not always safe to swim with sea lions, especially in mating areas, where the big sea lion bull could turn quite nasty. He showed us a huge scar on his thigh, which he got when rescuing a tourist, whose guide had let them snorkel in dangerous waters.

When we were not eating, sleeping, snorkelling or visiting islands, we spent our time on the sun deck. Again because of the design of the boat, this was huge and we lazed around on deck chairs, reading, sunbathing or looking out for wildlife. The captain of the boat knew all the good places and there was always one of the crew on 'wildlife spotting duty' who hooted the horn if they saw anything of interest.

They had somehow managed to spot a pair of rare sunfish who were rolling around near the surface. These are shy creatures, usually spending their time in deeper waters so this was quite a treat. Apparently they can sometimes be spotted off the Cornish coast, but not often. We saw a couple of schools of dolphins one of which consisted of hundreds of dolphins jumping alongside and underneath the hulls. There was a net across the front of the boat, linking the two hulls together and we all lay on this, "oohing" and "aahing", as they jumped right underneath us. They were definitely showing off and were leaping a few metres out of the water. It was a magical experience and was one of the highlights of the eight days.

It didn't take long for the question of 'tipping' to arise. How much and to whom. The 11-crew members worked their bollocks off all week (apart from Nancy, our stewardess, of course). They were constantly cooking, cleaning, making ongoing repairs, helping with the diving and snorkelling, not to mention sailing all night so we could arrive at a new island first thing in the morning. They did all they could, and more, to make sure the trip was as enjoyable and rewarding as possible. So should the majority of the tips go to them or to George, our guide, who had spent the whole week entertaining us, sharing his knowledge and enthusiasm with yet another group of tourists who he will never see again? Etiquette said it should go to George, but the rest of the crew deserved it just as much. Any tips given to the crew would also have to be shared out among them and wouldn't really amount to very much. George's clothes suggested he would take no harm if we didn't tip him too much – the designer labels, Calvin Klein shorts, Nike socks and RayBan sunglasses told us this. Most of our money went to the crew.

We could go on and on (and on, and on) about all the animals that we saw, the beaches we walked on, the waters we swam in, the islands we explored, the pictures we took, the history of the islands, the food we ate and the people we met. Like the trip though, we have to stop somewhere and for us this meant going back to the mainland. A week on the Galápagos had been great, but we felt that the luxury had made us soft. It was like we had not even set off from England yet, the butterflies in our stomach were back. We would soon be back on the mainland, and fending for ourselves again.

Had all that money been worth it – yes, every penny, and given the chance we would definitely go again.

# Beautiful Faces in Otavalo

After reading our guidebook, we had become convinced that we were going to be ripped off every time we stepped into a taxi. We stood, with phrase book in hand, by the side of the road and extended our arm. It took about 5 seconds for a yellow car to screech to a halt at our feet. The friendly looking face at the window told us that a ride to the main bus station, the Terminal Terrestre, was going to cost $3. Reading straight from our book, we proudly presented our new word, "demasiado" (too much). The driver looked at us as if to say, "You're taking the piss aren't you?" and with a shrug of his shoulders, put on his indicator and started to pull away. In a split second we agreed that $3 was a fair price, hailed the taxi back and crammed in, our rucksacks piled high on our laps. We were still too paranoid to put them in the boot. The bus station was on the other side of the Quito and it took more than 20 minutes to drive there through the Monday morning rush hour traffic. It was $3 well spent.

The Terminal Terrestre in Quito was as rough as our guidebook suggested. The taxi driver dropped us next to a policeman, giving him a discreet nod, as if to say, "Keep an eye on these two". The Terminal is a gloomy, urine smelling maze of small tobacconists, newsagents, sweet stalls, ticket kiosks and homeless people. As we walked up and down the different levels in an attempt to find a kiosk to buy our tickets for Otavalo, we would catch an occasional glimpse of the policeman, who had obviously decided that we were best not left on our own. We were too scared to ask anyone for help, and avoided eye contact with everyone. Eventually we figured it out. As we passed the lines of kiosks for the second and third times, it seemed like everyone was shouting their destinations at us. Easy. We decided that heading in the direction of a young lad yelling, "Otavalo, Otavalo, Otavalo" was a good enough indication where the right bus would be. Skilfully fending off other Otavalo touts, that magically appeared when they realised where we were heading, we negotiated buying a ticket and made our way towards the bus.

As we followed our young tout towards a set of barriers, we were stopped by a couple of security officials, who demanded a handful of small change. We automatically doubted their integrity, assuming it was for beer money, or the Christmas light funds. Right in front of us were parked a long row of buses, but unless we paid a 'departure tax' we would not be able to board our bus. All we wanted to do was to get through the barrier and away from the foul smelling, scary labyrinth that lay behind us, and we happily handed over our loose change. We really didn't care whose pocket it ended up in, as long as we could get to Otavalo.

As we pushed our legs through the 'Departure Gate', and felt fresh air again, our tout grabbed our bags and shoved them into the hold underneath a bus. There was nothing to tell us otherwise, but we assumed that it was the correct bus for Otavalo. Stressed and flustered we climbed onto the bus, expecting it to be full and ready to leave at any moment. All the seats were empty, and we had to wait another ten minutes before the next passenger arrived. She was an Aussie, called Jill, who looked absolutely petrified and probably would have thought the same about us if she had been there ten minutes previously. The bus tout had not managed to prise her rucksack away from her and she sat down next us, bear hugging her belongings.

With only a handful of passengers on board the bus driver finally decided he could not delay his departure any longer and eventually crawled out of the bus station. Before we had even left the main bus compound the tout was screaming, "Otavalo", at every moving thing, including a homeless man slumped unconscious on the pavement. Out of sight of the station, the bus stopped and a whole load of passengers piled in. They obviously waited around the corner so they could avoid paying the Departure Tax. At least by boarding at theTermianl we had been pretty much guaranteed a seat. It took an hour to reach to the edge of Quito, by which time the bus was full (and overflowing).

The small town of Otavalo lies between Quito and the Colombian border. Before we left the UK we had promised our families we would go no further north than Otavalo, although we were very tempted, having heard so much about the Colombia's beauty. Our friend from home, Matthew, who inspired us to make the decision to go to South America, said Colombia was one of the most fascinating countries in the world. He has spent about seven years travelling the globe, and is regarded as an authority and oracle on where to go and where to avoid.

Famous for its market, Otavalo is Ecuador's main ethno-tourist centre, where local Otavaleños gather to flog their produce. The success of their distinctive handicrafts, particularly their weavings, has made them the wealthiest Indian group in Ecuador, and probably the whole of Latin America. They are very shrewd business people, taking advantage of the busloads of tourists that descend on the town every day. The most popular day for the market is a Saturday when crowds flock to the town to spend their dollars on typical South American hats, gloves, scarves, bags, jewellery, rugs, blankets, carvings, pictures and jumpers. We chose to avoid the weekend and go during the week when transport, accommodation, restaurants and the market is generally quieter, and much cheaper.

Otavalo has more to offer than just a market, and the surrounding countryside is a great place for walking. By the time our bus arrived the market traders had already started to wind up for the day and so we headed out of town to explore the nearby hills and lakes for the afternoon instead.

We had agreed to meet up with Jill, the Australian on the bus. Convinced she was going to get mugged, she was really keen to go for a walk but too scared to go on her own. Jill, who was in her fifties, was one of many women (mostly middle aged) we met in South America, who were travelling alone. Surprisingly enough we encountered very few single men.

Unfortunately Jill did not trust our map reading, and even after we explained we both had geography degrees (and our guidebook detailed a simple and clear route), she proceeded to ask, in English, every person we passed if we were on the right path. Her command of the Spanish language was worse than ours; at least we knew how to say, "Hello".

Our walk took us along the old railway line, up past a couple of waterfalls at Peguche and onto the top of the hill looking down over Otavalo. The only thing that really spoiled it was the amount of litter just dumped by the road, in streams or just blowing around the countryside.

We passed through a small village on the edge of Lago de San Pablo. Jill asked a local farmer where the lake was, even though we could see it in front of us, the farmer looked at us all, as if to say, "Who's yer mate?"

Considering our guidebook had warned us of occasional robberies we felt really welcome and safe. A group of young children started following us, skipping, laughing and pointing. They were fascinated by us and started to sing "I Love You, I Love You", in English. All the farmers working in the fields and the women washing clothes in the streams were very polite to us, waving and smiling as we walked past.

Jill looked increasingly pale and terrified. Deciding the adventure had come too much for her she eventually jumped onto a bus back to town. We were really near to the outskirts of Otavalo, but she was convinced we were going to get lost. Maybe it was just our conversation that she had had enough of. Admittedly the person writing the guidebook had got bored and was a bit vague on which path we should take over the hill. There were plenty of routes to choose from, and we made it back to our hostel without too much trouble.

Otavalo is not the prettiest of towns, the result of a poorly planned rebuilding programme that followed a devastating earthquake in 1868 which destroyed many of the buildings. The laidback atmosphere in the town and the locals made up for its poor architecture.

Otavaleños, especially the women, are undoubtedly the most beautiful and distinctive looking people we came across in the whole of our trip, with pretty faces, long, dark hair, perfect skin and mischievous sparkling eyes. They were all immaculately dressed in their traditional clothes - the women in beautifully embroidered blouses, long black skirts, with their necks and wrists adorned with heaps of thin gold and red strings of beads. The men made less of an effort, with their long dark hair tied in ponytails, three quarter length white trousers and dark felt hats, they too were unmistakable. We desperately wanted to take photos of the local people, but could not bring ourselves to do so. Groups of American tourists would surround an Indian lady or child, all pointing their cameras at their faces and making them pose for their picture. We would have been intimidated if it was aimed at us, and we felt that it was rude. Even asking for their permission was an intrusion. Just because everyone else took their photo, did not give us the right to do the same.

The Otavalo market is an impressive sight, stretching over three large squares and all along the sides of the streets that linked them. The following morning we arrived early when most of the vendors were still setting up their stalls. We pretty much had the entire market to ourselves, the only other tourist being Jill. Luckily all the stallholders were too preoccupied hanging up rugs, hats, ponchos, and hammocks to pay us much attention. We were hassled a bit, but our new phrase of "Sólo estoy mirando" (I'm just looking) rolled off our tongues, and managed to avoid the majority of the persistent stallholders who were convinced their 6ft square rug would squeeze easily into our rucksacks.

The temptation to buy loads of great stuff to take home was unbearable. We had to keep reminding ourselves that we still had over two months to go, and our rucksacks were already overfilling with swimming costumes, fleeces, long johns and waterproof trousers. We figured that there would be lots of other markets to go to, all selling the same things, throughout the whole of South America. Some of the crafts from Otavalo seemed to be sold everywhere, even in Chile, but generally what we found was that the styles, designs and colours changed when we went to different markets. We eventually decided that if we saw something we really liked we would just buy it, because the chances were that we would not be able to buy it anywhere else. Abbey, on our Galápagos boat, had been kicking herself since leaving Cusco because she had not been able to get hold of an Andean cross anywhere else.

We did buy some simple oil paintings from a lady, whose husband and son had painted. She was overjoyed that we liked them and even more ecstatic that we bought three of them. Three paintings must have been a record, because her hands were shaking with joy as she gave us our change. She very proudly rolled them up into a cardboard tube for us, which we carefully carried in our rucksacks for the next three months. Sadly, when we opened the tube on our return one of the paintings was ruined by cracks in the paint.

Of course we couldn't resist getting a colourful woollen hat, complete with ear warmers. If we had known how popular they became in the UK the following winter we probably would have bought a few more.

We took a stroll through the locals market that sold fruit, vegetables, meat, clothing, hardware and general tat (like cheap plastic shoes and pirate DVD's). Ecuador's equatorial climate means that a huge variety of fruit and vegetables are grown. Mountains of peppers, avocados, lettuces, tomatoes, pineapples and bananas filled the stalls with vibrant colour, rather like the hats, rugs and blankets in the craft market. The butcher stalls, in contrast, were particularly grim, limbs being hacked with rusty blades, blood pouring over the benches and half skinned animals lying rigid in wheelbarrows. Small cafés served revolting looking bowls of brown or grey broth, and we made the excuse that eating soup for breakfast was just not right.

Travellers we met told us how great some of the food was from these stalls and that they had eaten delicious pig roasts, soups and drinks from the markets. We were being very careful with what we ate or drink, probably over cautious. Although, it was these more adventurous travellers who seemed to be rushing to the toilet every five minutes. We met one couple who had ended up in hospital because they were so ill from eating food from a market stall. Before we left England, a work colleague had mocked us about having loads of jabs, telling us there was no need to have a Hepatitis vaccination, because there wouldn't be in a situation when we needed to use a needle. The couple that

36

ended up in hospital didn't have any choice, because before they could say, "No", a needle had been stuck in their arm and they were attached to a drip to try and re-hydrate their bodies. They said it was all very clean, but if they had been anywhere other than Quito they may not have been so lucky.

We kept to one of the local specialities of the region – pie. As we sat eating the delicious, and rather impressive sized slices of lemon and apple pie we watched a local T.V. programme showing a live debate about how the Otavaleños should make more of an effort to welcome foreign tourists. The lady behind the counter must have been listening because she decided to come and chat to us in an overfriendly kind of way. When she served us, only five minutes previously, she had been as miserable as sin.

As well as being nice to tourists, part of the 'action plan' to encourage tourists to visit the area was to tidy up the town. After seeing the litter strewn along the road and streams the previous day we thought this was an excellent idea. The local council had obviously figured out, that "first impressions do count", but judging by the amount of rubbish lying around, it was going to be a long task.

From the café window we could see the goings on in the markets. By 11am, the buses had started arriving from Quito and the tour groups descended on the town. The market traders were having a field day, bartering with the tourists over hammocks and dodgy wooden carvings.

Not normally an activity that provides entertainment, we watched in amazement at a man having his shoes shined. He was wearing light brown walking boots – the popular material type, which looks a bit like suede. He picked up a paper and started reading while the shoe-shine boy got on with the job. We watched in horror as he applied the thick black liquid polish to the boots, which soaked straight into the material. The shoeshine boy realised he had reached the point of no return and just kept rubbing in more and more polish. Feeling the polish soak through the boots and onto his feet the man peered at his feet, and a look of incomprehension spread across his face. All he could do was finish reading the paper, resigned to the fact his boots were now totally ruined.

After our first walk to Lago de San Pablo, we were keen to see a bit more of the surrounding countryside. A trip to the Reserva Ecologica Cotacachi-Cayapas, an ecological reserve sounded good. Our guidebook and the local tourist information office both recommended it, informing us it was safe to go to the area. After the warnings of armed robberies, we still thought it best to leave all our belongings and valuables in the hostel and we headed out of town on a bus to the village of Quiroga.

The bus tout must have guessed where we were planning to go and hurried us aboard. When the bus dropped us at the village plaza the tout rushed across the square towards a queue of 4WD jeeps (known in Ecuador as a "caminetta"). Rather than leave us stranded he made sure we had onward transport to get to the lakes and advised us we needed to be in the village by 5.45 to get the last bus back to Otavalo.

When we told our caminetta driver we were planning to walk around the lake, he told us we did not have time and it was "no es possible". He told it would take at least five hours to walk around. We arranged for him to pick us up at 5.30pm, which gave us less than 4 hours to do the walk.

With the challenge set, we headed along the path at a steady pace. Forgetting we were at about 3500m asl, our lungs started to burn. The views were stunning. On one side we had a view of a beautiful volcanic crater lake, and to the other side we could see across the lush Otavalo valley and to the mountains and volcanoes beyond.

In terms of flora and fauna, Ecuador is renowned for its biodiversity and is one of most mega diverse countries in the world, with approximately nine different species per square kilometre. Seeing as the country is only 256,370km2 in size (about twice the size of the UK) that means there are 28,000 different species of animals, insects and plants. The route was lined with an abundance of flowers, and we saw at least ten of the 3500 species of orchids and a few of the 4500 species of butterfly that exist. There are supposedly 1600 species of birds as well, but none of the condors our guidebook had promised to us were flying that day.

There were no signs of any armed robbers either, only a couple of scary looking children who were killing small birds with a catapult.

By the halfway point we were exhausted and it was a case of carrying on around the lake, or turn back along the route we already knew. We decided to go forwards, determined to prove the caminetta driver wrong, and managed to make it back to our pickup point in a record time of 3.5 hours. We were totally knackered but it had been worth it.

# Cotopaxi

It was dogs, and not badgers like at home, that appeared to be the prime targets for passing motorists. On the road between Otavalo and Latacunga, we spotted six rigid bodies on the side the road. Based on the number of dogs hanging around on the verge, waiting in the hope of scraps of food being thrown out of car windows, we were surprised that the tally was not higher. Admittedly the dogs paid little attention to the traffic, their over active hormones seemed to distract them from the wheels that thundered towards them.

Latacunga is the capital of the Cotopaxi Province, with some 55,000 inhabitants. Walking across town, from one sprawling market to another, it felt a lot bigger. It is not the most invigorating of towns; the amount of litter and dust blowing around didn't improve our initial impressions.

Only 30km from the town centre, is Cotopaxi, often described as being the "Earth's highest active volcano" (5,900 m or 19,350 feet asl). This is technically not quite right; in fact we have identified at least seventeen other "active" volcanoes over 6,000m asl (one at nearly 6,900m asl), many having erupted in the last 20 years.

Known as the 'Avenues of the Volcanoes', the central valley stretching from Quito south towards Cuenca is one of the world's most seismic hotspots. Along with numerous volcanic cones and lakes formed within volcanic craters in this region, there are also many active volcanoes, including Cotopaxi.

In the last 300 years Latacunga town centre has been destroyed three times by volcanic eruptions. The last major explosion occurred in 1877, when the heat from the eruption caused the volcanoes glacier to melt. A huge and very fast moving mud flow, travelling at nearly 2 million cubic feet per second, engulfed Latacunga, killing hundreds of people. Although the volcano's activity is zero at the moment and other eruptions are not expected for at least a couple of decades we could not get it out of our minds that, should this spectacular peak blow again, it is calculated that it would take less than 5 minutes for the devastating pyroclastic flow to arrive and totally destroy Latacunga. In the knowledge that Cotopaxi could blow its top again soon, perhaps this is why the local town planners had not bothered to reinvest too much money in improving the town centre.

The only decent thing about Latacunga is that it is ideally located to use as a base for exploring the surrounding countryside. We decided to use the town as a jumping off point to visit Cotopaxi and a few remote villages nearby.

In order to take a closer look at the Cotopaxi Volcano we booked a day trip that gave us the opportunity to go part way up the mountain. Walking to the very top would take two days and involve a very steep and challenging climb over the glacier. We settled for a day trip to the Jose Ribas refuge hut instead. Climbers use the hut as a refuge, gathering there before making their attempt on the summit.

Up to this point on our trip, the highest altitude we had been at was 3500m asl, when we had visited the *Reserva Ecologica Cotacachi-Cayapas* near Otovala. To help our bodies acclimatise to the altitude we decided the best approach was to introduce higher altitudes gradually. Most climbers who are training for mountain expeditions prepare themselves by climbing between lower and higher altitudes, spending a few days at different base camps so they can get used to the lower oxygen levels. Obviously we were not quite in the same league, but we were still going to be visiting some of the highest cities in the world and we wanted to enjoy them. Getting to the summit of Cotopaxi was a bit ambitious but by climbing to the refuge we would be going to an altitude of 4800m asl, our highest yet.

Our guide, Catherine, was from Glasgow, of all places. Catherine was trying to earn some extra cash so she could continue travelling around the world. It was strange listening to her speak Spanish, which had a hint of Scottish in her accent. It was marginally easier trying to understand her Glaswegian accent than Spanish, but not a lot.

After driving through the National Park up a long winding road we arrived at the start of our walk. It was a bit of a cheat really because the car park is at 4600m and we only had to ascend another 200m or so before we reached the refuge.

On the drive up, we did not manage to see any of the Park or the mountain, because the fog was so thick. The fog had turned to snow by the time we reached the car park. Alex, our driver (a Benito del Torino of *Traffic* fame look-alike) had not seen the snowline so low at this time of year, but abandoned us all the same to go and collect some climbers who were hoping to attempt the summit that night.

Wrapped up in our thermals and fleeces, we had been sweating when we left Latacunga. It was a different story half way up the mountain and after struggling into our waterproofs and extra pair of gloves we stepped out into the fresh snow. The two Danes, Thomas and Jo, who were also on the trip, dressed in their thin designer tops and plastic cagoules looked a bit concerned and were shivering before they even got out of the truck. The wind was blowing straight through us, the air was thin and the snow falling heavily.

Catherine took us up the easy route – zigzagging up the mountain, rather than straight up. She had taken someone up the direct route earlier on that week, and they had vomited. The weather conditions did not improve and a mixture of snow, sleet and hail swept horizontally across the slope. We could only see a few metres in front of us and had to stick close together so we did not loose sight of each other. Walking directly into the wind, the hail stung our bare faces, and the snow covered us in a white shroud. There was some respite when we zigzagged the opposite way up the path, but it was only for a few minutes until we reached the next switchback and we were facing into the wind again. The track was slowly being covered, with small drifts forming on the edge of the path, and in places we found ourselves standing up to our knees in snow. There was certainly no way we would have found our way up to the hut on our own, we could hardly see the path never mind the refuge.

After less than ten minutes Thomas was struggling to walk and had started to stagger and shiver uncontrollably. The affects of altitude sickness, or *siroche* as they call it in South America, are far more pronounced over altitudes of 3000m asl where oxygen levels are greatly reduced and Thomas' body couldn't cope with the lack of oxygen.

If it wasn't for the terrible weather conditions we could have stopped and waited for him to get his breathe back, but hanging around for 15 minutes was not an option. He was starting to become irrational and insisted we carry on walking and said he would catch us up. We decided to turn around and take Thomas back down the mountain. He would never make it, the altitude and sub zero temperatures had taken their toll. The two cigarettes he had insisted on smoking before we had left the pickup had probably not helped. By the time we reached the car park 5 minutes later, Thomas was almost back to normal. His fingers were still freezing, but after a drink of water and a short rest he was keen to attempt walking to the refuge. Luckily Catherine dissuaded him, leaving both of them in the safe hands, and warmth, of a bus belonging to another tour agency.

For the second time we set off up the mountain, this time up the shorter steeper route. It was tougher, but at least the wind was not whipping snow directly into our faces like the more exposed zigzag path. All three of us were struggling to walk, and every 30-40 paces we had to stop to get our breath back. As we got higher up the mountain the number of paces became less and less between each rest. Catherine, who did the walk every other day found it no easier and told us that the air felt thinner than usual because of the cold temperatures. We couldn't even admire the view, which was non-existent. The car park had long since disappeared into the fog and snow. Eventually we caught a glimpse of our destination, the climbers hut. The last five big steps up to the front door made our lungs burn. We had made it to 4800m asl - the same altitude as Mont Blanc, the highest mountain in Europe.

Our clothes were drenched, but thought we better take some layers off so we 'could feel the benefit' when it came time to walk back down again. Catherine had lugged a rucksack full of food up with her, and it would have been rude if we did not eat some of it.  We were pretty exhausted and every mouthful was an effort to chew.

The only other people in the hut were the refuge warden and a couple of climbers from Derbyshire.  The previous night, they had attempted to climb to the summit, but unfortunately had not made it.  The tour agencies were too costly and so they had made their own way there, planning to follow the route the organised groups took up the glacier.  All the tour guides had turned back after about an hour of walking because the weather was so bad.  Without any tracks to follow they could not risk going on their own and followed them despondently back down to the refuge hut.  They were totally gutted, having spent the last of their money to get there.  The forecast was no better for the next few days and the only thing they could do was drown their sorrows in a fresh cup of tea, resigning themselves to the fact they would have to pack their rucksacks and start walking down the mountain.  Unlike them, we were pleased we had managed to get this far.

We didn't hang around too long at the refuge and we were soon putting back on our cold, wet coats and gloves - yuck.  We met a few more groups attempting to reach the hut, but surprised to see that they had even got past the car park.  Given the awful conditions they did not stand a chance in the weather. One of them was wearing high heels, and an umbrella that someone was carrying had turned inside out as the owner battled to keep a hold of it.  The effects of altitude were apparent as someone staggered dramatically past us with blood pouring from his nose.

The walk back down was so much easier and we almost ran down, jumping from drift to drift.  Without the breathing difficulties we had experienced on the way up it was only a 5-minute jaunt back to the car park and not the 40 minutes it had taken us to climb to the hut.  Thomas and Jo were sheltering behind a bus when we got to the car park and looked extremely pissed off, and cold. Thomas had fully recovered from the effects of the high altitude and was annoyed with himself for not making it to the hut. They had been abandoned by the pickup truck we had left them in, the driver desperate to leave before he got snowed in.

Alex, with our lift back to Latacunga, had not arrived yet so rather than hang around, getting cold, we started walking down the road to meet him. The driver of the other pickup had been right when he told Thomas and Jo that the road had become almost impassable and large snowdrifts blocked the way. Vehicles coming up the hill were struggling to get around the sharp corners and were skidding as the tyres tried to grip on the snowy surface.

Alex passed us, but all the seats were filled with expectant climbers, staring hopefully out of the steamed-up windows. Their journey was going to be in vain, there would be no conquering of the summit that evening for them.

Alex came back to collect us and we all piled gratefully into the back of the truck, and he drove off carefully down the hill. A car coming towards us was too impatient to wait for us to pass them on a wider section, forcing their way past and pushing us into a deep drift. The pickup was well and truly stuck, the wheels buried deep within the snow. No matter how hard we pushed it was not going to budge and the smell of burning clutch started to fill the air. The 4WD behind us attempted to drag us out, but to no avail, the wheels spinning the pickup into an even deeper hole until the towrope snapped. A tourist bus (looking totally out of place in the white wilderness) queuing behind us luckily had a stronger rope and enough power to pull us out.

As we drove out of the Park we caught a final glimpse of Cotopaxi through the fog and snow. Low cloud swirled around the peak suddenly broke away revealing a beautiful symmetrical cone, topped with snow. It was the perfect image of what a volcano should look like. Unfortunately the show only lasted for 10 seconds, not even giving us enough time to get our cameras out.

According to our diaries, the most annoying person we encountered on our travels was an American lady called Anne who we met on the hostel rooftop in Latacunga. We had gone up there to recover from our day out and to try and catch a glimpse of Cotopaxi at sunset. We were pleased to see it was still covered in a blanket of fog. Anne cornered us, and within two minutes of striking up a conversation we were itching to get away. We had no chance to get a word in edgeways and it was no surprise to us to learn that she was a teacher, the way she talked down at us. She spoke as if she knew everyone in Ecuador, personally, even though she had only been to three places - Latacunga, Guayaquille and Zumbahua, speaking with much authority on each of the places. She was travelling with her husband, but he had buggered off for two weeks to do some exploring on his own. We could see why. After talking to us continually for an hour or more about her trip, she just stopped and walked away, as if the lesson had finished. We wrote down a few snippets of information, as any recommendations from other people were always useful. We were not really interested to know where we could buy the cheapest water in Zumbahua, but thought her recommendations on where to stay and how to get there might be handy.

One of the great things about travelling is the people you meet along the way and we already had a list of e-mail addresses of people to keep in touch with. Most of them we would probably never contact again, a few have since developed into ongoing friendships. On Anne's instigation, we exchanged e-mail addresses, knowing in the back of our minds that we would never hear from her again. She would never hear from us either as it didn't take long to 'lose' the bit of paper with her details written on.

# Quilotoa Circuit

"Zumbahua, Zumbahua, Zumbahua" the tout screamed from the bus.

Excellent, we thought, as this was exactly where we wanted to go. Zumbahua was the first village on our way around the Quilotoa Circuit, a popular circular route that would take us into some remote Andean countryside. It was also perfect timing, the bus was just pulling out of the Terminal Terrestre and we would have had to wait another hour until the next one departed. It also meant we would get away without paying our Departure Tax (was this our first sign of becoming tight). The tout was well trained in spotting potential customers. Before we knew it, our bags were on the roof and we were shoved through the door and squeezed in. It was too late to change our minds, but wished we had waited for the next bus.

It looked as bad as a London underground tube train during Friday rush hour, with faces squashed against the windows and people rammed along the aisles. Cramped in the area between the driver and the door, perched on a couple of seats and the engine cover, there were 18 passengers. The rest of the bus wasn't much better but we managed to squeeze our feet into the only available floor space. Straddling the aisle, Vicky wedged herself between the seats. Years of practice standing on the school bus meant she was able to balance without having to hold on, which was lucky because there wasn't anything to hold on to. Skilfully swaying with the movement of the bus around the corners she was able to stay upright. Caius was hovering on one foot, keeping steady using his head to wedge himself in. Stood underneath the skylight, it meant he had something to rest his head against, and the extra headroom was also a definite bonus, at least he could stand up straight. The downside was when the bus braked, or accelerated, his head propelled forwards or backwards, and he ended up with dents and bruises on his head from butting the edge of the skylight.

There were a couple of other tourists on the bus, but they had seats. Admittedly they looked almost as uncomfortable as we did, crammed into particularly small looking seats. There was not a cat in hell's chance that we were ever going to get a seat, but it looked like we had the slightly better deal. We nodded appreciatively to each other and a look of sympathy for our equally uncomfortable positions passed between us. At least they had a view of the passing countryside, but only if they kept wiping the heavily steamed up windows clear. The only way for us to see anything apart from the carpeted bus ceiling was to crouch down and usually involved having to stick our bums in someone's face. The breathtaking views our guidebook had promised us turned into gasps of amazement when we saw how close the driver was to the edge of road, and how far it was down the cliff to the river below. It did not help matters that the driver had a particularly bad cold and was concentrating more on emptying the contents of his nostrils, not to mention counting his money and sorting out his paperwork, than he was on the mountain road ahead.

Two hours and 57 km later we arrived on the outskirts of Zumbahua. Our rucksacks were lowered from the roof and were replaced by live sheep and pigs hoisted on rope up the side of the bus. At least they would have more room than we had.

Stepping over piles of rubbish, excrement and green slime we walked down the dusty track into the village. The locals hanging outside their front doors stopped whatever they were doing to stare at us. It was not the warm welcome we had been anticipating. Emotionless eyes peered at us from weathered faces that were wrapped heavily in scarves to protect themselves from the dust blowing down the street.

We tried to be positive, but our first impressions of the village were not great. All the buildings looked extremely run down, many had broken windows and doors hanging on one hinge, rubbish and dust swirling around, and dogs crapping in the street. The buildings had not seen a paintbrush for many years, but seeing as they were all covered in a layer of dust it would have made little difference.

Being one of only two hostels in the village the Hotel Ora Verde was not difficult to find. It was just one of many dilapidated looking buildings that ran around the edge of the square, with a broken illuminated sign hanging limply outside. For only $3 each (the cheapest yet), we couldn't really complain, but we did. Looking at the sheets we decided that sleeping bag liners were definitely required. The description that Anne, our American 'friend', had given to us portrayed a nice, relaxing, comfortable family run hostel with a café and shop downstairs where we could stock up on supplies.

The café turned out to be the local greasy spoon and after witnessing the hygiene levels, and the 'chef' preparing the food we decided we were no longer hungry. A bottle of Coke each would "keep us going" until suppertime. We cleared some slime off the tabletop and sat down to watch life go by. It was market day and there was a constant flow of people coming in to get some knuckle soup or chicken and rice. It was also a popular haunt for dogs, which would come inside searching for scraps and dropped dinners on the floor. At least the owner didn't need to clean it. To show their appreciation they would cock their legs and piss against the door on their way out.

The market was not really geared up for tourists, which is what we had expected. It was mostly selling meat, fruit and vegetables for the locals and was the weekly gathering where people could exchange goods and gossip - there was a definite feeling of unwelcoming eyes boring through our heads as we wandered around the stalls.

All the stalls were set up in a huge dusty square. A road ran around the square and was filled with trucks, buses and small jeeps that were in the process of loading up people, animals and sacks of produce. The market had been going since the early hours and by mid-afternoon they were starting to pack up to go home. Most of the traders still had a good few hours of travelling ahead of them. Llamas were packed up with provisions and lead out of town. Sheep,

49

pigs, cows and goats were being rammed into the back of trucks and on the top of buses. If the meat stalls selling brutally butchered limbs, heads and tails, with guts sprawled out over the surfaces all covered in swarms of flies, wasn't enough to turn you into a vegetarian, then watching all the animals being piled on top of one another into the trucks would be the deciding factor. There were legs and heads sticking out from all directions, but when another trader came along trying to hitch a lift the driver always seemed to be able to find room for a few more.

The traditional Andean music that the guidebook had promised turned out to be ice cream van music blaring out of a loudspeaker. There was no escaping the noise, even in the small graffiti covered church.

To escape from the noise and the unfriendly bustle, we decided to take a short walk out of town. There was even more rubbish on the roadside than there had been in the town centre. It was all piled up in ditches, with toilet roll and bits of nappies draped over the bushes. Heaps of plastic bottles and drinks cans were piled underneath the bridges and in the streams. The only traffic along the road were a few jeeps that sped passed on their way to Quilotoa Lake.

The valley was wide, very dry and heavily eroded, the stream cutting a deep gorge up the middle. Nestled at the head of the valley, hemmed in by steep green fields, Zumbahua looked an idyllic place from a distance, but we could still hear the tinny music, and small dust whirlwinds were visibly swirling above the square. We only walked a short distance along the road, but did not feel very safe, so headed back into town.

We were met by a randy donkey who was chasing his female friend through the market. This did cheer us up a bit, and we began to see the funny side of our situation: stuck in a village with nothing to do, nowhere to eat in and the prospect that we would have to go to bed when it got dark at 6 o'clock.

We sat ourselves in the small 'grandstand' at the side of the market square to watch the last of the stalls packing up and the final truck trundle out of town. The music had finally stopped, sending the village into a less frantic, more peaceful state. The sun had finally decided to shine and it seemed like the whole of the village had come to sit on the grandstand to enjoy the warmth of the rays.

The main square was full of rubbish left over from the market – rotten fruit and vegetables, a few bones, cardboard, empty bottles, piles of straw, hay and sweet corn husks littered the ground. It was good to see that the local council had employed a few people to sweep the rubbish up and within a few hours it had been piled into a corner of the square. No doubt it would end up in the stream on the outskirts of town. The strong, cold wind had not abated, and with the stalls now gone it managed to find even more dust to swirl around the town and into our eyes.

The reason why the 'grandstand' had been built soon became apparent, as a couple of nets were erected across the square right in front of us. It was for a game of volleyball, a sport that seemed to be extremely popular in Ecuador. There wasn't normally a dedicated court in most villages and we often saw nets hung across the middle of the road that then had to be removed to let buses and trucks through.

Set slightly higher than the usual volleyball net, it was difficult for the Ecuadorians to even reach the bottom of the net, never mind get a ball over it. It was not just the net that differed from the usual volleyball game. The ball was more like a heavy football. Caius was lucky not to end up with broken wrists when he attempted to knock a stray ball back into play. The players used the tips of their fingers and their fists to push the ball over. With only three players on each side the teams were rushing around the court, but the shots were much more controlled and diving on the ground to get the ball was out of the question. Trendy sports gear was not an issue; the players wore what they had left the house in that morning – leather brogues, woolly jumpers, hats and jeans. The fact that they were running around at 3500m asl didn't seem to be bothering them in the slightest and we watched them play for almost three hours – winner stayed on. Money that had been made on the market earlier in the day was being used to make bets and a large number of notes were exchanging hands with the 'bookie'. The veteran team, all aged about 45 held the court of about two and half hours until they started to flag and conceded a game to some 'youths' (aged about 30). The older team were not happy with the result and were desperate to play another game even though it was starting to get dark and no one had any money left to gamble.

Surprisingly enough there were a few other travellers staying in the village (in the other, more upmarket, hostel) and we kept bumping into them wandering around the square. They too were desperately trying to find something to do and eat. Any moral support in the 'gringo' corner was greatly appreciated, especially after being stared at all day, and we were pleased when three other tourists joined us on the grandstand. Two brothers, James and Kelvin along with James' Kiwi girlfriend, Jo, were in Ecuador buying ethnic handy crafts to take back to New Zealand to flog at hugely inflated prices. Kelvin had already been in South America for over a year and had met up with his brother to assist with bartering at Otavalo market.

After spending the entire day in Zumbahua we knew that there was little chance of eating that evening. The greasy café at the hostel only served meals during the daytime and so we bought some very nice chips from one of the ladies who were frying food on their small stoves at the edge of the square. She was very pleased to see us, especially when we went back for seconds.

The only thing left for us to do was to go to bed – the time on our watch read 6.30 pm. The hostel owner let us sit in the café and have a cup of tea. He had closed for the evening, but was eating his supper with his young disabled daughter. We had seen her earlier on in the day, sitting in a high chair staring out of the window, chewing on a chicken thigh. She was aged about six and spent the entire day colouring in, and laughing and smiling at all the customers. Her father obviously adored her and even though he had been really busy serving food all day he made sure he sat with her that evening, playing games and chatting before she went to bed. Her mother was nowhere to be seen, but he seemed to be doing a remarkable job on his own, as well as running a café, shop and hostel.

Kelvin, James and Jo went off in search of food. About five minutes later they turned up at the café, still hungry after their packet of chips. The adjoining shop sold all the essentials like pasta, rice, potatoes and canned tomatoes, but with nothing to cook them on they were pretty useless.

Together we decided that the best thing to do was to have a drink and our hostel proprietor happily sold us a bottle of rum and coke. We were interested to see what effect alcohol would have on us at such a high altitude. The first few glasses didn't seem to make much difference but after another hour of drinking we started feeling a bit tipsy. This probably had very little to do with the altitude, the real reason for our merriment being the fact that we were onto our second bottle of rum.

There was plenty to talk about because, although Kelvin and James had emigrated to New Zealand, they were originally from Cornwall and had been brought up only a few miles from where we lived. Before we knew it we were trying to buy our third bottle of rum, but the hostel owner would not sell it to us because it was getting late and he wanted to go to bed. It was 9.30pm. Staggering upstairs we concluded that we were totally pissed and it was all because of the effects of altitude – nothing to do with the fact we had not eaten all day and had just polished off two litres of rum.

We fell asleep to the noise of dogs fighting, the hostel sign squeaking in the wind, our stomachs rumbling and the room spinning. We woke up early with the sun pouring in through the window. The dogs were still fighting, the sign was still squeaking, our stomachs were still rumbling and the room still spinning.

In our drunken state we had somehow managed to wangle a lift to Quilotoa Lake in a minibus owned by the other hostel. The only disadvantage was that we were leaving at 8am, but it was better than our other option - one of the suspicious looking caminettas that had passed us by the previous day.

Luckily we discovered an open shop before we left and stocked up on supplies of bread, chocolate, fruit and water. Caius had only gone into the shop to buy some bread, but the girl in the shop kept handing him things to buy and before he knew it he had a bag load of goodies.

We were keen to leave as soon as possible and arrived at our pickup point 10 minutes early. The dust was still swirling around the square and women were already starting to set up their stoves to sell chips. Two young boys hung around, eyeing up our rucksacks. Painted on the wall next to where we waited was a picture of a big rotten looking tooth - it was the local dentists. If the rest of the village was anything to go by, never mind the smashed windows and the dodgy mural, this was not the sort of place we would ever even want our worst enemies to go for root canal work.

It was a shock, but no surprise, to learn a week later that a Dutch man and his young daughter had been brutally murdered in the stream gorge on the outskirts of village - right next to the track we had walked along. It happened only a few days after we had visited Zumbahua and the thought that anyone could do such a thing really upset us, especially as it was only for the sake of a few dollars and a camera.

We had stayed in Zumbahua for less than 24 hours, but that had been more than enough. The minibus was full, 11 travellers, all of whom were relieved to be leaving for Quilotoa.

Officially Quilotoa volcano is still active, but seeing as the last major explosion was nearly 1000 years ago it was unlikely we were going to get engulfed by lava flows and falling rocks. We only found out afterwards that the only threat from volcanic activity is from the build up of gases from the lake, which can supposedly kill people and animals.

When the volcano last erupted, the top was 'blown off' leaving a huge crater, one and a half miles wide. Inside the crater is a lake, Laguna Quilotoa. Its beauty attracts many tourists, especially at weekends when Latacungans head out of town for their Sunday drive.

Volcanic deposits form very fertile soils and the pyroclastic flows, following Quilotoa's eruptions, have filled the local valleys. Unfortunately the sediments are also very soft and the river has quickly cut down through the deposits to produce deep ravines and gorges several hundred feet deep. As we travelled the short distance to Quilotoa from Zumbahua it became more and more apparent how severely eroded the landscape was. Fields of maize and wheat crumbled away into the deep gorges.

Zumbahua was a metropolis compared to the village of Quilotoa, which consists of only a couple of shacks and a car park. With nowhere to buy any rum we were glad we had not spent the night in Quilotoa. At over 3850m asl, Quilotoa is almost 400m higher than Zumbahua. It does not benefit from the shelter of the surrounding hills, and felt even more exposed, windy and cold than Zumbahua had. Touts bombarded us, with arms full of warm clothing as soon as we arrived, but we had seen them coming and had put on our hats and gloves before we got out of the bus.

We left our rucksacks in the safe hands of a local artist, who probably hoped we would buy some of his paintings on his return. The artwork from the area is known as Tigua and is supposedly very famous, but we weren't inspired.

From the rim of the crater we looked down on a beautiful emerald lake, 300 metres below. Dropping down over the rim and into the crater was like entering a different world. Sheltered from the cold wind, it was extremely tranquil and with the full heat of the sun on our faces we soon ditched our hats and gloves.

With the help of a five year old boy we were guided down to the lake. He was the coolest guide we had met so far and led us down the easiest, quickest paths to the bottom. He didn't say very much, but we put our trust in him, following him regardless. At the edge of the lake he left us, without pestering us for any money, to join his mum, the local pedalo operator.

Kelvin brewed up a cup of coffee and we sat at the edge of the lake soaking in the sun and the stunning scenery. Looking in the water we could see the reflection of the steep sides of the crater, which contrasted starkly against bright blue sky. Out of the wind and dust, and at a slightly more agreeable altitude, the air felt fresh in our lungs. Even more agreeable was our picnic, especially as we not eaten properly the day before.

We found a piece of wood on the lakeside and started up a game of cricket. A group of kids, who were being treated to a school outing, quickly joined in. They didn't have a clue what to do to start with, but once they worked it out they were desperate to have a go at batting or bowling. Not surprisingly, they didn't like being fielders. The concept of waiting their turn was a bit alien to them and it always seemed to be the same kids scrabbling for the ball and bat.

When the game fizzled out, the kids attacked a dustbin, fighting over the empty water bottles we had thrown away. They were obviously a valuable commodity judging by the scraps that were breaking out over an empty 'sin gas'. They let the rest of the rubbish fly around the lakeside and looked at us strangely when we tried to get them to chase after it to put it back in the bin.

Before we left the lake we tipped our little guide - he was ecstatic. We made our own way back up the crater, desperately trying to remember the route our guide had taken. Walking back up was extremely hard work. The path was soft and sandy and we kept sliding back down. Our 'altitude training' on our trip up Cotopaxi seemed to help a bit, but the climb was still very tiring. An hour after setting off from the lake we arrived back at the rim of the crater, hot, sweaty and very dusty. Kelvin, Jo and James had sensibly opted for the easy option – a donkey ride up to the top.

Generally the public transport around the Quilotoa Circuit is a bit erratic and our plan was to catch the daily bus to Chugchilán. We had met a couple that had missed the bus the previous day because it was early, so just in case we headed over to the bus stop half an hour before the bus was due. We didn't fancy spending a night in Quilotoa or, even worse, another night in Zumbahua. Two hours later we were still waiting on the side of the road. We didn't really mind because the scenery was fantastic. The sun was warm on our faces, and we lay on the grass absorbing the view across to the snow-capped peaks of the Valley of the Volcanoes.

The only seats left on the bus were right at the very back, which on a normal bus on paved roads would not have been a problem. After about five minutes being thrown around on the hard seats we were all feeling a bit queasy. Judging by the piles of vomit on the floor, we had not been the first passengers to sit at the back of the bus that day and it quickly dawned on us why there had been plenty of spare seats.

The journey to Chugchilán took an hour, and was pretty terrifying. Amounting to no more than a dusty track, the 'road' was severely eroded by rainfall, leaving small rivers crossing over the road. The water had also stripped away most of the side of the track making it desperately narrow. On top of that, parts of the road had collapsed down the side of the mountain, leaving gaping holes at the edge. In some places the bus appeared to be much wider than the width of the road and we are sure the wheels went over a few times. The drop over the edge was a couple of hundred metres and we were pleased it was not the wet season, much preferring to bump around rather than slide down the hillside.

Chugchilán is a far more attractive place to stay than Zumbahua. For such a small village and with probably the worst transport connections we had encountered, it boasts some of the best accommodation in Ecuador. Just outside of the village is the popular Black Sheep Inn, but at $18 a night (each) we decided to give it a miss. The only way the other hostel owners can compete with the Black Sheep is to provide high quality accommodation, but at more affordable rates. There are a number of excellent hostels to choose from and we got the last room at Mama Hildas ($10, including breakfast and evening meals). It was either the fact that we had not eaten properly for a couple of days or that the food was totally delicious, but we managed to polish off four bowls of lentil soup that evening (plus the other two courses). This was to be the best hostel we stayed in on our entire trip. Our room had beautiful views across to the Quilotoa crater, the showers were hot, the food was fantastic, the hammocks in the wonderful garden were great to relax in and the comfortable common room had a nice warming wood burning stove. The social area was a great place to play cards and swap 'where to go / not to go' stories with other hostel guests. And what a difference to the shit hole we had left at 8am that morning.

That night, beer in hand, we saw the biggest, brightest full moon we had ever seen - magical. We stood gawping at it for some time and the memories of Zumbahua faded to the back of our minds.

Chugchilán is a great place to spend walking, horse-riding, or just relaxing. The horses looked more like Shetland ponies (only thinner) and we opted for a walk to some Incan ruins instead. The trek consisted of a 10km hike up hill to about 4000m and a 10km hike back down again. As we walked up the mountain track, the views got better and better. Perched on the hillside were small thatched houses, orchids filled the hedges and in the lush green fields farmers were going about their daily chores. Young children and roaming llamas strayed out into the road to meet us.

Each house we walked past seemed to own a ferocious dog. Most of them appeared to be just warding us away from their 'territory', but we did not want to take any risks. Another guest at the hostel had been bitten twice, on the same day, by different dogs and had to go back to Quito to get a post-bite rabies injection. We were glad we forked out £100 each for our rabies jabs before we left - at least it would give us enough time to get to a big hospital if we needed to.

We carried sticks with us in case we needed to fend the dogs off, but waving sticks at them just made them bare some more teeth and foam a bit more. Someone had told us that pretending to pick up stones helped. We thought it was a bit odd, but as the dogs approached us, teeth still bared and mouths still foaming, we bent down to gather some stones off the ground in the faint hope it would work. That was the last we saw of the hounds, they turned and fled with their tails between their legs, yelping as if in pain. We did not even need to throw the rocks at them. This was a good trick and saved our legs many times that day.

At the top of the hill we did not actually see the Inca ruins we had set out to find. The fantastic view along the Avenue of Volcanoes was enough to compensate for missing out on the ruins. Even though we had to take the same path back down to Chugchilán the walk was just as interesting as on the way up. By the time we got back to the hostel, after almost seven hours of walking, our feet were burning. A well-deserved beer soon relieved us of the pain. Relaxing in the hammocks in the hostel garden we watched our first condors soaring way above our heads.

People tend to stay in Chugchilán for longer than they planned. This is partly due to the fact that it is such a great place to stay, but also because it is almost impossible to leave using public transport. Every day, there are two bus services that operate from Chugchilán to Sigchos. Unfortunately, they both depart at 3 o'clock in the morning, and no one seemed very keen to drag themselves out of Ecuador's most comfortable beds to catch them. There were four other hostel guests who had ended staying an extra night because they had missed the bus – both of the buses had decided to leave 30 minutes earlier than they were supposed to.

The journey is apparently a total nightmare, with the buses racing each other to try and be first to arrive at the next stop. We reckoned that they used to depart at a sensible time of day (about 9am), but over the years they left earlier and earlier each day to give them an advantage over the other bus.

The other travel options were to pay a huge price for a caminetta, hitch, walk or go on the milk float. The recommendations that Anne, the American from Latacunga, had so far turned out to be pretty crap and we were a little bit dubious about her suggestion of catching the milk float. It had been mentioned in our guidebook, and it left at the more sociable hour of 9am, so decided to give it a go.

It turned up on time, which was a good start, picking us up right outside the hostel. We climbed in and with the memory of the condition of the road from Quilotoa to Chugchilán still fresh in our minds we secured our bags as best we could.

The milk float was more of a large truck, rather than a traditional milk float. A huge plastic barrel had been fitted in the back to store the milk in. Also in the truck was an assortment of tyres, plastic diesel and oil containers, and bottles of LPG. The truck stopped every 500 metres, or so, to collect or sell milk to people on the roadside. The impression Anne (our American 'amigo') had given us was that she just plonked herself on some old tyres and didn't move until she arrived in Sigchos. We probably did not have to, but we helped to lift the buckets of milk up into the truck and pour it into the barrel. Any help, even just unscrewing the lid of the barrel was gratefully received from the 'milk boy', whose job it was to fill the barrel.

Milk was collected from anyone who happened to be waiting on the roadside. Sometimes an old woman or young kid would appear from out of nowhere with a small metal bucket filled with the creamy liquid. Where there were a few more houses, or in the small villages a crowd would congregate around the truck. The containers they used to carry the milk varied considerably: nice shiny metal buckets, black water buckets, used water bottles, or old oil and petrol containers. The people were paid by the driver depending on how much milk they were adding to the barrel. If there were any disputes over the quantity, the driver would climb out and get his own bucket out to measure it out properly. Whatever he said went, no more arguing.

For most of the journey we were the only passengers, but as we got closer to our destination it became apparent that the milk truck also doubled as the local bus/taxi service, picking up anyone who happened to be loitering at the side of the road. At one stage we were made redundant from our job as 'barrel opener' when one of the regular passengers took over our duties.

Clinging onto the edge of the truck, we trundled along the bumpy road. Each time the truck pulled away, a stream of dust enveloped the truck and we had to duck onto the truck floor to avoid getting a mouthful of dirt. A grey sludge soon developed on top of the milk, but nobody seemed too bothered by it. As the barrel got fuller and fuller, the milk started to leak out of the top, especially when we went over a particularly big hole and around sharp corners. It dribbled across the floor, soaking into the bottom of our rucksacks.

After two hours of being thrown around in the back of the truck, we arrived in Sigchos.  We were absolutely filthy and looked like we had been working up a chimney, but it had been great fun, and it had only cost us a dollar.

We only had to wait half an hour or so until our bus for Latacunga turned up, which we thought was pretty good timing.  After buying our tickets, the driver took our bags and loaded them into the boot of the bus.  Raring to go, we piled in and made ourselves comfortable.  After about ten minutes of sitting on the bus it dawned on us that we were not due to depart for another two hours.  The 2:30pm service advertised on the wall outside the bus company's ticket office referred to the buses operating on Mondays and Thursdays.  It was Tuesday – so much for good timing.

Sigchos was a pleasant little town, with a lovely laidback feel to it but didn't have huge amounts to offer in the way of entertainment, especially to keep us occupied for two hours.  Sitting on the wall, watching life go by was the best pastime, but seeing as most of the residents of Sigchos were taking a siesta there wasn't a lot to watch.

To while away a few minutes Caius kindly offered to help an old lady carry her bags across the road.  Bent double from the huge bag of spuds she had hoisted onto her back, the only courteous thing to do was to offer to help her with the other sack.  She was about 70 after all and she was only going about 50 metres down the road.  This was easier said than done, and he quickly regretted his decision as soon as he lifted up the sack - it weighed a tonne.  Desperately trying to grip on to the sack he followed the little old lady down the road, panting and wheezing, his arms shaking from the exertion.

The bus driver and his wife took pity on us and invited us to their favourite local eatery for lunch.  We were a little unsure to begin with, but it was probably the cleanest 'locals' restaurant we had encountered so far.  The meal was a typical lunchtime set menu  - soup with a chicken foot and other unidentifiable bits of meat floating in it, followed by rice with chicken, and all washed down with some freshly squeezed orange juice.  Costing only $1.10 it was a bit of a bargain, even though the waiter had assured Caius it was 'sin carne' (without meat).

Compared to our trip we had taken earlier that morning in the milk float, the bus journey to Latacunga was fairly uneventful. Saying that, the scenery was still fantastic, with the tortuous road taking us along high mountain ridges, down through the valleys and across bare mountain plains. By the time we arrived in Latacunga it was dark, we had been travelling for over 12 hours and we were pretty shattered.

Because we had been the first passengers onto the bus, our bags were right at the very back of the hold. After almost dislocating his vertebrae carrying the old lady's sack of potatoes Caius still hadn't learnt his lesson and proceeded to help unload the boot so we could get to our bags quicker. This time the sack was not heavy, but the fact that it was stained red, with blood pouring from the bottom almost made him vomit. He dragged our rucksacks out, vowing never again to help anyone with their luggage.

# Baños

One of the great things about going on holiday is planning a route. Even before we had finally decided on South America, we pored over atlases and through guidebooks to find the places we wanted to visit. We found that brochures for the organised 'adventure holidays', companies like *Exodus* and *Travelbag*, were a good source of information and they gave us some ideas for which towns to visit. Based on the fact that Baños featured in all of the tour itineraries we decided that it was probably worth a visit.

For the most part, and particularly in Ecuador, the Andes actually consist of two, and not one mountain chains. Separated by an enormous valley are two parallel ridges of mountains that stretch down the centre of Ecuador from Quito to Cuenca.

Baños is located to the east of the central Andean valley. In order to get to the town you have cross the range of mountains that separate the Andean highlands from the jungle lowlands. The majority of the routes over the mountain chains are infrequently travelled and notoriously treacherous passes. Baños is one of those rare places where the main access road is in pretty good condition and the descent is not too dangerous. It was still fairly steep, the road hugging the side of the mountain. We wound our way down the valley, dropping over 1000m in elevation in less than an hour. Because it is so accessible, Baños has inherited the name "the gateway to the Amazon". Beautifully placed in a deep valley, surrounded by lush green slopes, with an agreeable sub-tropical climate it is very touristy, and is particularly popular as a holiday and weekend resort for Ecuadorians. Luckily it was neither a holiday, nor a weekend, but there were still plenty of tourists milling around.

Lying only 8km away, towering above the town centre is the crater of Tungurahua volcano, literally meaning "throat of fire". In 1999, after eight decades of being dormant, the volcano sprung back to life, threatening a major eruption, (its first since 1916). Based on the fact it would take only 15 minutes for hot lava to engulf the village if the volcano erupted, 20,000 residents of the town and surrounding area were evacuated by government troops. Fortunately, for the town, Tungurahua only spewed out quantities of ash and steam instead and the locals were able to return to their homes.

The residents still live with the threat of a major eruption and only a couple of weeks prior to our arrival it had blown its top, spreading a layer of dust for miles around and destroying many farm crops in the area. There are actually two main roads that lead from the Pan-American to Baños, but the other one had been closed until further notice, because of damage caused by the blast. All up-close volcano trips had been cancelled, and our hopes of getting a glimpse of its smouldering peak were dashed by low cloud and drizzle that had descended on the town.

Baños has an abundance of cafés, restaurants, hotels and tour agencies. As one of the easiest places for tourists to access the Ecuadorian jungle, the streets are lined with tour companies offering jungle trips, white water rafting, mountain biking, horse riding, hiking, climbing, volcano spotting and quad biking. We opted for none of the above, instead choosing to spend our time in Baños relaxing, eating cake, drinking coffee and soaking in the hot baths. Not surprisingly it is these hot baths that give the town its name.

Thermal springs at the base of Tungurahua supply the baths with hot water and glacial melt waters provide the cold. The pools looked particularly murky and we were reassured it was all the volcanic minerals that made the water a brown muddy colour. We spent an hour relaxing in the baths, watching the locals - who swear by the waters restorative properties - taking their daily dip. We watched in amazement as one man, who was obviously not content with soaking in the baths, proceeded to do some sit-ups and press-ups at the side of the pool. Between hot soaks we 'refreshed' ourselves by bravely standing

64

under a cold shower. The shower was really a glorified drainpipe poking out of the hillside, pouring freezing cold water directly onto our heads.

Baños is also famous for making toffee, a local speciality. It is sold on small stands in shop doorways and being tourists we felt obliged to buy a few packs. Wandering around with our teeth firmly stuck together we bumped into a couple of French girls we had met at Mama Hildas, in Chugchilán. They appeared extremely thankful of our generosity when we handed them three-quarters of a pack of the local delicacy. We were more than happy to get rid of the gross lump of sticky sugar we had purchased.

On the bus out of Baños, the bus conductor tried to diddle us out of our change. Normally if they did not have enough change when we paid for the ticket, they would give it to us once they had collected the rest of the fares. They usually wrote on the back of the ticket how much we were owed. On this occasion, the tout did not even give us a ticket or the change that was due to us. When we asked for it he told us that the cost of the fare was the full $5. We knew roughly how much it should have cost so we stood our ground, arguing with the embarrassed looking conductor. All the passengers were staring out of the window and we were holding the bus up at the side of a busy road. He told us that we had paid the standard price, but when we asked a couple of other gringos how much they had been charged, which was substantially less, he backed down and gave us the correct change. It was a minor victory and served him right for trying to rip us off.

Vicky Brewis & Caius Simmons

# JC and the Devils Nose

We arrived in Alausí after a long and windy journey. The brakes on the bus didn't sound like they were up to the job and after a several hundred-metre descent the smell of burning brake pads was quite sickening.

The town of Alausí perches on a large terrace, deep within the Chanchán gorge. The focal point of the town is a huge colourful mosaic statue of Jesus Christ. Towering over the streets J.C. dominates the view across the valley and to the mountains beyond.

The streets were quiet, tidy and laid-back, and it was hard to believe that it was once a thriving holiday resort and major transport hub. Lined with numerous dilapidated hotels, the wide main street, (a dual carriageway to be correct) is over half mile long and an indication of the town's affluent history. Today these hotels are not what you would call 'Grand', their huge facades are crumbling, the windows broken, the woodwork rotting and the doors barred shut. There was evidence of this former grandeur in the small hostel we booked ourselves into. With a nice sunny, flower-filled, cobbled courtyard and a wooden balcony running around the side, it had similarities with a Mediterranean French villa. The beds had seen better days, probably about 70 years previously, but our room was basic and clean.

The only other landmark to suggest that Alausí was once the Ecuadorian equivalent of Blackpool is the train station. Consisting of only one platform, a small ticket office and café, this station comes alive three times a week when the train travelling from Riobamba to Sibambe passes through. This was the main, and only, reason we had come to Alausí as we planned to catch the train the following day for the last section of the journey down the gorge to Nariz del Diablo (Devils Nose).

We spent that afternoon doing the only thing there is to do in Alausí – nothing. After walking up to pay our homage to J.C. and to take in the views of the Cerro Gampala Mountain, there was only the small market to explore and then have a drink in the only open café.

With some free time on our hands we took the opportunity to change some money at the one and only bank. The currency in Ecuador is the dollar, the notes being the same as those in America, but the coins are specially minted for the Ecuadorian monetary system. In 1999 the Ecuadorian economy plummeted in value, the result of a poor return on crops, flooding due to El Nino, and the depressed oil market of 1997-98. Throughout 1999, Ecuador saw a 70% depreciation of its currency, the Sucre, causing the banking sector to collapse, and default on loan repayments. A desperate government 'sold its soul to the devil' when in 2000 it was forced to 'dollarise' the currency in an attempt to stabilise the economy.

Even though the larger dollar notes, like $20's and $10's, are valid currency in Ecuador they were not widely accepted. If something cost $7 and you handed over a $10 note, the shopkeeper would often look at you in disgust, shrug their shoulders, huff and expect you to pay with the correct monies. We reckoned that they hoped we would just say, "Keep the change", but if you stood there long enough they would miraculously produce the change and usually had a drawer full of $1 notes and coins.

Our reason for the trip to the bank was solely to get some smaller denomination notes. The cashier disappeared behind the counter and returning with a big smile on his face he passed us an immaculate 5 Sucre note. The cashier asked if we had any coins from England. Delighted by our Ecuadorian note we rummaged through our pockets, handing him about £1.80 in change to add to his collection. He had not seen all of the coins before, so was just as pleased as we were. Calculating that the 5 Sucre note would have only been worth about 2p, the cashier definitely got the best deal.

The Ecuadorians didn't really care less what state the notes were in, as long as they got paid. Most of the dollars looked they had been used to clean the floor with and one couple that we met insisted that they cleaned their hands with wet wipes after they handled money. This was taking it a little bit to the extreme, but we could see their point.

We broke our vow and took a photo of some local people without asking their permission. It was from a distance and we just couldn't resist. A truck loaded with wooden tabletops from market stalls, with the traders perched on top, passed by. As the truck accelerated, the tabletops all slid out the back, along with all the people. It wasn't funny really, but we couldn't help laughing and Caius just had to catch the moment on film.

The Indian ladies who had slid out of the back onto the street hadn't thought it quite as amusing as Caius had. Either they believed in divine retribution or they put a curse on him, because within 10 minutes of taking the photo his stomach started feeling a bit dodgy. It probably had more to do with the hot baths at Baños rather than a curse, but whatever it was he spent the whole night sitting on the bog with a classic case of simultaneous upstairs / downstairs symptoms. Luckily the sink was right next to the loo, so he only needed to lean forward when he got the urge to vomit.

By the morning Caius was feeling a bit better and all he could was cross his fingers (and legs) and hope he would last the two-hour train journey without needing the toilet.

Buying a ticket for the train took longer than getting through U.S customs, the 'Station Master' insisting we wrote down all our personal details. What our age and eye colour had to do with catching a train we were not quite sure of, but it took nearly 10 minutes to buy two tickets – the previous customers were held up for 15 minutes (the people at the back of the queue were concerned they were all going to miss the train so started timing him to calculate if they were going to make it to the train).

Leaving at 7am, the train travels from Riobamba along the same valley we had driven through on the bus. Once a vital link from the Guayaquil on the coast, to Quito, nowadays the service only operates for the sake of tourism.

When the train arrived at Alausí, the roofs of the carriages were covered in tourists, some Ecuadorians, but mainly foreigners. They had been on the train for 4 hours and the novelty of a roof top journey was beginning to run a bit thin for most of them. It had been freezing cold when they left Riobamba, and sitting on a hard, bumpy tin roof had not been as enjoyable as they had anticipated. Still, there was no chance anyone was going to relinquish their spaces, but we managed to squeeze onto the roof. If Caius was going to be sick, at least he could do so over the edge of the roof.

The one-hour journey from Alausí took us down 1000 metres, deep into the Chanchán gorge, to the Nariz del Diablo (Devils Nose). This is a small hill at the end of the gorge, which supposedly looks like a persons nose. To get around the base of the 'Nose' the track switches backwards and forwards, the train changing directions in order to get down the steep slope. The train track runs along the side of the valley, with a sheer drop into the gorge below. We later heard many stories that the train had a habit of derailing, but luckily not on this section of track.

Touts carrying water, juice, crisps and sweets didn't miss the opportunity and they stumbled up and down the moving carriages in the hope of selling their wares. The touts were followed closely by a couple of dexterous train conductors, who were clipping tickets. There was certainly no chance that we could have jumped the fare.

At the bottom of the hill, the train turned around and we came back up again. For $8 each we agreed the train ride was expensive, but fun. Our bums and backs ached and we were glad we didn't have four more hours sitting on the roof back to Riobamba.

The next part of our journey out of Alausí was probably the scariest bus ride we experienced. The scenery was stunning, what we saw of it. We were too busy concentrating on the road to take any of it in.  We had become used to travelling along mountain roads, with 1000 metre drops down the side, but not at the speed the bus driver decided to travel at.  What made it worse was that we appeared to be racing another bus in an attempt to arrive first at the next bus stop.  The driver took no notice of the fact that the road was not straight and even though he couldn't see if anything was coming towards us, he was overtaking cars and trucks on corners.  With a classic overtake on a blind bend our bus managed to pass the other bus, winning the race to the next town.  When we arrived at the bus stop the tout was out on the pavement shouting, "Vamos, Vamos!" ("Let's go, Let's go!") and pushing passengers up the steps onto the bus as quickly as he could.  It was only a minor victory because the other bus passed us, and the race started all over again.  A few kilometres down the road, we overtook it for the last time.  It had stopped to load huge sacks on to the roof and there was no chance they would be able to catch us up again.  The other driver and tout looked disheartened, as they knew they had lost the race.

Relieved to have arrived at our destination in one piece, our knuckles slowly returned to their normal colour.

# Ingapirca

We didn't hang around to see much of El Tambo, literally jumping straight on a bus for Ingapirca. We were on a mission to get there in time to see Ecuador's most famous archaeological site, and we needed plenty of time to walk around the ruins before it got dark.

The young school kids on the bus stared quite intensely at us. This had probably something to do with the fact that our heads were touching the ceiling, even though we were sat down. We were getting quite used to this, but on this occasion the bus was exceptionally small and we looked even more conspicuous than usual. In these situations the hardest thing to do when you are being stared at, is not to stare back.

One of us must have made eye contact with the old man in front of us (he was making a special effort to turn around to catch our attention) because he decided to strike up a conversation with us. We were sat right under the radio speakers, which were blasting the theme tune to the Flintstones (a pleasant change from pan pipe music) and we couldn't hear a word he said to us. Not that this made any difference because we didn't understand what the old man was saying anyhow. We judged by his expressions whether we needed to nod a "yes", shake a "no" or laugh. Vicky thought he was talking about his clothes (Ropa), while Caius thought he was gabbling on about Europe (Europa). In these situations we felt particularly ignorant and wished our conversational Spanish was better. Although, based on the amount of spit being projected from his mouth when he was speaking, we agreed that we probably wouldn't have understood him even if he spoke English.

We had built an image of Ingapirca in our minds and our expectations were that of a large Incan settlement, not dissimilar to Machu Picchu. Our excitement didn't last long and as we unloaded our bags from the roof of the bus all we could see were some ruins that looked like a small fortress. We wondered if the rest of the site was spread in the valley on the other side, but we're slightly disappointed to discover that it didn't. The phrase, 'What you see, is what you get', came to mind. Some outstanding Inca stonework, with its trapezoidal shaped doorways and niches made up for the fact that the ruins were not as extensive as we hoped they would be.

Administered by the local community, the site is dominated by a large elliptical platform structure, the Temple of the Sun. We couldn't figure it out, but the museum gave the impression that the Temple had recently been "rebuilt" as a research exercise. Much of the original stone was pinched after the Spanish conquest to build local houses with. We felt slightly "done", coming to an Incan archaeological site, whose main feature had been built in the last 20 years. Admittedly the stonework was amazing. If we did smoke we would not have been able to get a cigarette paper between the stonework it was so close together. This was our first experience of this unmistakeable Inca style.

After further investigation we soon realised that this site was the most significant Inca site in Ecuador, rather than the largest, as we first thought. The site was originally an important settlement for the native Cañari people whose occupation lasted for some 500 years before Huayna Capac, the Inca Emperor, seized the site about 500 years ago.

After about 20 minutes of strolling around, we were ready to buy the T-shirt and the video. The last of the tour buses had long gone and apart from a couple of grazing llamas we pretty much had the site to ourselves. We took a small circular walk past a few other Inca features; a ceremonial altar for sacrificial purposes, a royal throne carved out of rock, and a cliff face that looked like it had a persons face carved in to it. Our imagination was obviously not as good as the Incans; it was a good job our guidebook told us what they were all supposed to be.

Walking back to the village we encountered a very old wizened, toothless lady, accompanied by her sheep and dog.  She started chatting and cackling away at us and pointing out across the fields.  We employed exactly the same tactic as we would have done if we had met someone like this in the UK - we just smiled and nodded and said, "muy bien".  She seemed very happy with our response, cackling to herself as she hobbled away.  We tried to imagine what she had been trying to tell us and the best we could come up with was, "My husband has just fallen in a mine shaft, you can help me rescue him if you like, but I am not too bothered if he gets out because he never washes the dishes anyway"

Apart from the Inca ruins, Ingapirca does not have a great deal to offer and we could see why people took advantage of the day trips or only visited the ruins as part of a tour.  With this fact in mind, the restaurant owners see little point opening for the evening and as our stomachs started to rumble, memories of Zumbahua came back to us.

There was a menu displayed outside a building, the door was open so we went in and sat ourselves down at a table.  The owners were very surprised to see us - the lights went on, the table quickly laid, and the fire stoked up.  We opted for the traditional meal consisting of potato and bean soup followed by chicken and rice.  Well there wasn't really an option, it was more a case of "do you want it or not".

The owners son, who was about seven years old acted as our waiter and barman while mum was out the back slaughtering another chicken.  He was desperate to make our stay perfect, insisting we had a straw with our beers and running back and forth with napkins, salt and pepper.  He actually couldn't reach the table yet which proved problematic when he was putting our plates in front of us, managing to spill half a bowl of soup right into Caius' lap.  We got the impression that the food had been cooked specially for us and the thought crossed our minds that we had perhaps just eaten their supper.  When we enquired how much the bill was, the owner just stood there with a blank expression on her face, desperately trying to think up a price.  She could have quite easily charged us a fortune and we would have never known, but as it was she only asked for a few dollars. After all their efforts, especially her son, the least we could was leave a good tip, which was highly unusual for us. They waved goodbye from the door, grinning like they had just won the lottery.

If anyone tells you that travelling is full of fun and excitement, where every night is party night, don't believe them. With no volleyball to watch and nowhere to buy any rum and coke we headed back to our hostel, where we sat in our cold, dirty, dark bland room playing cards until we could justify going to bed at 7.30pm.

# Cuenca

The only memorable part of the bus journey from Ingapirca to Cuenca was that the bus broke down 100 metres short of the bus terminal, dumping us on the main road leading into town. The walk into the centre wouldn't have been too bad if we weren't lugging our rucksacks with us and by the time we reached the hostel, on the other side of town, we had built up a bit of a sweat and our necks were aching.

Conveniently located right in the centre of town our hostel, *El Monasterio*, with its fantastic views across the rooftops, was an excellent choice. From our room we could see down into the cloisters of El Carmen Alto where nuns live in isolation. From what we could see they appeared to spend their time, not in prayer, but tending to their flower gardens and vegetable patches. The hostel's balcony overlooked the San Francisco Plaza and church and we also had great views of the beautiful blue domes of the New Cathedral.

Typified by cobblestone streets, towering cathedrals, marble and whitewashed buildings, and red tiled roofs Cuenca certainly deserves its status as a UNESCO World Heritage Trust site. Its beautiful colonial architecture is kept in immaculate condition and it was the first place we had visited where a conscious effort was being made to clear away rubbish, with dustbin lorries emptying bins each evening and morning.

We arrived on a Saturday and we're surprised to see that the majority of the shops were closed, as were all the museums. Traders in Cuenca stick rigidly to traditional opening times, closing early on Saturday and shut all day Sunday. We couldn't go shopping, or visit any museums, our only option was to spend a couple of days in cafés, ice cream parlours, looking at the views from our hostel balcony and writing up our journal.

Even most of the cafés and restaurants we wanted to go to were closed for the weekend and we walked across town (more than once) in an attempt to find a place serving decent coffee. Despite being on the doorstep of the best coffee producing countries in the world all we had been offered so far were cups of instant Nescafe and mugs of a foul tasting brown liquid, usually with floaters in it. According to an ex-New York Police Commissioner, Raymond Kelly, "[neighbouring] Colombia has probably the best cocaine, the best heroin, and the best marijuana in the world. And the best coffee." It was a shame they hadn't exported any of these excellent coffee beans a few miles across the border into Ecuador. The best coffee beans, like the drugs, are exported to US and Europe where the best prices are to be had. Of all the places on offer in Cuenca it was a German run café that finally satisfied our desire.

By day, Cuenca is a bustling city, even on a Sunday when local people travel to the centre to visit the Cathedral, amble around the streets and get family photos taken in the main square. As soon as darkness fell, the streets became deserted and all the people and cars that had been clogging up the streets earlier on in the day just disappeared.

Just like most regions of the UK, areas of the Andes can be distinguished by the clothing its inhabitants wear. In Britain its kilts for Scotland, wellies in Wales, short skirts in Newcastle, shell suits in Liverpool, tweeds in Yorkshire, suits in London, black and gold rugby shirts in Cornwall. In Andean America it is the style of hat that points to a particular region. Since the 1930's hats became common attire in South America. Though the origins are not fully known they were possibly adopted from western miners or railway workers. In northern Ecuador the hats are a variation of the Panama hat, becoming more bowler in shape the further south you travel. In some regions of Peru they resemble top hats (which is entertaining watching them squeeze into minibuses), others have mini-bowlers, precariously perched on the back of the head, and in

Bolivia some looked like upside down dustbins. Overall though, for some reason, the bowler hat did seem to be the most popular.

The Panama hat is one the biggest and most famous exports from Ecuador. The hats are not from Panama as many people are led to believe, they actually originate from the area around Cuenca. Workers on the Panama Canal wore the imported hat to protect their heads from the sun, and thus the Panama hat got its name. Seeing as we were in the city where the majority and the best quality hats are made we were disappointed to find that all the factories and shops were shut for the weekend.

In a moment of madness we decided to check out the local hot baths and caught a bus to the suburbs of Baños on the outskirts of town. There was a variety of different baths at the complex to choose from and in our confusion we bought a ticket for the wrong one. The lady in the kiosk had assured us the water was 'caliente' (hot), but when we dipped our toe in we discovered it was 'mucho fria'. We didn't fancy spending the afternoon in a cold swimming pool with a load of screaming kids so joined the queue again at the ticket kiosk to try and get our money back. Every time we reached the counter, an irate mother would jump the queue, pushing us out of the way. This happened a couple of times, by which point we were getting pretty pissed off and forcibly pushed the next one out of the way. We got a ferocious stare, before she pushed in behind us without further comment. We were really pleased with ourselves because we managed to negotiate, in Spanish, a refund and then buy some new tickets for the steam baths.

From a distance the hot pool didn't look too bad, apart from the fact it was really busy. It was Sunday and we had forgotten that our guidebook had warned us it was really popular with Cuencans, especially at weekends. We couldn't bring ourselves to ask for another refund.

After a closer inspection we saw that the baths were dirty and smelly (nothing to do with minerals and sulphur), and they were obviously being used, literally, as a bath. There was a soap scum around the edges and stray floating hairs everywhere you looked. Things weren't any better when we got into the brown scummy water and it was not really a pool where we could relax. Not only were the kids determined that we should swallow as much water as possible by splashing it in our faces, but the water was not very hot either.

Seeing as we had made the effort to get there, we decided to give the steam sauna a visit. The women's sauna was a room carved out of the hillside, where hot water was pumped along channels and pipes, filling the cave with hot steam. The women lounged around on benches and plastic chairs, occasionally dousing themselves, and everyone else in the room, with buckets of cold water. Vicky described it as OK, rather than nice. Caius described the men's sauna as totally gross, rather than OK. It was full of fat men wearing skimpy fake Speedos, strutting around the room. They all had an unnatural fixation with rearranging themselves and rubbing their groins. One man had taken the opportunity to have a shave. It felt more like being on a Japanese torture programme than in a hot steam room.

Remembering how uncomfortable the walk across town had been with our rucksacks we caught a bus from our hostel to the Terminal Terrestre. It was Monday morning rush hour and the bus was mostly full of smart, business like people. Although there were a few seats available, we decided to stand near the rear doors, rather than struggle taking our rucksacks off. Considering there was plenty of space on the bus, it suddenly felt very crowded. Looking behind him, Caius noticed a couple of men fiddling with the straps on his rucksack. At the same time another man snuck around the front of him, and was feeling for his money belt. They had blocked Vicky off so she couldn't help and the men started circling around Caius in an attempt to confuse him. Luckily he quickly realised what was going on and shouted, "OIY" as loudly as possible. All the other passengers turned around to see what all the noise was about and the ticket man headed towards us, by which time the bus had pulled up at the bus stop and all three men jumped off. They stared at us from the pavement as if to say, "Next time". Feeling rather shaken, we did a quick check, but luckily nothing was missing.

# Valley of the Immortals

Known as the "Valle de la Juventud Eterna" (meaning Valley of Eternal Youth or Valley of the Immortals), Vilcabamba is a tranquil and sleepy little village in Southern Ecuador. Researchers have reported that an unusual number of townsfolk live to be over 100 years of age, the latest count is 60 out of the 2000 population are centenarians. Some, it is estimated, have reached the grand old age of 135. The prolonged existence has been mainly explained by the near-perfect all year round climate, deep family roots, low fat diets, little stress, a simple life and a hard work ethic. We reckoned it was due to the uplifting properties of the local bottled water, aptly named Viagua.

Attracted by the prospect of a good, long life, there is also a huge influx of westerners, mainly French and Germans, who have brought with them their own problems. Lack of close family ties and the stress from business ventures will undoubtedly start causing an imbalance in this fragile human ecosystem and affecting the areas impressive statistics.

However the westerners have also brought some good things to Vilcabamba – namely decent food and accommodation. The first place we came across was a café, owned by a French lady, and whilst enjoying some of her excellent bread and cakes we noted how quiet the town was.

Filled with an abundance of flowers, the central Plaza is neat and tidy. With not much better to do, the townsfolk lounge around it enjoying its peaceful surroundings. It is very much a frontier town, the wooden buildings were more like something out a Western film and just to make it even more authentic there were people wearing cowboy hats and leather chaps, riding around on horses. It all appeared to be part of everyday life in Vilcabamba, and nobody took any notice of these pseudo-cowboys as they rode around the square.

Just as we remarked that we had not seen many old people hanging around the church bells started to toll, the church doors were thrown open and people poured out into the square. Leading the way was a priest, closely followed by pallbearers carrying a coffin. The procession quickly walked around the square and up the hill towards the cemetery. So much for "eternal youth"

Vilcabamba is also a favourite weekend getaway destination for Ecuadorians and we were spoilt for choice on accommodation. Recommended by numerous people, we settled for Hotel Izhcayluma, situated a couple of miles out of the town centre. With it's own restaurant, bar, pool table, along with great views and comfy hammocks outside the rooms it was easy to see how people couldn't help but relax.

Two gay Bavarian men own the hostel; both sporting particularly dodgy beards. They had come to Vilcabamba in search of a peaceful lifestyle. Unfortunately for them they own one of the most popular hostels in the area and spend their entire time trying to find rooms for guests without reservations, serving meals in the restaurant and organising traveller's social lives.

A few people staying at the hostel were there specifically to sample the hallucinogenic properties of the San Pedro (or San Pedrillo) cactus, which grows locally in the valley. Apart from perhaps reading the *Gringo Trail*, these travellers had not done their research very well, and they could have gone anywhere in South America to sample it. For some travellers this is the only reason why they visit Vilcabamba. One student in particular stood out, he was very pleased with himself as he bragged how he had been tripping for the past three days. The drug had obviously affected his hearing, as he spoke so loudly so that everyone could hear his tale. Nobody was particularly interested apart from the hostel owners because he had stayed with them for almost 10 days, clocking a particularly large tab on food, beer and massages.

It would have been quite easy to spend a few days reading, playing cards and lazing around the town, but we decided we should explore some of the local trails close by. Bordering the Podocarpus National Park, the land surrounding Vilcabamba largely consists of private Nature Reserves, which are easily accessible from the town. One of the most popular of these is the track leading to the nearby mountain, Mandango. The route was dusty, and the surrounding slopes were particularly barren and dry. Apart from a few trees and thorny bushes, there was very little vegetation. Our lungs benefited from being at a much lower altitude (1500m asl), and it didn't take us long to climb to the small cross at the top of the hill. Needless to say, the views across the valley were fantastic. The lower slopes were very green and fertile, but scorched by the sun the higher peaks were looking very brown and frazzled. So far on our trip, all we had seen were lush green fields and wooded glades but the landscape had started to change, the parched fields surrounding Vilcabamba were a good indication that we were heading into drier regions.

Beyond Mandango was a bigger hill, with an even bigger cross on top. This mountain consisted of a sheer cliff, with a small hill perched on the top. We figured that we could get to the top because we could see people walking around the cross. On the far side of the hill we found a path up the escarpment. We negotiated the first section, which was not too bad, a little steep and dusty, but at least there was a proper path. After much scrabbling we made it to the top of the escarpment and all we had to do was walk up the less steep section to the cross. In order to reach this path, though we had to walk around the edge of the cliff face. Caius' fear of heights suddenly made a guest appearance – his mind deciding that his body was not going to go any further and he just froze on the side of the path, unable to move either forwards or backwards. Caius hadn't even seen the path, or the drop, but his instincts said it was steep and dangerous. There was no way he was going to go any further. After about 10 pathetic minutes, his adrenalin levels subsided, and he managed to make it to the bottom of the cliff, and solid ground again.

We were quite excited about our plans for the following day – a horse trek – that was, until we saw the horses. The horses were not the strongest beasts we had ever seen, or the biggest. Our feet didn't quite scrape along the ground, but they weren't far off.

Caballos Wilson was our guide and he took us into the mountain foothills and to a nature reserve owned by his family. There was a minor language problem, not just because of our poor Spanish or because Wilson didn't speak English, but because Wilson wasn't the chattiest of guides we had come across. We tried to strike up a few basic conversations, but in order to prolong his life he appeared to be conserving his energy by not talking.

We spent the morning exploring the hillsides around Vilcamba, up and down steep paths, through rivers, past sugar cane plantations, up and down more steep paths, through more rivers, and past more sugar cane plantations. Taking into account the speed the horses were going we probably could have walked the trek quicker. We could have avoided suffering from painful arses if we walked. The horses tired quickly and towards the end of the trek they had to keep stopping halfway up the hills for a rest. We trotted (more of a quick walk) into town and tied our steeds to a wooden rail outside the tour agency. A slatted, wooden swing door wouldn't have gone amiss. After four hours of sitting on the saddle we were as exhausted as the horses and vowed never to subject ourselves to the torture again.

We could see why people spend longer in Vilcabamba than they intend to, but luckily for us the weather turned unusually cold and cloudy. After our walk and horse ride all we could really do was relax in the garden, which wasn't a very appealing option when it was raining. We decided we had 'done' Vilcabamba and it was time to move on to the next stage in our journey – Peru.

# Peru

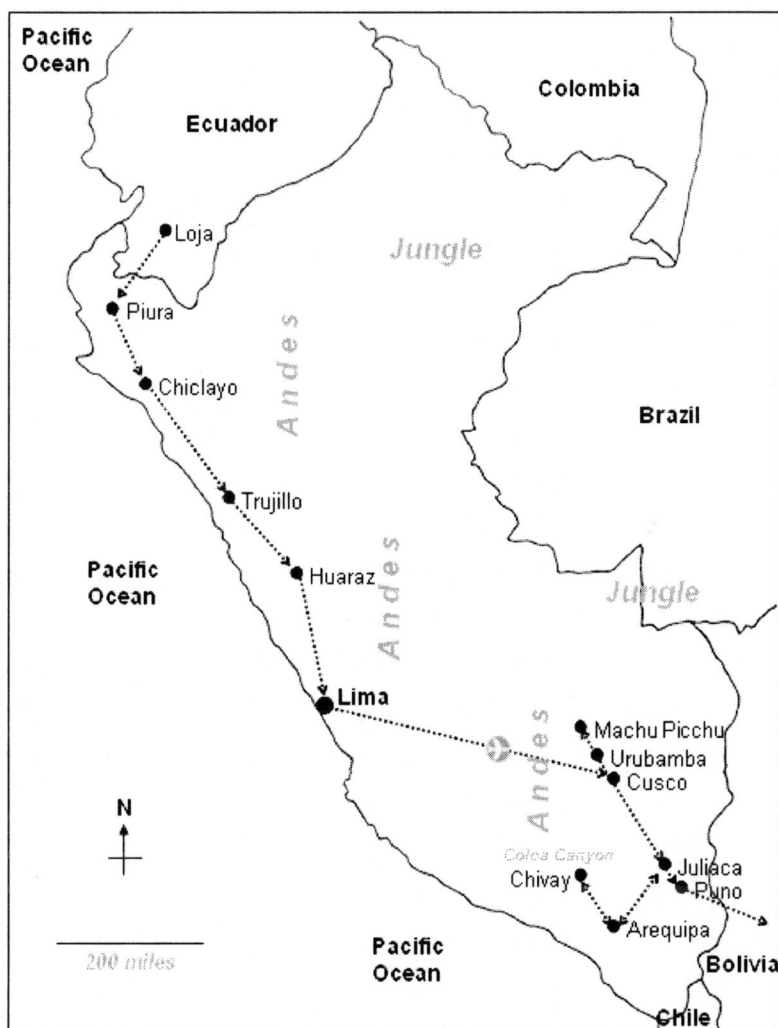

Pacific
Ocean

Ecuador

Colombia

Loja

Piura

Jungle

Chiclayo

Andes

Brazil

Trujillo

Pacific
Ocean

Huaraz

Andes

Jungle

Lima

Andes

Machu Picchu

Urubamba

Cusco

N

Colca Canyon

Chivay

Juliaca

Puno

200 miles

Arequipa

Pacific
Ocean

Bolivia

Chile

(not to scale)

# Crossing into Peru

There were plenty 'words of wisdom' concerning how to, where to, how not to and where not to cross the border into Peru. We consulted our list from Charlie and Abbey and taking their advice caught the bus from Loja to Piura.

The journey was no different than any other we had taken, but for some reason it seemed longer, hotter and more uncomfortable than any we had been on so far.

The bus was particularly knackered, the brakes emitting a horrible burning smell every time we went down a hill and there was a disconcerting knocking noise when we went over about 35mph. The noise was so bad, even the driver got out to investigate where it was coming from. Apparently one of the wheels looked a bit loose, but they decided just to risk it.

The touts who got on the bus were even more annoying than usual. At one point there were 21 vendors on the bus, a bit of an overkill, but very hilarious to watch all the same. We could have easily eaten a four-course meal if we had bought something from everyone. For starters we probably would have chosen corn on the cob with a bread roll on the side, followed by chicken and rice or if we fancied, we could have had chips instead of rice, with bags of sweaty salad to accompany it. For dessert we would have opted for a tub of fluorescent jelly or perhaps a cup of the pinkest ice cream we had ever come across. If we were still hungry after our gourmet meal we had a fruit bowl right next to us; oranges, pineapple, apples and an endless supply of mandarins. For drinks, we were also spoilt for choice; water (with or without bubbles), cola, fanta, sprite and bottles of what the South Americans refer to as gaseos, fizzy drinks in a variety of colours which all taste like Tizer or Irn Bru. We were quickly put off our meal by the man selling mandarins, who had rolled his t-shirt right up to his nipples, exposing the most enormous, flabbiest, sweatiest gut imaginable. Vicky was overjoyed when he stopped right next to her, while the other vendors squeezed by, shoving his belly into her face.

Our bus kept stopping at military checkpoints, hanging around until either our, or the bus drivers, documentation were verified. It didn't quite make sense that the military were only interested in our documents, rather than the Peruvians, who are their main threat. In the past Ecuador has lost quite a bit of its territory to Peru and they were at war together as recently as 1999. Tensions are still fairly high, and the army actively protects its borders, especially as there are oil and gas fields along the boundary.

Perhaps it was our nervous expectation of what Peru had in store for us that made the journey drag on. Whatever it was it didn't make the bus go any faster and it took us over five hours to reach the border town of Macara.

There were a couple of other tourists on the bus, and this was also their first border crossing in South America. No one really knew what to expect, but it wasn't very difficult to work out. The Macara – La Tina border crossing consisted of a few buildings, which house the Ecuadorian and Peruvian immigration and customs officials. A wide river separates the two countries and the bus driver dumped us at the end of the bridge, promising he would wait for us at the other side.

The only problem we had with the crossing was the mosquitoes. Dusk was not the best time of day to be standing next to a river, filling in immigration forms, when all our insect repellent and long sleeved tops were on a bus parked up the road. The mosquitoes were particularly enjoying the fresh blood, and we were slowly being eaten to bits. Luckily the formalities were quite straightforward, taking no more than ten minutes to cross over the bridge. Desperate to get back to the safety of the bus, we almost forgot to remember the fact that we had just left Ecuador and arrived in a new country, Peru.

# Piura

As we drove along in the dark, there was no way of knowing what the Peruvian countryside had to offer us. How we thought it differed from Ecuador we weren't really sure, but it was a new country so it had to be different. Arriving in Piura, we discovered the first difference between the two countries. No *Terminal Terrestre.*

The bus drove directly to the company's depot rather than to the main bus station, like they had done in Ecuador. The depot just happened to be in a middle of a dark and gloomy industrial estate on the edge of town. Great, stuck in a new country, without knowing where we were or where we were going. We had absolutely no choice but to catch a taxi. It seemed that all the local drivers had known a bus was due in from Ecuador and they were already waiting at the depot. Keen to get their greedy hands on our business, they were physically fighting over us before we had even got off the bus. The concept of waiting for our bags appeared totally alien to them and they seemed more than happy for us to leave our rucksacks on the bus just so they didn't miss out on the fare.

Joining forces with a Sicilian, called Andreas, we selected the least pushy of all the taxi drivers - the quiet one at the back of the queue. Andreas, a student based in London, sported an impressive bushy beard and a large wide scar running the length of his forehead. Because of his height (6 foot 8 inches) Andreas encountered a few problems travelling on the buses and to guarantee a seat where he was able to stretch his legs out he would have to book a few days in advance to make sure he had a front seat or the middle back seat. Having suffered a particularly uncomfortable journey from Loja, with his legs crushed up against the partition at the front of the bus, Andreas was not in the best of

86

moods. Towering, like a giant, several feet above their heads, Andreas was not going to put up with being hassled and the taxi touts clambering for our business all caught the wrong side of his fiery Latin tongue.

We told the taxi driver to take us to the hostel we wanted to stay at. Nodding agreeably, he floored the accelerator, but instead of taking us to where we requested, he took us to his own choice of hotel at the other end of town. Judging by his selection he obviously thought we were wealthy. Arguing with him got us nowhere. We had been warned about taxi drivers that took you to a different hotel because they received a commission if you booked in. We were more pissed off with his underhand tactics rather than the hotel itself, which turned out to be okay.

As we filled out the relevant paperwork, the hotel proprietor asked Andreas how he scarred his forehead. Andreas leaned over the counter and whispered, "Mafia". We laughed, but the owner cowered away with a surprised look on his face, especially after he saw Andreas write down his nationality as Sicilian. The price of the hotel, which we had been arguing over, suddenly became quite reasonable; the 'gringo tax' disappeared before our eyes, and we were all upgraded to their best rooms.

Andreas' conversation with the hotel owner reminded us of a story about the time when a friend, who also just happened to be travelling in Peru, was asked by a fellow bus passenger if he knew the Queen of England. "Si, si", said Matthew, jokingly. "I have tea with her from time to time". The other passengers started grilling him, "What she is like?", "How well do you know her?", "Do you know her children?", "What is her house like?".

We didn't have any of the local currency, the Peruvian Sol, and we doubted the few scruffy dollar notes in our wallets would get us very far. Heading for a bank, with Andreas as our security, we took our first trip through a Peruvian city. It had a familiar central plaza and a cathedral - so no real difference from any other Ecuadorian town centre. Walking further into Piura, it was blatantly obvious that we were very much in a new place, with different cultures and traditions. The main contrast between Peru and Ecuador was, being

9.00pm, the town was buzzing. People were sat in bars and restaurants, and the roads were full of horrid little yellow taxis, which hooted endlessly. In Ecuador at the same time, the streets would be deserted, not a soul to be seen, even on a Saturday night.

It didn't take long, five minutes to be precise, for the beeping taxis to get on our nerves. We hoped it was just an oddity peculiar to Piura as we didn't fancy putting up with them for a whole month.

There was one noticeable thing that hadn't changed, the national dish. It just so happened to be chicken and rice. There was one additional bonus that the menu offered - a new beer to try. After a month of drinking litre bottles of very good Ecuadorian Pilsner, we progressed onto one of Peru's locally brewed beers. We were pleased to discover in Peru, we could sample a different beer in every region. The beers are imaginatively named after the town they are brewed in, so, with a bottle of *Piura* in hand we tried to work out how much we had just paid for our chips and beer. How many dollars in a pound, how many sols in a dollar, how many pounds to a sol? The joys of a new currency.

It took us most of the following morning to sort out how the bus system worked so that we could leave town for our next stop, Trujillo. Not having a central bus station meant that we had no way of knowing where to catch a bus from. The hostel staff were useless, the tourist information office was closed and our Rough Guide was hopelessly out of date. Eventually, we found a bus company (just around the corner from our hostel) who ran a service to Trujillo, but their one-bus-a-day was sold out for the next few days. We were so used to being able to jump on a bus anytime we wanted to in Ecuador. It hadn't occurred to us that we might need to consider booking a seat in advance. Our travel plans for Peru were quite simple – get to the Cusco, via Huaraz and Lima, as soon as possible so we could spend a leisurely three weeks in Cusco, Arequipa and Lake Titicaca. At this rate it was going to take at least three weeks to reach Cusco.

We stood out on the street, trying to make up our minds as to what we were going to do. An endless stream of hooting taxis didn't help our stress levels. The more we tried to ignore them, the more we could hear their incessant and inane beeping. They tried to get our attention even if we just wanted to cross the road. Stopping on a street corner, to work out where we were, was fatal. Not only that, but they hooted at us even if they already had passengers in the car.

Finally, we worked out we could get a bus to take us half way to Trujillo, to Chiclayo, and they left every hour. We thought it odd that no one suggested that we split the journey up. When we came to catch a taxi to take us out to the bus depot, which just so happened to be conveniently located at the opposite end of town, we had great delight in specifically selecting the one taxi driver that didn't beep at us.

At the bus station we had to book our luggage in, as if we were flying somewhere. Unlike Ecuador, there was going to be no slinging the rucksacks on the roof with the hope that they would arrive at our destination intact. Peru was far more organised and had progressed onto a cloakroom type system for handling the baggage. Each bag had a numbered tag stapled to the straps, and a corresponding ticket was given to us as a receipt. In theory, we would be able to exchange our ticket for our own rucksack at the other end.

When we handed the money over for our fare, we were allocated a seat, and when we sat down in our seat the conductor came around and ticked us off a register. It was totally different to the bus system in Ecuador and it all felt a bit alien. The strangest phenomenon was the fact that the bus left the depot bang on time. Nobody stood or sat in the aisle, there were a few empty seats, no touting from the front door and, to our disappointment, no vendors. All these little Ecuadorian peculiarities had made travelling on the bus fun and we missed them.

Vicky Brewis & Caius Simmons

# Colonic Irritation

The scenery in Northern Peru was totally different to what we had seen so far. Only the previous day, we had been driving through the high Andean mountains along windy, treacherous roads. In complete contrast, the Peruvian countryside was like being in the middle of a flat desert, not a mountain in sight and surrounded by a dry and barren wasteland. A very narrow strip of this desert like landscape hugs Peru's coast for hundreds of miles, reaching down into Northern Chile and beyond.

Despite all the engine fumes, and dust blowing in from the open windows, we found it a lot easier to breathe. Being so close to sea level, the air was thick with oxygen, and it didn't feel like something, or someone, was leaning against our ribcages every time we breathed.

Arriving in Chiclayo, our half way town, we got off the bus, booked straight on to another, and left immediately. It took us only seven hours to get from Piura to Trujillo, Peru's third city (after Lima and Arequipa) - the same time it would have taken us if we had caught a direct bus service. We were extremely pleased with ourselves for beating the system, but it made us realise that travelling around Peru was not as straightforward as it was in Ecuador. Unfortunately, we would no longer be able to walk down to the bus station and get straight onto the bus we wanted to catch. Forward planning was needed, and this also meant learning a new repertoire of phrases so we could book bus tickets in advance.

The name of the hostel we booked into in Trujillo, the *Hostal Colón*, should have made us realise it was a bit of a shit hole. It soon dawned on us that our guidebook was horrifically out of date and what was once, "A pleasant place with simple rooms" was now, "A piss hole of a place with shabby rooms". Our room stank of damp, the water soaking through from the shower room next door pouring down the black mouldy walls. The thought occurred to us that we could have just walked out and gone somewhere else, but the hostel further down the road hadn't looked much better.

As we were booking in we noticed a young Peruvian couple come in, giggling and laughing. We thought it odd that they didn't have any luggage with them, but they had definitely booked in because the woman behind the counter handed them their quota of toilet paper. We saw them leaving a few hours later, with stupid grins across their faces. Not only were we staying in a complete shit hole, but it was the local knocking shop too.

To make up for our dire accommodation we treated ourselves to a night out at the cinema. The only film showing in English was *Charlies Angels 2*, (with Spanish subtitles). We had been told quite a few stories of travellers going into watch a film, only to find out it was in Spanish and they didn't have a clue what was going on. The usher must of thought us a bit strange when we asked her about four times if the film was definitely going to be in English.

The screen was slightly elongated, making it appear squashed, which in turn made the cast look short and fat. Caius was hoping it would make the Angels a bit more 'buxom', but much to his disappointment it didn't really work. What made the film more amusing was listening to the locals roar with laughter at the not very funny bits. The volume was so loud it distorted the sound through the speakers so when the loud action bits were going on we couldn't work out was being said. We felt sorry for the people reading the Spanish subtitles, because you couldn't really read them properly because they were written in white, which just so happened to be the colour of the background for large sections of the film.

The two stars we awarded the film, put it in our "crap" category. We actually upgraded it from a one star, "total shite", category, just because we were happy to be entertained in English.

Back at the stinking pit of a hotel, the room smelt worse, and even the bed felt really damp. We sprayed our insect repellent around the room to try and improve the stench of rotting walls. It was definitely a sleeping bag liner night. We had brought them with us for when it got really cold at night, but the only times we used them was if the sheets on the beds were really grotty. The last bed that justified their use had been at the Ingapirca. By our calculations, on average, we would end up staying in a shit hostel every two weeks. Admittedly, this was much better than we first thought as we had the idea that all of the accommodation would be poor quality.

As we lay in bed all we could hear was "beep, beep, beep, beep". Bloody taxis.

At 2 o'clock in the morning a cockerel, that happened to be sitting outside our window, decided it was time for everyone to get up. After about an hour he stopped. By this time we were wide-awake, and rather than counting sheep to get back to sleep, we counted taxi beeps out on the street. We timed the silence between beeps, working out that the average length of peace and quiet was two seconds. It was three in the morning, the town was deserted and the taxi drivers could think of nothing better to do but beep their horns – aaaargh.

One of our main aims once we arrived in Trujillo was to get out of the place as quickly as possible. From what we had seen of the Northern Peruvian lowlands we weren't wildly impressed and couldn't wait to get out of town to head back into the mountains. Unfortunately for us, being 28 July, it was Peru's National Independence Day (from Spain, 1821) and meant that a four-day long holiday was about to begin. We read the guidebook with despair, as it advised not to try and bother to travel over the period as Peruvians take the opportunity of a holiday very seriously. They especially liked to go to the mountains, in fact to Huaraz, the same place we were headed to.

It was Saturday and we had left it a bit late to try and travel anywhere. We decided it would be like trying to get a train on Good Friday, back at home, a journey that should be avoided at all costs. After trawling around all the different bus companies, we finally found a night bus that left the following evening. Result. It was not ideal as we really wanted to see the view of the mountains on the way up, but at least we were getting out of town. Night buses were popular, especially for the longer journeys because it meant the locals could avoid paying for an extra nights accommodation. We also discovered that, like Britain, the cost of travel on Bank Holidays is extortionate with prices becoming heavily inflated.

Trujillo had come highly recommended from various guidebooks and other travellers we had met. "You must go", they raved, "There is loads to do and plenty of interesting archaeological sites and beautiful buildings". They were right. The city does have many graceful old churches, and colonial buildings with grand balconies and windows, all of which were pleasing to the eye, but it was not the sort of place we felt we could relax in. We were touted endlessly, mostly by taxi drivers and men on street corners wanting to exchange US Dollars into Sols. Beggars on the street thrusted their hands at us expectantly, the streets were busy and smelly, and we never really felt very welcome or safe. An English girl we met had been verbally abused several times in the couple of hours she had been in Trujillo. This was definitely one advantage of not speaking the language, which was, we didn't know if we were being insulted.

After having made a special effort to visit the town we thought the least we should do was check out some of the archaeological sights for which Trujillo is famed. There was only one problem – we needed to catch a 'beeping' taxi.

Within seconds of putting our arm out, a taxi pulled up beside us. We asked "Quanto Es" (how much?)

"20 sols", the driver replied expectantly.

"Es muy caro" (it is very expensive). No bloody chance is what we were really thinking.

"15 sols", was his response

It worked, shall we try it again. There are plenty of other cabs to choose from if he says no, "Demasiado" (too much).

"10 sols", he said, still smiling.

"That's more like it, shall we get in.  Yes, why not", we said to each other.  We didn't fancy walking all the way across town for the third time in one day to catch a bus.

Sensing our hesitation, he said, "6 sols".

Fine, silly bugger, we were quite happy with paying 10.  Jumping in, we couldn't help but smile to ourselves.  This was more like it.  In Ecuador we had never managed to barter a taxi fare down once.

The Chan Chan site was miles out of town and it took about 20 minutes to get there.  Our trust for taxi drivers was not very high, especially as we had knocked the price down so much.  Images sprang to our minds of being taken down a dodgy road and being mugged.  With a slight sense of relief, we were dropped at the site, feeling a tiny bit bad having doubted his integrity and that our fare would have just about paid for the petrol.  Then we remembered that he had probably kept us awake the previous night, and forgot to give him a tip

Chan Chan was the capital of the Chimu Empire, which was the largest urban civilisation of its kind in pre-Colombian America.  The Chimu society reached its pinnacle in the 15th century, just before the Incas turned up on the scene.  In fact, the Chimu Empire was so powerful and resilient that the Incas only managed to take control of their territory 60 years prior to the Spanish turning up.

Archaeologists are continually unearthing new sections of the huge adobe city which, over time, has become buried beneath the desert.  The city centre consists of many elaborate flat-roofed buildings where the nobility would have lived, surrounded by beautiful ornate temples.  After nearly a 1000 years, the mud walls still show signs of intricately decorated markings, with criss-cross diamond-shaped lattices, geometric and animal designs adorning most buildings.

Unfortunately, the mud walls are very prone to weathering, especially from wind and rain.  The Peruvian Pacific coast is the home of the notorious El Niño current (named after the Christ-child, because of its tendency to appear during the Christmas period).  The impact of El Niño affects the climate worldwide, and usually leads to torrential rain and flooding along this desert coastline. Although the rain is not very frequent, when it does arrive it has a devastating effect on the fragile adobe structures and details. The rain has ruined large sections of the site.

The ruins of Chan Chan were impressive, and we felt that our visit to Trujillo had been worthwhile.

According to our guidebook there were a few other adobe structures to visit. We consulted the map and decided that one of them was just up the road from Chan Chan and was well within walking distance. The book and map didn't describe the area we needed to walk through and there was nothing to suggest it wasn't safe. The first indication of what the area was like was the graffiti and large murals sprayed onto the front of shops and houses. Pictures of cockerels suggested cock fighting was popular. Our suspicions were confirmed when we met two young lads carrying battered and cut up cockerels. We hoped one of them was the cockerel that lived outside our hotel room.

The locals all stopped and stared at us, and didn't make any effort to move over when we walked past them. It was not the friendliest of neighbourhoods and we wished we had caught a taxi or bus. Eventually we arrived at the archaeological site, which was right in the middle of a housing estate. It was interesting, but not worth the walk, or the nagging doubts that we might have been beaten up

We bumped into a couple of American girls we had met in Vilcabamba. Like us, their plans had also been scuppered by the public holidays and they were stuck in Trujillo waiting for a bus to take them to Lima. They seemed to think that Trujillo was great and weren't too bothered about having to spend a couple of extra days in the town. When we enquired which hostel they were staying in, it transpired they weren't actually in the centre of Trujillo, but staying in the beach resort of Huanchaco.

It was then that we decided we'd had enough of the heat, dust and archaeological sites and decided to give the ruined temples on the other side of town a miss in favour of going to the beach.

Vicky Brewis & Caius Simmons

When we arrived in Huanchaco, we realised why everyone had been raving about Trujillo. They had obviously not been staying in the city centre, but at a really nice, clean, friendly and picturesque beach resort with good seafood restaurants and decent accommodation. What the hell were we doing staying in the centre of a polluted town in a brothel when we could stay at a beach resort in a comfortable hostel? Unfortunately, the hostels were either all full, or only wanted bookings for 3 nights or more, because of the holiday. We were stuck with Hostal 'lower intestine leading to rectum' at night, but at least we had found somewhere nice to spend the day.

Huanchaco is a friendly fishing village, with a huge sandy beach, stretching for miles, and a great spot for surfing. The surf was excellent, with cool dudes travelling the breaking waves along the whole length of the beach. We sat in the sun and watched holidaymakers having surfing lessons on dry land – bizarre, but very amusing. They probably didn't look quite as odd as we did in our walking boots and trousers, sat on the beach in the burning heat of the midday sun, while they were able to cool off in the clear blue ocean waters after their lesson.

The fishermen of the village still use the traditional, handmade totora reed boats. The design of these curved, peapod-shaped boats has changed little from those used by pre-Inca fishing tribes and there was obviously a technique to manoeuvring them without drowning. These boats are called caballitos (little horses) because of the way they are ridden, the fishermen straddling them rather like a surfer would while waiting for the next set to arrive. A couple of tourists entertained us as they struggled to get past the breaking waves, their hired caballitos being swamped by the endless rollers. They soon gave up, totally exhausted and drenched.

The fisherman had been out that morning and bucket loads of fish, crabs and shellfish were being sorted and sold along the beach.

One of the culinary specialities of South America is *ceviche*, raw fish and seafood marinated in onions, chilli, garlic and lemon or limejuice. Being on the coast, we decided that it would be one of the safer places to try it, rather than

96

high up in the mountains where we would not know how fresh the fish would be. The touts outside the restaurants were out in force, and became chums with Caius because he was wearing a Billabong sweatshirt and they kept shouting comments at him, like, "Hey dude, we love surfing, do you?".

We picked our restaurant, and chose our *ceviche* - one normal and a mixed shellfish one. The mixed dish consisted of raw shrimp, mussels, oysters, lobster, octopus and a shellfish with a green phlegm coloured centre. We closed our eyes as we tucked in. The taste made up for its presentation, and soon our plates and beer bottles were empty, except, of course, for the lettuce leaves. There was no way we were going to risk eating the salad just in case it had been washed in tap water and might make us ill. We were not convinced that eating *ceviche* was a good move and planned the rest of the day around being close to public conveniences just in case.

The taxi driver who took us out to the bus depot did not understand our Spanish so we showed him a map, pointing at where we wanted to go. "Si, si", he nodded happily and drove off at high speed. We smiled. Thank goodness pointing is an international language understood by everyone. It did not take long for our smiles to fade. Even though we did not know the city as well as the driver did, having a good sense of direction, we felt we were going the wrong way. After about 10 minutes the driver stopped to consult the map again. It turned out we were at the furthest point possible from our intended destination. As we drove back the opposite way he explained he did not have his glasses on, and could not see the map properly. This was not very reassuring as he swerved in and out of the traffic, beeping as he went.

Our guidebook outlined the risks of travelling on certain routes, where buses had often been stopped and ransacked by Sendero Luminoso (Shining Path) rebels. We hoped this information was as out of date as the rest of the guidebook. Even though the road to Huaraz (pronounced a bit like "your ass") was a little way from the problem region we were still a little bit nervous about travelling at night. It was our first night bus and we didn't really know what to expect. Our nerves were shaken further when the conductor came around with a camcorder and videoed everyone on the bus. Did they know something we didn't? The bus was then boarded by 4-armed police officers, in full body armour, and took the seats directly behind us. Our imaginations worked on over time, planning what we would do if there were a shoot-out between the police and the rebels. Luckily we were able to relax a bit more when the guards got off a few hours later at a checkpoint.

# Up Huaraz

We arrived in Huaraz at the same time as the first glow of daylight crept over the mountains. We sleepily watched the sun cover the snow-capped peaks, towering high above the town, with a scarlet glow. Set at an altitude of over 3000m, wedged between the two mountain chains of the Cordillera Negra (black mountains) and the permanently snow capped peaks of the Cordliera Blanca, Huaraz has been nicknamed the 'Switzerland of Peru'. Unfortunately, we were too knackered to really appreciate the stunning sunrise.

There was no way we wanted to stay in another complete shit hole of a brothel like the hostel in Trujillo so we had phoned ahead to ensure we got booked into a decent hostel. As all the buses had been fully booked, we reasoned that the accommodation would be to. We arrived at *Jo's Place* the same time as a couple of other tourists. They looked totally despondent when they were turned away in favour of us. All pleased and smug with ourselves, we fell into bed and within seconds we were asleep.

A night bus sounds like a good idea but it was so uncomfortable we only managed to get a few hours of sleep. We were so tired that we didn't even notice that the bed squeaked – it was so bad that every small breath was enough to make the springs groan. After a few hours, the squeak became unbearable so we took the mattress off to try and sort it out. We were obviously not the first people to have done this because there were extra pieces of wood nailed underneath, bits of paper stuck in the joints and cardboard spread over the boards in an attempt to stop the racket. It was a small price to pay, though, to stay in a nice hostel. At least it wasn't damp and, more importantly, we couldn't hear any hooting taxis.

Not surprisingly the owner of the hostel is called Jo, a Brit who moved to Huaraz to hike, climb and set up a hostel with his Peruvian wife. The common room was full of photos of them both grinning and looking extremely cold and tired on the top of various mountain summits. Whether you wanted to go climbing, trekking, catch a bus up to the next town, or just do a couple of day walks, like ourselves, Jo had all the information we needed.

From Huaraz, you can count 20 snow-capped peaks over 5000m asl, of which the most notable is Huascarán (6,768m), the highest mountain in Peru. We couldn't see all of the mountains from the hostel rooftop, but the views across to the Cordeleria Blanca were totally hypnotising all the same. At whatever time of day, but especially at sunrise and sunset, they looked magnificent and we could see why people were taken with the urge to climb them.

The hostel (and all the other hostels in Huaraz) was full of teenagers who were taking part in Team Challenge. After spending a week in the jungle and a week on the coast, they were preparing for their ultimate challenge, a community project in a remote mountain village where they were going to build a bridge. We decided that we both obviously went to the wrong schools, because the only times we ever got to get out of the classroom was to do a shop survey or look at coastal defence systems. A trip to South America – no bloody chance. We also doubted that they realised how lucky they were to have been given such a fantastic opportunity. Their main concern, apart from helping sort out food, transport and equipment, was finding the soap. All we could hear from the showers were calls of, "Where's the soap?" or, "Pass me the soap". When they woke us up one morning at 6am, shouting for the soap, we had to stop ourselves from telling them where they could stick it – "up Huaraz!!!".

The town is a good base for exploring the surrounding mountain ranges and the main street is full of tour agencies offering guided mountain tours in the Cordilleras, mountain biking, white water rafting and trips to glacial lakes. With the hope of conquering a mountain, most people head to Huaraz to go climbing.

One of the other hostel guests, an Austrian, had just come back from an expedition to climb Huascarán. He hadn't quite made it to the top, but considering he hadn't really done much climbing before, getting to within 100 metres from the top was something to be proud of. And he was glad to be alive. Reading the newspaper, he had just heard the news of two Israeli climbers who had died attempting another nearby summit, Alpamayo. With this in mind we decided that a couple of local walks would be the extent of our activities in Huaraz.

It was tempting to wake up the 'soap boys' who had disturbed us the previous day, but thought better of it as we sneaked out at dawn. We needed to catch a *collectivo* to Llupa, a small village on the outskirts of Huaraz, where we could join a trail leading to a glacial lake.

Rather than use smaller buses, like we had done in Ecuador, for the shorter journeys in Peru we came to rely on *collectivos*. To refer to them as mini-buses would perhaps be a bit of an overstatement. *Collectivos* are more like converted delivery vans, similar to the mini-Bedford vans with the sliding side door, or like some of the large people carriers. In the UK they probably seat no more than eight people, but in Peru there are usually enough seats for about 15 people. Although, there didn't seem to be a limit on how many passengers they could carry, basically the more the merrier. We always ended up completely wedged in that there was never any need (or provision) for seatbelts. Because they had quite high roofs, standing room was available, but only really possible for kids and adults under 4ft 8in, i.e., a high proportion of Peruvians. The westerners had to be content with trying to ram their legs in behind the tightly packed seats.

There was no *collectivo* waiting at the designated bus stop / street corner, and we plucked up the courage to ask a loitering taxi driver where it was going to depart from. He tried to convince us that there were no buses to Llupa and we would have to pay his extortionate fare in order to get there. We figured that asking a taxi driver had not been the best person to advise us. Convinced there was a bus service to the village (because Jo had said so) we pestered someone else, who kindly pointed us in the right direction. The scheming bugger of a taxi driver hadn't had it in him to tell us that the *collectivo* left from the next block down, just a couple of hundred feet from where we had been standing.

Our bus ticket cost six times more than any of the other passengers and it felt like everyone was out to rip us off that morning. The price of the bus ticket wasn't going to break the bank, but their attitude towards tourists started to give us a nasty impression of how Peruvians operated. It seemed that some, but not all, were out to exploit tourists and if they could get away with it, so much the better. That's not to say it doesn't happen in the UK, but paying twice as much as you should for a pasty or parking in St Ives during the summer pisses us off as well. At least in the UK everyone is charged the same price.

The *collectivo* driver kicked us out at Llupa and we started walking up a small winding track towards the next village, Pitec. The path was surprisingly busy, with children running down to school, farmers moving donkeys and sheep, and women heading to the streams to wash clothes. As we walked up the hill, we were accompanied by stares and giggles from everyone we passed.

Seeing as our dirty washing bag had far exceeded the size of our clean clothes bag, and we had reached the 'recycling pants' stage, we didn't really have much option but to wear shorts. If being tall, white and blonde wasn't enough to attract attention to ourselves, wearing shorts made us stand out from the crowd even more. The village of Llupa obviously hadn't seen bare legs for some time, especially legs as white as ours. From their reaction we guessed that wearing shorts in winter was not the 'done thing' to do.

Further up the path, a small girl stopped us to ask the time. She looked very flustered and was obviously late for her class. Asking us the time was just her rouse to start begging for money, but she had chosen the wrong people to ask. Firstly, we didn't want to encourage begging. Secondly, we didn't have much change left after paying over the odds for our *collectivo*. And, finally, we were starting to get sick of people asking us for money. Only the day before, when we had gone for a walk to the viewpoint overlooking Huaraz, an old man

102

and his son had accosted us. Dressed in smart trousers, jackets and shoes, they approached us, hands extended and muttering Spanish at us. We had pretended we didn't understand that they wanted money, smiled at them and wished them an overly enthusiastic 'Buenos Dias'. Before they had realised what was going on we were half way down the hill.

The village of Pitec consisted of a couple of small huts and a car park. Because the bus only went as far as Llupa we hadn't even realised that the road went further. Small bus and truckloads had driven all the way to Pitec to drop off groups of organised tours. After having the track all to ourselves for most of the morning we were joined by about 50 new walkers.

Our pace was slow but steady. Because we had been walking for a while, we knew what our bodies could cope with at the high altitude, which was approaching 4000m asl. The fresh legs quickly overtook us, but they were the hares and we were the tortoises, and it didn't take us long to overtake them again. Up, up, up we walked.

The path at Llupa was lined with small fields, overgrown hedges and tall shady trees. As we walked further up past Pitec and onto the exposed hillside, the vegetation thinned, the trees became less frequent and more stunted, the grass became browner, the rocks increased in numbers, the path got steeper and the amount of oxygen slowly decreased.

We had to keep stopping for short rests and more water, but as soon as we got our breath back we were off again. With renewed oxygen in our blood and our lungs full of air, the first few minutes of walking felt fairly normal. It didn't take long to tire again and the desire to stop for another rest occupied our minds. We set ourselves goals, like walking to the next tree, or to a rock we could see at the top of a particularly steep section. As we climbed higher the gaps between each rest seemed to get further and further apart, when in reality they probably got closer together.

The last section of the path followed alongside a small waterfall and after scrambling up the path, clambering over cliff faces and rocks, we eventually arrived at a corrie lake (4465m asl) called Laguna Churrup. This was the highest altitude we had walked to (Cotopaxi didn't really count). Our legs and lungs were burning, and we were exhausted. We felt good at having made it all the way and somewhat smug, when, an hour later the other walkers arrived.

A large glaciated mountain rose up behind the lake, with a dusting of fresh snow covering its flanks. The sapphire blue lake looked almost inviting, its tropical colour tempting us to dive in. Vicky managed to drop our only piece of change into the lake and we watched the big silver coin catch the light as it floated just out of reach to the bottom of the lake. After dipping our toes into the icy waters we decided there was no chance of us going in to retrieve it. We could have easily sat by the lake soaking in the sunshine for the rest of the day, but it was going to be a long walk home because our *collectivo* fare back to Huaraz unfortunately lay at the bottom of the lake.

With each footstep we took back down the path, our lungs sucked in more oxygen, and walking became easier and easier. We tried to convince the people walking in the other direction that it wasn't far and to keep going. Three Austrian lads, struggling, gasping, spluttering and sweating profusely looked totally despondent when we told them how far they still had to walk before they reached the lake. They were on the edge of giving up and turning back and we took solace in the knowledge that we had not been quite in the same state as them on our way up. A little further down the mountain we met three Austrian girls, who were looking quite tired, but laughing and having fun. They too were depressed when we informed them they still had about an hour to go, but their spirits lifted when they heard their boyfriends were not far ahead and in a terrible state. They set off, with even bigger smiles on their faces, determined they were going to get there before the boys.

Huaraz is obviously the place to go for volunteering work in Peru. Back in Llupa we met a girl who was helping to teach at the village school. The conversation turned to the heat of the sun and the fact that we had been piling on the factor 30 to make sure we didn't burn. She told us the kids in school had been a little bit confused by this concept and thought that if they put suntan cream on it would make their skin go whiter!!

Waiting at the bus stop were a group of volunteers from England. They were with an organisation called madventure.com, a relatively new voluntary organisation, based in Newcastle-upon-Tyne. It offers gap year opportunities to students and people taking a career break. Volunteers are able to combine helping a local community with a trip abroad. This group were building a very wonky looking wall outside the village school. Considering most of Huaraz was flattened by an earthquake in 1970, it was unlikely that their wall was ever going to survive even the smallest of earth tremors.

Luckily the volunteers believed our pathetic story about dropping our bus money in the lake, and we negotiated a small loan to pay for our fare (about a pound). Having been in Llupa for a couple of months they 'knew' the *collectivo* driver. Rather than charge them six times the fare, they got a special rate because they were helping out at the school. This was still three times what the locals paid.

As we drove into town, we pointed out all the houses with a red and white Peruvian flags, or bunches of flowers hoisted on a pole outside the front door. We thought it was to do with the Independence Day celebrations, but one of the volunteers explained that they were watering holes, and the flags meant the houses were open to anyone who fancied a pint of Chica, a fermented native maize beer.

# **Smelly Lima**

After our bus journey to Huaraz we were determined not to travel by night again unless we really had to. Everyone we met told us about the fantastic scenery and we didn't want to miss out on seeing the mountains for a second time.

We were bound for Lima, the capital of Peru. To be more accurate we were heading for Lima airport so we would catch a plane for Cusco. What we really wanted to do was to catch the train from Lima to Huancayo on the world's highest passenger railway line and then bus it to Cusco.

We had read that the train has to negotiate 9 switchbacks, go over 61 bridges, through 68 tunnels, runs over 298 km of tracks and reaches a height of 4,843m asl. An investment of $35 Million by the World Bank in 1995 planned to get a regular passenger service up and running again, instead of the train just transporting freight. It was probably not the best $35 Million the World Bank has ever invested. Four years later the service was suspended following a strike when the strikers ripped large sections of the line out. Although the trains have resumed, we could hardly call the one-day a month trip, "A regular service". Unfortunately we didn't really have the time to wait three weeks for the next train. We weighed up the other options: 22 hours on a bus which went through the Shining Path territory notorious for armed bus robberies and hijacking or, a one hour flight over the Andes. We felt we were cheating a bit, but after staying longer in Northern Peru than we originally planned, we didn't want to spend a whole day sitting on a bus and opted for the plane from Lima.

Our bus headed out of Huaraz and onto the vast, arid, empty plain that lies between the mountain ranges of the Cordillera Blanca and the Cordillera

Negra. In Ecuador, this central valley, which is filled with sediments from the surrounding mountains, had been highly populated and heavily cultivated. At much higher altitudes this enclosed valley is referred to as the Altiplano, literally meaning, 'high plain' and unlike Ecuador there wasn't a village or a potato to be seen.

We wondered if we could see the mountain, Siula Grande, where climbers Joe Simpson and Simon Yates made their perilous and disastrous ascent of the formidable peak. Along with Bruce Chatwin's, *In Patagonia*, and numerous copies of Harry Potter, Joe Simpson's book *Touching the Void* was among the most popular books we had found in the hostel and café book exchanges.

Leaving behind the chains of snow capped mountains we cut across the Cordillera Negra and headed west back to the coast. For over two hours the bus wound its way down a deeply cut valley. We sat glued to the window watching the scenery change with every switchback. Instead of getting greener as we headed towards the coast it became drier and drier. The mountain faces were bare rock, incapable of supporting anything apart from a few cacti. Contrasting with the sandy rocks and the bright blue sky were the green trees and crops that were growing close to the river bed. It was more of a small stream rather than a river and beyond the narrow floodplain it was back to rocks, cacti and dust. A few flowers in a garden and piles of bright red, green, purple, yellow and orange peppers drying in the sun were the only thing to remind us that colour existed in this bare landscape.

The mountains and rocks ended abruptly and we were suddenly on the coastal desert. The bus driver decided that one of the nice looking villages dotted along the side of the river wasn't good enough to stop at for lunch and he chose a really grubby, piss smelling truck stop instead. He locked us out of the bus for an hour so he could eat his free lunch. Along with the rest of the passengers we huddled up behind the bus to avoid being covered in dust that was being spewed up from the Pan-American.

For the remainder of the journey we kept getting tantalising glimpses of the sea. The road crossed the desert, occasionally travelling along a narrow road that had been cut into the huge coastal sand dunes. Rising above us was the massive slope of the dune. Below us, beyond the steep cliff, was the longest beach, and waves, we had ever seen. The desert gave way to rubbish tips and then into the overflowing shantytown settlements on the outskirts of Lima. The shabby corrugated buildings, burnt out cars, smog, piles of rubbish, dirt and obvious poverty were a sobering sight.

Crawling through the traffic clogged roads we reached the centre of the city. Views of grand government buildings, impressive churches and grand squares were not enough to tempt us to extend our stay. We were relieved to think that we had only 12 hours to spend in Lima, and most of that time would be spent asleep. We are the first ones to admit we were being chickens, but we are chickens that prefer to be roaming around the countryside rather than cooped up in a cage with hundreds of other chickens.

The hostel we stayed in was stuck in the middle of a quiet housing district, away from the main tourist areas. Not all the stories we had heard about Lima were bad, but they weren't that good either. It was late when we arrived and we didn't fancy exploring Lima in the dark. Eventually though we had to step out of the safety of the hostel into the dark streets and walked a couple of blocks in search of food. Pizza Hut was our only option. We didn't care - at least it wasn't Macdonalds. Still hungry after our extremely expensive, measly pizza we returned to the hostel to watch Manchester United hammer Juventus (4 – 0).

Okay, so we hadn't really given Lima the benefit of the doubt, but we didn't really care. We were heading to Cusco, and that meant we would be going to Machu Picchu. The best view we had of Lima was undoubtedly from the plane window, but even better were the spectacular views of the Andes. All the passengers sat in silence, mesmerized by snow capped peaks, which seemed close enough to touch.

# Cusco – Inca Capital

The city of Cusco sits in a beautiful setting in the Andean mountains, at an altitude of 3400m asl, a height that left many fellow passengers breathless as they stepped of the plane. As we were waiting for our bags we were serenaded by a bunch of poncho clad pan pipers, hands fully extended while they played. Touts quickly descended on us like a swarm of bees. Even after saying "no", we still managed to find ourselves sitting next to a tout in our taxi who pointed out sights of interest as we headed towards the centre of town. We engaged ourselves in a long and boring conversation about the weather, not giving him a chance to get a word in edgeways. Desperate for an opportunity to give us his sales pitch, he hovered around as we were booking into our hotel. Eventually collaring us, he tried to flog us a tour on the Inca trail, a bus trip through the Sacred Valley and a visit to the jungle. We were trying to enjoy our first cup of coca tea (a pile of leaves in a cup filled with boiling water – it smelt rank but did not taste too bad), and the last thing we wanted to do was think about what trips we wanted to go on. Eventually our tout got bored, storming off in a huff and back to the airport to await the next flight arrival.

We arrived in Cusco at the worst possible time of year, when the streets, hotels and museums were full of Americans and Europeans, mostly on large guided tours. These were the first tourists, rather than travellers, we had really seen for weeks. With so many tourists around, the chances of us bumping into someone we knew was quite high. The closest we got to a 'coincidence' encounter was not the usual story of meeting a sisters house mate, or a work colleague that knows one of your old school friends, but more the fact that we lived in the same town. It was enough of a 'coincidence' to start a conversation with Nicky and Caroline while we were having a drink in a really hideous English style pub – The Cross Keys. The pub sold European and American beers, but we didn't think the Guinness would have travelled well and kept to the local beer, Cusquenan, instead. Mounted on the walls were photos from the UK, Premiership football scarves and a large wide screen TV showing sport highlights. They even had pool tables and served roast dinners. We could see why it was so popular.

Nicky and Caroline had been working in a local orphanage for a few days, had squeezed in a trip to Machu Picchu and were busy trying to sort out a trip to the jungle. An organised tour was too expensive for their budget, but as they walked out through the tour agency door a jungle guide walked in and told them if they made it to a specified meeting point he would show them around for the fraction of the cost. Their rendezvous point was right in the middle of the jungle, which involved catching a bus, then a truck and a couple of boats to get there on a specified day. When they told us their plans we were not entirely convinced, but with a clink of glasses we wished them the best of luck all the same.

We also bumped into Sherri and Brett, (from the Galapagos) who had just returned from a trip into the jungle. It just so happened to be Brett's 32nd birthday as well, so any excuse for another beer to catch up on all their travel stories. They had just got back from the Manu National Park, famed for its bird life and diversity of wildlife. Over 1,000 different species have been recorded in the Park. The bus journey from Cusco into the Amazon basin took several days and sounded absolutely horrendous. When they got there they didn't see many birds because of the density of the vegetation. Brett was still managing to take over 100 photos a day on his supersonic digital camera, claiming that most of the pictures were rubbish. They looked pretty impressive to us and we really hoped that even one of our photos would come out as half as decent as theirs.

They were a bit disappointed with their jungle trip and really wanted to fly to Puerto Maldonado to visit a shaman and hopefully see some better wildlife. Fate was not with them and they were unable to get a flight for over three weeks. We hoped the DIY Shaman kit (coca leaves, dream-catchers and a couple of coloured beads) we had bought Brett for his birthday made up for missing a shamanic ceremony. It was probably a good omen that they didn't go because both of them had also picked up a particularly bad bug from their jungle expedition. Something to do with drinking the dodgy water from the river they reckoned.

We left Sherri and Brett to go to a posh restaurant alone to eat cuy (or guinea pig). Peru is the home of the guinea pig, and has been reared as a food animal by the Andean folk for thousands of years. It was fitting that they were to try it on Brett's birthday, as cuy is generally eaten on special occasions. Inspired by some really nice chicken and bean stews we had tasted we were tempted to give it a go, but the temptation didn't last long. We had seen cuy being cooked on market stalls and in restaurant windows and it reminded us of road kill, complete with head and splayed legs. We had also been put off by the many travellers who had tried it, at great expense (about $10 each in Cusco), and had told us there was not much meat in a cuy and consisted of nothing more than a deep-fried bag of bones, spread-eagle style across a large plate, together with rice and fries. Its flavour is said to be like that of rabbit or pheasant or chicken, no one seemed entirely sure, but it was still not as nice as any of these. Sherri and Brett later informed us it had been OK, but after drinking one too many beers they couldn't really place the flavour precisely.

It is impossible to walk 10 metres through the streets of Cusco without being hassled by someone. It is a real shame as it ruins the ambiance of the place. We were constantly harassed by street vendors to buy postcards, chocolates or fags, have a shoeshine, or take a taxi ride – the touts would not take "no" or "fuck off" for an answer. We wanted to shout at them all, but most of them were just kids who were trying to earn a meagre living. The most frustrating ones were the deaf people, who could not hear you say "no" and would hang around while we ate, loitering at the end of the table, with their hands limply extended and a pathetic look upon their faces.

As time went on, our boots got dustier and dustier, and we were attracting the attention of more and more shoe shiners. Young boys seemed to appear from every side street, shouting a very bored, "Shoeshine" as they spotted even the smallest speck of dirt on your shoes. We would reply, "no gracias" and they would reply, "only one sol, shoeshine" again. This dialogue would go on a few more times, round and round in circles, until they got bored and left. They appeared to work in teams and as soon as one walked away another quickly replaced them, "Shoeshine mister?"

"No gracias".

"Only one sol, shoeshine?"

"No gracias".

"OK, shoeshine?"

Aaargh. After a while we ended up giving in and at one stage Caius had one boy cleaning a shoe each, surrounded by a dozen more of them who were desperate to clean his shoes again when the other two had finished polishing.

We experienced a new pest that we had encountered before, but not to such a great extent - restaurant touts. They were ten times worse than those that you find in Europe hanging outside the doors, thrusting menus into your hands. Nothing would deter this new strain of super pest, and they even chased tourists down the streets. It amazed us why they had not learnt that British (and probably most Europeans and Americans) hate being hassled. We prefer to be left alone to look at the menu displayed outside to try and get a feel of the restaurant before making our decision. It was no great surprise that the busiest restaurants, as well as having the best reputation for good food, did not have touts hanging outside the entrance. One evening, after having looked at the menu in peace, we decided to go into the restaurant and we're bombarded from all directions by a bunch of touts from other restaurants, who literally tried pulling us away from the door. They really started getting on our nerves and we felt like punching them.

Cusco was stressful and after one afternoon of being there we were desperate to escape. The only thing that made our visit bearable was that it is such beautiful city.

Vicky Brewis & Caius Simmons

# Inca

The Incas adopted Cusco as its sacred capital in AD 1438, giving it the name Qosqo, meaning 'bellybutton' or 'navel of the world'. Its rise in popularity as an important centre coincided with the emperor Pachacuti coming to power, at a time when the Incas were really making themselves known throughout South America.

Even though the Incas were around for over 300 years, the mark they made on the history books was only really during the last 100 years of these. Prior to the Inca Empire, it was different cultures that dominated society - the Moche, Nazca and Tiahuanuc. Each culture was characterised by their architecture, ceramics, jewellery or textiles, which are marked with their specific symbols and patterns. These cultures coexisted simultaneously for hundreds of years, usually peacefully, but in later years the Tiahuanuco culture became particularly dominant throughout most of Peru. Various tribes developed within these cultures and internal war faring soon caused the Tiahuanuco culture to slowly disappear. It was replaced by a number of small empires along the coast, the most notable being the Chimu who constructed the Chan Chan complex near Trujillo. Inland, three tribes developed, including the Incas who, under the rule of Manco Capac established themselves at Cusco around AD1200. It took the Incas over 200 years to develop from a large tribal unit into an Empire.

Once established, the Inca Empire quickly became the largest and most powerful ever witnessed in South America. The name Inca originally applied only to the Emperor, but nowadays refers to the whole nation of some 20 million Indians. At their peak, the Incas ruled over territory stretching 5500km from southern Colombia to the Maule River in central Chile, and eastwards as far as the fringes of the Amazon Basin.

Many aspects of the organisation and structure of Inca society were inherited from previous cultures. Using the existing cultures and tribes, utilising buildings and towns, the Incans developed on what was already there. That's not to say the Inca's relied totally on what had been before them and they set about constructing huge fortresses, urban and agricultural centres and temples.

The Incas have become world famous for their impressive architecture. They developed a system of carving massive, multi-angled stone blocks with remarkable precision. The stone used was often very hard igneous rock, like granite, which is particularly difficult to cut. Although these blocks are all irregularly shaped, they interlock perfectly. The walls were designed to withstand the considerable seismic activity common in the Andes.

Wandering around the city centre we caught glimpses of this famous Inca legacy - cobbled streets lined with the remains of the exquisite Inca architecture. In many cases more modern buildings had been constructed right on top, and next to the Incan stonewalls.

When the Spanish arrived in Peru in 1526, under the command of Francisco Pizzaro, it heralded the demise of the Incan Empire. Impressed by the extensive mineral deposits of the Inca Empire, Pizzaro sailed back to Spain to recruit an army of fortune hunters. The Inca were warriors, with a strong and powerful army but they were no match for the 160 Spanish guns Pizzaro had enlisted and they quickly crushed a 40,000 strong Inca force.

In 1532, the Inca leader, Atahualpa was ambushed and held for ransom, but even 20 tons of silver and gold failed to buy the release of the captured Inca leader. In 1533 Atahualpa was 'tried' and executed. By 1535, the Inca society was completely overthrown. In the same year Pizzaro founded the city of Lima, which quickly replaced Cusco as the major economic centre for the Andean nations. The new Inca ruler Manco Inca managed to escape from Cusco with an army of 50,000 and held out until 1572 when the resistance ended with his capture and beheading after a failed rebellion. (Many people believe that Manco fled to Wales to buy a horse, ending his life *In-Caerphilly*).

In the process of defeating the Incas, the Spanish managed to dismantle most of the Incan temples, fortresses and fine buildings. The introduction of their own architectural ideas involved knocking down structures and using the stones for their new buildings, often just placing their new buildings on top of existing foundations.

This is no more apparent than at the church of Santo Domingo. Also known as Coricancha, it is a fine example of the Spanish culture imposing on Incan history. The church comprises of a wonderful courtyard, in the centre of which is an octagonal grey-stone coffer. Known as the Cusco Car Urumi (the Uncovered Naval Stone), it supposedly represented the centre of a field planted by the Incans with corn fashioned out of pure gold. The stone was particularly symbolic and had been surrounded by numerous Incan temples. The Spanish proceeded to build the church around it, plundering the 55kg of gold that once covered the stone. The Inca site was forgotten until an earthquake in 1951 that demolished the church, exposing the earthquake resistant Inca block foundations beneath it.

# Around Cusco

Cusco is not just all about the Incans. There are countless museums, colonial houses, churches, cathedrals and important structures that kept us occupied for a couple of days. An overdose of depressing religious art was enough to drive us out of Cusco in search of more ruins and rocks. We didn't have to go far to see even more Inca remains, many being on the outskirts of the city and the surrounding countryside. It also meant we could escape the shoeshine boys and restaurant touts for a few hours.

Sacsayhuaman (pronounced sexy woman) is a short, steep walk from Cusco, and discounting the slog up the hill it is probably one the easiest Inca sites to visit from the city centre. Some say the literal meaning of the name is *Satisfied Falcon* or *Speckled Head*, others call it the *City of Stone*. Its use, like its literal meaning, remains unsure.

The Sacsayhuaman site is dominated by a series of 3 parallel zigzag terraces, each terrace being 15 metres high and 300 metres wide across the hillside. The shape is thought to either signify the jagged teeth of a Puma or to symbolise lightening (again no one really knows). We decided that we would need a lot more coca leaves before we saw any puma teeth. Whatever they were supposed to represent, they were very impressive. Even looking at them from a distance it was difficult to get a view of the entire length of the terraces.

It is estimated that with ten to twenty thousand men continually mining, transporting stone and constructing the walls it would have taken about 100 years to build. It is not just the pure size of the site that impresses, but the way the gigantic lumps of granite fit together perfectly without the aid of any mortar. The stonework is truly amazing and it was literally impossible to slide our penknife blades in the gaps (probably because over the years, 1000s of people have filled any gaps with bits of paper and snapped penknife blades).

To give an idea of how massive these rocks are, many weigh about 200 tonnes and the largest, standing over 8 metres tall, weighs over 300 tonnes. The construction makes Stonehenge look like children's building blocks.

Destroyed by the Spanish, little remains of the buildings, and tourists and archaeologists alike are left to speculate what the function of the ruins were. Unfortunately the Incas had no written language and their history was passed down through the generations through word of mouth. Archaeologists have uncovered a number of knotted pieces of rope, which are believed to have been used as a system for recording information. How these worked has not been fully understood yet, so remains fairly useless as a method for unlocking some of the mystery associated with the Incas. Interestingly these braided knots are compared to the symbols used in Chinese writing. According to Gavin Menzie in his book *1421 The Year China Discovered the World*, and other associated research, it is suggested that the Chinese, in around 1422 AD, may have visited the Incas. It is therefore possible that in the future more information may be gathered about the Incas from ancient Chinese documentation and manuscripts.

It seemed that every place we visited was filled with speculation about when, what and who used the buildings/structures. The guidebook writers must make a fortune and get away with writing just about anything. A new book seems to be published every year, each with new and ground breaking theories.

One such place, where the guides can get away with saying what they please, is *Qenko* (meaning zigzag), a heavily eroded butte of limestone close to Sacsayhuaman. Believed to have been a religious shrine it has been carved inside to create a dome filled with caves, passageways, hidden rooms and seats. On the top of the dome deep narrow zigzag channels have been cut. Inca priests are thought to have poured chicha or animal blood down these channels during annual ceremonies (religion has a lot to answer for). Depending on which channel the blood went down determined the success of the harvest and the fortunes of the Inca people for the following year. We tried to figure out what all the carvings signified. In the end we resorted to eavesdropping on an English-speaking guide who was deciphering the lumps of rock and carvings as images of Llamas, Pumas and Condors. We were starting to think that the Incans spent most of their time taking mild hallucinogenic drugs, because what we saw was an eroded limestone rock with some bits carved out of it.

The Incas didn't just build fortresses and religious temples, but also a network of administrative centres, storehouses, way stations, baths and provincial cities. They also built 25,000 miles of stone-paved roads to link them all together. (Even though they built this extensive road network, they preferred to travel by river, *In-ca-noes*). A small journey further out of town took us to an Inca outdoor shower, Tambo Machay, and then to a hill top fort or hunting lodge, *Puka Pukara* both of which were built specifically for high nobility. Just because they didn't consist of massive walls or have some bizarre religious association, most of the guidebooks had written that they were not very interesting sites and we were able to enjoy them without being swamped with large tour groups.

The bus back down the hill cost us twice as much as it cost us on the way up – special 'Gringo Tax' again. The 'Gringo Tax', as we had come to call it, was the additional cost that South American business people add onto their goods and services especially for tourists. It is not a fixed amount, and varies from place to place, depending on the mood of the vendor. It is not restricted to market stalls and street vendors, but applies for all bus companies as well, in fact anywhere where a fixed price is not being advertised.

Shortly after we had arrived in Cusco we booked ourselves onto the Inca trail to Machu Picchu, but had to wait almost a week before our departure. The commercialism, and cost, of Cusco became really frustrating, and there was no way we would last until our departure date without seriously hurting a restaurant tout. It was the perfect opportunity for us to explore the local countryside and we decided to spend a few days in the Sacred Valley.

Known as Vilcamayo to the Incas, the Sacred Valley has the Rio Vilcanota-Urubamba as its central feature. The river flows through Urubamba, past Machu Picchu and down into the Jungle and the Amazon basin. The Sacred Valley only officially runs between the two Inca fortresses of Pisac and Ollantaytambo, an 80km section of the river scattered with traditional settlements and interesting sites.

Getting out of Cusco also meant we could grab a few days of rest and recuperation before starting our walk to Machu Picchu. Vicky had managed to pick up a cold from somewhere, and the warmer weather and lower altitude would be a welcome change from the cold air (and tight chests) in Cusco.

# The Sacred Valley

Still trying to get the hang of how the Peruvian bus system operated, it was a surprise for us when we turned up at the bus compound and had to queue to buy a ticket. Not only that, but the queue was quite orderly and civilised. Once all the seats were full, the bus company wouldn't let any more people on and we drove out of town with a respectable amount of leg room and no armpits or arses shoved in our faces.

As soon as we got out of town, the bus driver stopped at every possible opportunity to let more passengers on. Eventually the aisle was so full that the people at the back of the bus started screaming and shouting at the driver not to let anyone else board. They started getting quite aggressive and it was a good job there were about 20 people between themselves and the driver. We have to admit that the journey was extremely uncomfortable and we ended up sharing our seat with a small child and a sack containing a puppy that yapped all the way.

We considered stopping off at the village of Chinchero along the way to look at the market, but there was no way we could have made it to the door. Judging from the demonstrative mood from the back of the bus, the amount of time it would have taken us to get off may have led to a minor riot. So we sat tight, with child on knees, puppy yapping, face squashed against window and clutching a rucksack that we had somehow managed to inherit.

At Urubamba everyone detangled themselves out of the bus, leaving us standing in the middle of a dusty bus compound to figure out that we needed to walk all the way back to the other end of town to find some accommodation. There wasn't a lot to choose from, settling for a lovely little hostel which we had all to ourselves. The look of surprise on the hostel owners face made us wonder when they last had anyone staying with them. It was a nice place to chill out, with beautiful gardens where we sat and watched hummingbirds gorging on the blooming flowers.

Urubamba is a laid back village, especially after the bustle and stress of Cusco. We walked around freely without being accosted to buy postcards or get a shoeshine. There was certainly no chance of us being hassled by restaurant touts, because there weren't really any places to eat. Lining the main road were a few large restaurants, but spotting the coaches parked up outside we guessed that this was where the whistle stop Sacred Valley tours from Cusco stopped for lunch.

Town itself didn't really amount to very much, with a daily market, lots of bakeries, a few general store shops that always seemed to be closed, and a handful of small restaurants which were also shut most of the time. Considering the size of the town, there were an extraordinary number of hairdressers. They were also about the only shops we could guarantee would be open, especially on a Sunday night when they all appeared full.

The good thing about Urubamba was that there wasn't a huge amount to do there. It certainly wasn't the place to sort out our e-mails and although it boasted a couple of internet cafes in its list of facilities, it took us almost half an hour to send one message. We joined the locals in the central Plaza, with its palm trees and fountain (that has a large phallic maize corn as its centrepiece), and watched life go by while we ate ice creams. In the two days we spent there, we only noticed a few other tourists. For us, Urubamba was a great place to hang out while everyone else was back in Cusco dancing the night away. Having travelled for over 6 weeks, it amazed us still how we didn't have to make too much of an effort to get away from the crowds.

From Urubamba we caught a *collectivo* to Ollantaytambo, a few miles up the road. Famed for its extensive Inca terraces and ruined temple-fortress, Ollantaytambo marks the lowest end of the Sacred Valley. Whilst in use, its function is thought to have been an administrative centre, but following the

Spanish "invasion" it was also used as an Inca stronghold after the fall of Cusco in 1536.

The village itself could be referred to as 'quaint'. A high proportion of the buildings are built on huge granite Inca foundations, with the distinctive, closely-knit, stonework that we became accustomed to seeing. The layout of the village still retains characteristics inherited from the Incas, including the notion that if you look at it from the air it supposedly resembles a piece of maize. Although Ollantaytambo is quite small it is really geared up for the tourists and is full of extortionately priced cafés, restaurants and shops. It is the nearest village to the start of the Inca trail and it is also a popular place to catch the train from to go to Machu Picchu. The number of hostels far exceeded those in Urubamba, as did their costs.

A couple of minutes walk from the central plaza we were wowed by an incredible set of grand terraces. The tall stone terraces probably acted as protection from possible invasions, but their primary function was most likely to have been agricultural. Like huge steps, they led to a temple/fortress construction on the top. One of the amazing things about these ruins were the massive red granite megaliths that were located way up the hillside, about 80 metres from the level of the village. It looked like the Incas had grand ideas for Ollantaytambo and were in the process of building a temple before the Spanish scuppered their plans. The smoothly cut stone faces imply that the temple would have had a significant religious status - the rule of thumb being, the better the stonework, the more important the building was. The huge slabs, weighing at least 100 tonnes each, originated from a quarry about three miles from the village. It would have taken some manpower to move them, but the Incans weren't stupid and supposedly diverted the river to help them get the slabs across the valley. How they got them up the hillside to the top of the site was probably not so easy.

On reaching the top of the terraces we sat and enjoyed commanding views of the whole village and up the Sacred Valley. It was easy to distinguish the smaller terraces along the valley and hillsides, many of which are in very good condition and still in use. We didn't get a chance to visit the salt terraces, which are still used today, or the nearby experimental agricultural terraces that form an amphitheatre, but the terraces were enough to show us that this valley was important agriculturally. The Incans developed complex irrigation schemes, setting up drainage systems and canals to help expand their crop resources. The highland areas today produce little more than potatoes, wheat and maize, but the Incans added to this list tomatoes, cotton, peanuts and coca among the many crops they grew.

Perched high on the hillside opposite the fortress are even more ruins. Bearing in mind that prisons during the Incan rule were of no use because their punishment usually consisted of death, the theory that they were used as granaries rather than prisons is more feasible. In fact the Incas had a particularly violent punishment system. If someone stole, murdered, or had sex with a Sapa (high priest) wife or a Sun Virgin, they were either thrown off a cliff, hands cut off, eyes cut out, or hung up to starve to death. "*Ama Sua, Ama Quella, Ama Lulla*", "Don't lie, don't steal, don't be lazy" was the philosophy of the Inca Empire, where laziness was a capital offence punishable by death. Funnily enough, this excluded priests and royalty. This philosophy is still apparent and despite being very poor, begging on the streets was not a common a sight as we had expected. It seemed to be restricted to very old, wailing women, all of whom were totally ungrateful of any gifts of food or money.

Unemployment was non-existent during the Inca rule, everyone taking part in building roads, fortresses, temples, drainage and agricultural systems. Rather than paying taxes, each Inca citizen was required to spend 7 weeks in the service of their Lord. Back in the UK, the average person works at least 21 weeks of the year just to pay their basic taxes. It is also believed they were the first people to introduce an *Inca-pacity* benefit into society – boom, boom.

We clambered up the mountainside to try and reach the other ruins, but the main route was mostly impassable as most of it had slumped down the hillside many years ago.

Huge amounts of grain would have been collected from the along the valley and stored in these buildings. Kept well away from the river would prevent it from getting wet and being so far up the mountainside meant there was little chance of it being stolen either. From this point we could see back across the village and to the ruins, which looked even more imposing. Our guidebook suggested that the terracing formed the image of a mother llama, with one of its young. If we squinted hard enough we could make out some agricultural terraces with a fortress/temple on the top and came to the conclusion that the author may have been under the influence at the time. This theory was more than possible and our reasoning was not unfounded.

Whilst walking amongst the ruins we spotted a group of westerners sitting on a ledge. With them was a 'god like figure, dressed in white robes, with a big white beard. They were sitting in silence, puffing away on a pipe that was being passed around.

Later that day we met a lady who was on, what we called, a 'Magical, Mystery Tour'. She was with an organised trip, spending three weeks in Peru visiting shamans and getting in touch with nature and the Incan ideology. The Inca had many shamans who believed in animal spirits living on earth, where a condor depicted heaven, the underworld by an anaconda, and the brother who resided on earth was the puma. An American wife of a University Professor she seemed content with visiting the ruins, enjoying the villages and scenery, but wasn't really into the shamanism, especially the drug taking that was all part of the experience. Her husband went off with the group and their guide and took huge amounts of hallucinogenic drugs. They were also mixing different drugs everyday without giving themselves time to recover from their last shamanic experience. Needless to say, after about a week they were all totally fucked up and couldn't stop tripping.

The highlight of any shamanic visit in South America is taking the ayahuasca. The shaman produces this from a cactus, found throughout the Andes, and when taken the effects can be particularly disturbing. The shaman should remain in full control and can snap his subject out when they are ready to leave the trip. The problem arises when the drug is taken without the guidance of a proper qualified shaman, and people can carry on tripping for several days.

All the guidebooks and travel brochures always contain the 'perfect photo'. Whether it is of people, animals, mountains or buildings, they are always photographs that you wished you had been able to get, but never do. We just happened to be in the right place at the right time in Ollantaytambo when school kicked out and the students were leaving to go home. Usually doubling as an animal lorry, their school bus was a small open topped lorry, a bit like an old military transport truck, with the cover rolled back away from the frame. Just when we thought it was full, and ready to leave, another group of kids would turn up and pile on. They were hanging onto to anything they could get a hold off. By the time they left, the truck was totally swamped, with legs and arms sticking up in all directions. Even as the truck drove off down the street more students were running along side, desperately trying to jump on rather than being left behind. Anywhere else in the world, the worry would be not just the number of kids on the bus, but if they were wearing seatbelts.

Our next stop at the other end of the Sacred Valley was Pisac, another quaint village famous for its market. It is probably among the best and most colourful in Peru and it is also one of the busiest. Unlike other markets we had been to, it did not really cater for the locals, existing solely for tourists, especially day-trippers from Cusco. A handful of vendors sat on the pavement selling peppers and tomatoes, but the large stalls selling local handicrafts and textiles heavily outnumbered them. The market seemed more compact than the Otavalo market, but there were a lot more tourists.

Trying not to catch the eye of any of the stall vendors, we moseyed around the labyrinth of Andean colours; reds, oranges and browns. We were almost halfway through our trip, which meant we could start considering buying things to take home. Showing any interest at all in any of the goods was fatal, the stallholder pouncing on you before you could move onto the next stall. The only item we ended up buying were a few brightly coloured locally made ceramic beads.

If we saw something we liked we invariably tried to knock of a bit of "gringo tax", although to be honest we didn't really want to barter the price too low. Quibbling over a few pennies didn't seem quite right. We had learnt to tell if we were being ripped off, and knew what the going rates were for most goods. We walked away from those vendors that were trying it on, who would usually shout after us, offering the goods at a fairer price.

Wandering around the market were local woman and young children dressed in traditional costume, with lambs or puppies tucked under their arms, or young llamas on leads. Every tourist they passed they would ask them if they wanted to take a photo of them with their fluffy cute animal. As soon as the photo had been taken, they would then ask for money. The tourists didn't have much option but to hand over some coins - they had been fleeced (literally). Maybe this was how all the books and brochures managed to get some interesting photos of people. There was no way we were prepared to pay for the privilege of taking a photo, and anyway the women were making enough money without our cash lining their pockets. Overlooking the square we watched these entrepreneurs in action and couldn't help but laugh at a particularly loud, arrogant American woman being collared. After making a small girl holding a puppy pose for her camera she turned to walk away, only to be chased after by the little girl with her hand outstretched asking for a dollar. A Peruvian Sol was obviously not enough for her. Not only that, but the three other women who had been sitting on the pavement in the background also insisted on being paid for their appearance. The cost of one photo was more than she would have paid for the actual camera film.

High above the village centre, and away from the hustle and bustle of the market, is a large citadel. Marking the southerly entrance to the Sacred Valley, this fortress would have been strategically important, monitoring the road that travelled between the mountains and the jungle.

The walk up to the ruins took us up through loads of terraces, and was quite exhausting, but the great panoramic views over the village and surrounding mountains made it worthwhile. Reaching the first part of the fortress we sat and appreciated the birds eye view high above the valley. From such a height we could see how fertile this valley was, a patchwork of fields spread out across the floodplain and terraces stretching up the steep flanks of the hills. Spotting a tractor in one field, we realised it was the first we had noticed in South America as most fields are ploughed by hand or using oxen.

This was just the start of the citadel complex and we kept discovering more and more with every corner we went round and every hilltop we went over. The Pisac fortress, terraces and settlements were a great place for exploring, following narrow paths around the edge of the steep cliff, up ladders and through small tunnels carved into the mountain. Around each corner was another fortress, temple or small ruined hamlet. In the centre of one ruin was a beautiful and precisely constructed religious centre, with smooth granite walls surrounded by sacred rocky outcrops, whose peculiar shapes and angles are thought to have aided in tracking important stars. A strange function, considering it is called Temple of the Sun.

Engrossed in exploring the ruins, we hadn't realised that the site had actually closed and the sun was starting to set behind the mountains. We didn't manage to see all of the buildings and could have easily spent a couple more hours wandering around the houses and temples, but our time, and light, had run out. It was dark, and we were shattered, by the time we got back to town. The market was packed up, all the stalls and tourists had gone, the main square eerily quiet.

We left Pisac over a kilogram lighter. It certainly had nothing to do with lack of food, because we had found a great restaurant to eat it. Nor did we have the return of the shits. Just before we left home, the new Harry Potter book had been realised. Seeing as J.K. Rowling had kept us waiting so long for book number five we just had to take a copy with us. It had seemed like a good idea at the time, but when we had both finished reading it, we suddenly realised how heavy and bulky the book really was. In Pisac there was a reasonably good book exchange where we finally got rid of Harry Potter, therefore taking 1kg off the weight of our packs. It was a shame to see it go, but Ulrike, the local restaurant owner who had acquired it had been waiting for it to be released as long as we had and certainly appreciated us relinquishing it.

Back in Cusco we re-packed our rucksacks for our trip to Machu Picchu. Our hotel had moved us to the front room, and we were kept awake all night with endless numbers of pissed people shouting out on the street and ringing the hotel doorbell all night. When the drunks quietened off, all that remained was cockerels, dogs and beeping taxis every other minute.

We were driven around Cusco collecting other members of our Inca group and it seemed to take forever to even get out of town. An hour after we had been picked up, it didn't surprise us when we found ourselves parked back up outside the front door of the hostel again. We wouldn't have minded so much if we hadn't missed out on our breakfast because the tour agency insisted on collecting us so early.

After stops for food, petrol, gas, tyre checks etc, we finally arrived in Ollantaytambo, for the second time. Unlike the beautiful sunshine we had enjoyed only a few days previously we were subjected to freezing cold temperatures and lashing rain. We considered going down to the train station to catch the next train for Machu Picchu. The thought only lasted momentarily.

The touts were clambering onto the bus before the driver even had a chance to turn off the engine. They were piled high with plastic ponchos, coca leaves and mass produced rustic looking walking sticks (a bamboo pole with a colourful looped handle). We thought our raincoats might be enough, but seeing as our Guide, Lobo, was buying a plastic poncho, we thought we better do the same. Maybe Lobo knew something we didn't. Caius chose a particularly fetching white poncho, which was far too short for him, and with the hood up it made him look like a member of the Klu Klux Klan. The touts must rub their hands with glee when it rains. After stocking up on extra coca leaves, we stood in a doorway trying to keep dry and watched the rain pour down in front of us.

Vicky Brewis & Caius Simmons

# The Inca Trail

The time had come to start walking the famous Inca Trail. You can now only walk the Inca trail as part of a pre-booked group with a guide. Only 500 people are allowed to start the three-day trail each day, including guides and porters. We thought that the trail would be packed with walkers, jostling for position along the path, but it was only when we stopped for a break or lunch did we realise that there were other groups on the trail.

The porters were all wide-eyed and fired up when we collected them, their cheeks bulging with coca leaves. There were 11 porters and 2 guides with us in our group, almost one porter each. They really appeared to enjoy their jobs, and were having a great laugh together. They do get a relatively good wage, compared to them working in the fields, but its still bloody hard work.

A couple of years ago, porters used to carry about 50-60kg each. Regulations now in force have improved their conditions considerably. At each checkpoint their packs are weighed, to make sure they are not carrying too much. Their maximum weight now is 30kg, which is still a hell of a lot but they all seemed to be coping okay. It was amazing to watch them run past, with sacks, food, pots, pans, sugar bowls, napkins, stools, tables, tablecloths, tents and cooking gas on their backs, which was all covered in a large piece of plastic that trailed behind them like a cloak. Having been along the path so many times, they were very sure footed. Watching them run down granite steps, two steps at a time, was quite nerve racking. They didn't bother with wearing boots, opting for sandals or no shoes. Quite often they are given boots by people who have finished the trail and have no further use for them, but they prefer not to wear them. We guessed that they probably wear them down the pub on a Friday night instead.

We had opted to pay a small amount extra to have our stuff carried by a porter. This sounds like a bit of a cop out but we thought we may as well take advantage of it and had sound reason to do so. Most of the people were carrying their own stuff out of pride - it was the Inca trail after all. By the second day most of them were struggling and got a porter to carry their stuff for the rest of the walk. After all we were at about 3000m asl and no matter how fit you are, altitude does have an effect. There were a couple of people who managed their packs all the way, mostly without any complaints, but the others who insisted on carrying their rucksacks all the way were totally exhausted and had not enjoyed the walk at all. They had spent all their time and energy concentrating on walking and had not had time to stop and appreciate their amazing surroundings. All their stuff had got soaking wet, but the porters made sure ours were kept covered and everything was bone dry when we opened the sack each evening. It was definitely worth it.

The porters took great pride in everything that they did. Running ahead of us, they would be ready for when we stopped, with a large tent set up with either popcorn and hot drinks for elevenses and afternoon tea, or hot bowls of soup for lunch. We don't think we actually saw anyone use them, but they also laid out bowls of water with soaps and towels for us to wash with. When we arrived at the campsites, the tents were ready, and our dry belongings lying in the tent. We could quickly change into dry clothes and sit admiring the views. The whole trip is designed so that the tourists only needed to walk and look at the scenery.

In the mornings our guide would wake us up at 6.00am with a cup of coca tea being passed into the tent. We were fed constantly throughout the day and were even given snacks just to make sure we did not starve. By the end of the fourth day we were stuffed and we could not even manage to eat a fabulous banquet the porters had prepared for us. The thank you presentation on the final evening was fantastic and the porters all looked really pleased with themselves.

At the end, the porters very shyly received their well-deserved recognition and tips. It is this extra bit of cash that makes all their hard work and leather soled feet worth their while.

As the Inca Trail is mostly within cloud forest, we should not have been too surprised to find it raining most of the way. Lobo buying a poncho had been the only indication of what weather was going to be in store for us. The rain we experienced on the first day continued on and off (but mainly on) for two days. Waterproof trousers had been great when we had been stuck halfway up Cotopaxi, but it was a lot warmer on the Inca Trail and although the trousers kept the rain off they trapped just as much moisture. Peeling off the waterproof trousers after the first day we decided that we were better off without the waterproofs as our trousers were so wet underneath. Shorts were a much better option and at least it meant we had dry trousers to change into each night. Some may have questioned our sanity as we stood on top of the Abra de Runkuracay pass (3800m asl) with heavy lumps of snow falling around us and our legs covered in goose pimples.

There are a number of other ruins along the way; ancient checkpoints, guards houses and small agricultural centres. Everybody in the group were so wet they couldn't be bothered to visit any of these ruins. We were already soaked and it didn't make any difference to make a detour for an hour or so to look at them. A few of us made it up the stairs to Sayamarca. It was so foggy we had not even realised that it even existed, and the view from it was not much better. We both said we could have been standing at any ruined site in Cornwall on a foggy day. By the time we made our way back down onto the main trail, the clouds cleared and the beautiful cloud forest materialised before us. The peaks that we had just walked down from were covered in a dusting of snow.

With clear skies came another menace – sand flies. They got into our hair, making our scalps irritatingly itchy. If we stopped for any reason, like to admire the view, take a photo, or have a drink of water, within minutes we were scratching every bit of exposed flesh.

The Inca Trail from Ollantaytambo is only 27 miles (43Km) long, which spread over three and a half days means it is not too strenuous and we had plenty of time to relax, take in the views, read, play cards and explore.

The trail is mostly stone paved and had been constructed as a royal highway to reach Machu Picchu. It is just one of the numerous paths built by the Incas that cross remote parts of the Andes. They had done a great job in constructing the route all those years ago and even though it has undergone restoration it was in excellent condition. There seemed to be little erosion, the restrictions on the number of walkers seemed to be working. One of the sections of the path was amazing, snaking around the edge of the mountainsides, through tunnels and over bridges. We took our time, enjoying the views of the snow-capped mountains of the Vilcabamba range and Salcantay. Standing on the watershed separating two mountain ranges, we felt the cold air of the Vilcabamba range on one side of the path, whilst on the other side of the path we experienced the warm air rising up from the valley below the Urubamba mountain range. It was a particularly strange phenomenon.

Not everyone who does the Inca trail are athletic, keen hikers. As long as you are relatively fit and can walk, then you would probably manage it. The most important thing is probably to take a few days to acclimatise to the altitude before starting. The trail crosses over three high-altitude mountain passes; the highest is "Dead Woman's Pass" at 13,440ft (4,200m). We had been warned that it was a tough climb, and we saw a number of people collapsed on the way up being administered oxygen. It was a long slog, but we all managed it to the top. The second pass was just as tough, shorter but steeper and we had to walk it first thing in the morning when our bodies were still struggling to warm up. It was interesting to see that the people who made it to the top of the hills first were the people who had not just flown into Cusco, but had been at a high altitude for a few weeks or more. Even though we were not running alongside the porters, our walk the previous week in Huaraz had definitely helped us to acclimatize to the altitude.

If going up the hills wasn't going to wear us out then the going down them would. We passed down hundreds of granite steps, some of which were carved out of the rock face. This was just as tough as going up hill and no one seemed to escape getting sore knees by the time we reached camp.

Debbie and Lucy, two Brits, who had been travelling around the world for a year, introduced us to their marking system for the toilets. Each toilet experience was marked out of 10, ten being the best. Marks were knocked off for dirtiness, lack of toilet roll, seat, door or even toilet. Their worst ever toilet was in Thailand - ours was yet to come. They rated the toilets on the trail quite low, but we thought they were being a bit harsh; at least there were some toilets to use.

Part of the new regulations mean you have to camp at assigned campsites, which usually have rudimentary facilities. This all seems a bit of a cheat and some of the sites even have showers, but it means that people are not going to the toilet wherever they feel like it, or washing in the streams. One of the toilets did have a number of points knocked off for the worst ever design; rather than having just a hole in the floor (which would have sufficed) a box had been thoughtfully built around the hole. Unfortunately it was too high and the hole set so far back that you had no option but to sit down. Squatting is the preferable option, and everyone before us had obviously felt the same. They had climbed onto the box and squatted either side of the hole, leaving their muddy footprints all over the loo seat.

# Mucho Poncho

No one seemed too bothered about the early start (4am) on the final day. We were all too excited and had been unable to sleep properly anyway – our dreams of seeing Machu Picchu were about to be realised. For almost the first time in four days it was not raining and the sky was full of bright stars. It was only now that it became apparent how many other people had been actually walking the Inca Trail. Joined by extra groups who were on a shortened two-day Inca Trail there suddenly appeared to huge numbers of walkers heading towards Machu Picchu. Looking in front and behind us along the path was a torch lit procession snaking along the side of the mountain through the woods. We walked in almost complete silence for a couple of hours, getting more and more excited. The hair on our heads stood on end from the anticipation, and not the fact that it had not been washed for 4 days. Heading towards Intipunku, the Sun Gate, we became agitated by slower walkers. As the sky became lighter and lighter, the whole valley below us was revealed to us as the sun started to rise from behind a mountain in the distance and we were anxious we were going to miss our first view as the sun rose up over Machu Picchu. We virtually ran up the steep steps to the Sun Gate. As we walked around the corner and looked down on the ancient citadel, our hearts dropped. The valley in front was filled with a mass of swirling cloud. We tried not to be disappointed, but after 4 days of walking in the rain to be greeted with fog was not what we had planned on.

Joe, an American in the group, chuckled to himself. He had not really been prepared for the walk, wearing jeans and trainers that got soaking wet on the first day. His attempts to carry all his kit did not last and he had resorted to hiring a porter by day two. He caught a cold and looked like he had not enjoyed the trek.  It was also very disturbing when he spoke, because his slow drawl sounded just like the character played by Billy Bob Thornton in the Oscar winning film, *Sling Blade*.  At any moment we expected him to say, "Ah, Huh, I Rekkun".  If he could see the funny side of the situation then we had no reason not to either.  There was nothing else we could do about it, but laugh with him.

We hung around at the Sun Gate, waiting for the fog to clear, but it was not looking very hopeful.  Our guide told us that he probably only sees Machu Picchu from that spot once or twice a year.  That is something they don't bother to tell you in the guidebooks or at the tour agencies.  Of course we had to take some photos, it was after all our first view of Machu Picchu.  We thought we might be able to use it for a game, a bit like pin the tail on the donkey.  As we descended into the clouds we glanced behind us to admire the valley and mountains from where we had come from which were now bathed in early morning sunlight.

After 30 minutes walking down through the fog we finally reached the photographers vantage point, known as the 'Hut of the Caretaker of the Funerary Rock'.  If you have ever received a postcard of Machu Picchu, it is likely that it was taken from this spot.  The fog started to lift and we got our first glimpse of the ruins.  There were the obligatory wisps of clouds clinging to the hillside making it looked really mystical.  An ideal photo opportunity, the only noise was from the clicking of cameras.

Maybe it was the angle that the photos had been taken at, but we imagined the ruins to be a lot bigger.  It is the location of the ruins that make them so important and not it's size.  The beautiful natural setting of Machu Picchu at 2,430 m above sea level, set amongst tropical mountain forest, is extraordinary.  The site lies in the middle of a saddle shaped ridge between two mountains.  No one knows what the Incas called their city, which has adopted its name from the mountain that rises behind the ruins, Machu Picchu (literally meaning 'Ancient Peak').  This mountain is just one of four ancient peaks that surround the ruins, the other three being Huayna Picchu, Putukusi and Pumasillo.  From the centre of the site, each peak points towards a specific direction, North, South, East or West. Blending in naturally with the landscape, its giant walls, terraces and ramps could easily be mistaken for the rock escarpments that it is built on.

It is easy to understand why these ruins went undiscovered for so long, it's remote location and its concealment ensuring that the Spanish did not know of its existence. If they ever did know, it was probably too inaccessible for them to have bothered with. For whatever reason, it luckily escaped the looting, plundering, burning and destruction that most Inca sites were subjected to during the Spanish Conquest. As a result, this has become the most significant and famous archaeological site in South America.

It was not until 1911, when a Yale University expedition led by a chap called Hiram Bingham, that the ruins at Machu Picchu were 'rediscovered'. Bingham paid a local Quechua man one sol (things haven't changed much since 1911), who told him that on top of the hill, out of sight was an archaeological ruin. He assumed it to be the site he was looking for, Vilcabamba (one of the last Inca strongholds), and so he actually discovered Machu Picchu purely by mistake. The site was totally overgrown with vegetation and although it had been abandoned by the Inca centuries before, a couple of local peasant families were living there.

The search for Vilcabamba continued for many years, until 1964 when Gene Savoy (an American archaeologist) unearthed the site at Espiritu Pampa. Hiram Bingham had already made it there not long after he had discovered Machu Picchu but had left it alone thinking he had already found the last Incan stronghold. In his excitement he forgot to log the exact location, and therefore it became 'lost' again. More recently, Peruvian and British explorers have discovered a number of other lost Inca cities all in the same area. Lying only 40 kilometres from Machu Picchu are one of these sites, Corihuayrachina. These ruins are even more sophisticated than Machu Picchu, suggesting a well-developed settlement. Included in the site are ruins of circular homes, storehouses, cemeteries, funeral towers, roadways, waterworks, farming terraces, a dam and a truncated pyramid.

138

Obviously, there has been a lot of archaeological exploration since the discovery of Machu Picchu and new things are always being excavated. In total, about 150 skeletal remains have been exhumed; the vast majority of these are females, with only about 20 males and four children. The large number of female remains was quite curious and has led to various theories, the most popular being that the last inhabitants of Machu Picchu were women, left by the men who had gone off to fight the Spanish, selected to stay to continue important ritual ceremonies. The theory of it being a glorified brothel is a great suggestion but, unfortunately, very unlikely.

The mystery surrounding Machu Picchu and its precise function is one of is greatest attractions and huge numbers of people believing it was a particularly important centre of worship and ceremonies come searching for a spiritual experience. Maybe it was the two dogs copulating in the main grassy plaza that distracted us, but it did not really feel that it was a particularly sacred place. Neither of us felt compelled to sit down and meditate, or take off our clothes and run around naked for that matter.

The majority of the site is split between agricultural terracing and buildings to accommodate about 500 people. Even though there are a number of temples and the usual stone alter that is illuminated by the sun during one of the Solstices, most of the buildings are very functional consisting of not just houses, but also workshops, storage areas and baths. Built at the height of the Inca Empire it was probably one of the most amazing urban centres, not the biggest, but certainly one of the most dramatic.

Machu Picchu is an exceptionally well-preserved archaeological site, with some fantastic granite stonework, locking together like a huge jigsaw puzzle (one stone had 34 interlocking angles cut into it). Anyone who has ever worked with granite will know that it is not only a very heavy stone, but also very tough and is takes a great deal of skill to cut it accurately. There are 3 granite quarries within the site, which must have been working full time to provide a constant supply of stone during the city's construction.

Our guided tour only took an hour and a half and by 10 am we were left to explore on our own. Vicky decided to climb up Huayna Picchu (Younger or Lesser Peak). This is the hill that is the backdrop for most of the photos taken of Machu Picchu and is almost 400 metres higher than the ruins. We had been warned it was not the easiest hills to climb and those with a fear of heights, including Caius decided to give it a miss. The route clings to the side of the mountain and there is an almost vertical stairway of about 50 metres carved into the rocky face. It was not too scary and there was a handrail much of the way to support and pull yourself up. The final climb to the top was with the aid of a rope, which someone had apparently recently misjudged and had tumbled to their death. The panoramic view from the top was worth the tiring climb, with Machu Picchu, the Urubamba Canyon and the snow-capped peaks in the distance. There were too many people hanging around at the top, determined to try and find the highest and most precarious rock to conquer. The walk back down was a little more disconcerting and from the top of some mini terraces we realised how steep it really was. The set of tiny steps we had come up now seemed even smaller and steeper and we realised there was nothing at the bottom to stop us from falling right to the bottom if we had slipped.

By the time we had reached the bottom, the ruins were crawling with tourists. Caius had managed to spend a relaxing hour wandering around before the train from Cusco had arrived. Even though there are restrictions on the number of people walking the Inca Trail, there are none on the number that can visit the ruins. From a height it looked like someone had been painting the ruins in splodges of white, blue, red, green, yellow and black. What we were actually looking at was a load of tourists wearing ponchos, shuffling around in their organised tour.

It had been a good idea to walk in shorts, while it was raining, but now we were lower down and it was warmer we were the prime targets for sand flies again. We were too engrossed in the excitement of going to Machu Picchu we had forgotten to put on any mosquito guard that morning. They were particularly attracted to our bare legs, which were soon covered in small, weeping wounds. Our early start had been worth it, but sharing the ruins with a couple of thousand other people (and sand flies) was not enjoyable, so we made our escape just as it started to rain - again.

Vicky Brewis & Caius Simmons

# Slippage

It is estimated that 400,000 people visit Machu Picchu every year, on average that's over 1000 people each day. There have been talks about closing the ruins to the public, because geologists and archaeologists claim that with the number of visitors, which is increasing annually, the site is being damaged. Many people are led to believe that the citadel is in danger of falling off the edge of the mountain into the River Urubamba in the next five to ten years because of amount of feet pounding the ruins and making the ground unstable. The volume of people passing through the ruins is only a minor problem when you consider the real reason for the experts concern.

Machu Picchu is located on a ridge between two mountains, Machu Picchu and Huayanpichu. This ridge, which is lower than the surrounding mountains, has formed due to the existence of at least five major geological faults and countless minor faults. The faults result in the ridge sinking lower and lower at an alarming rate of 1cm per month and taking the ruins with it. Most of the damage to the buildings just so happens to occur along these fault lines, where the distinctive close-knit stonework has moved to leave large gaps, big enough to slide your hand through.

UNESCO has already told the Peruvian government that if they do not take action to reduce the number of visitors they will put Machu Picchu on its list of endangered sites. They appear to be 'monitoring the situation' and along with a few warning signs they have also chalked a number of stones to help measure the amount of movement. The marks probably also mean they can rebuild the structure if it collapses. Continuing to let more and more visitors travel to Machu Picchu, the Peruvian authorities are insisting there is no need for panic.

As we sat and wrote this section of the book we learnt that 1500 tourists were trapped in the village near to Machu Picchu, Aguas Calientes, following a mudslide blocking all access and unfortunately killing a handful of locals. The Peruvian President was also there, apparently filming a documentary promoting the area for tourism. For them it was a well-timed bit of eco-tourism lobbying by Mother Nature. Machu Picchu is far too lucrative for Peru and if they ever close it, it would not only result in the downfall of hundreds of tour agencies, hotels and restaurants in Cusco, but also the bankruptcy of the airlines, the train line and the bus companies that operate to, from and around Cusco. The closure of the ruins would probably be enough to trigger a crash in the Peruvian economy.

Vicky Brewis & Caius Simmons

# Hot Water

For a small fortune, even by UK standards, a bus took us to the nearby town of Aguas Calientes.  This is the closest town to Machu Picchu, which at first appears to be a pretty miserable place - full of expensive hotels, tacky souvenir shops, busy restaurants, and American and European tourists.  Based on the horror stories about the thermal springs we decided to give bathing a miss.

We never found out if *Gringo Bill's* lives up to it's good reputation.  So much for making a reservation in advance - when we turned up, they didn't have a room reserved for us and they wanted double the price we had agreed over the phone.  The extremely rude receptionist assumed we would just put up with her offer, but we just walked away.  Later, overhearing a conversation between six friends, we listened to an almost identical story.  They were extremely pissed off because they had already paid for their rooms through an agency and '*Bill*' was insisting they coughed up for a room again.

*Los Cabaña* was a far nicer, and friendly, alternative.  After being so cold and wet, and not washing properly for four days, the shower was magic.  *Aguas Calientes* we were in, and 'aguas calientes' it was.  Standing underneath the hot, powerful jet of water, it was wonderful to feel the bones warm up again.  It was just a good job the soap and hot water ran out, otherwise Vicky would have stood there forever.

Against popular opinion, we quite liked Aguas Calientes, once the last train left and all the tourists had gone, that is.  The main street is, in fact, the main rail track, with shops, stalls and restaurants lining the platform.  As long as we stayed away from here we seemed to be relatively safe from being touted.

144

Strolling around the main square with Bobby (the Canadian), and Joe ("Ah, Huh, I Rekkun"), was more than a pleasant way to spend an evening, reflecting on our trip to Machu Picchu. Bobby taught us how to deal with any touts outside the restaurants. When they approached, he would say "Que tal?" (How are you?), which would really throw them, not knowing what to say, and leaving them completely speechless. By the time they figured out a reply, we had passed by and onto the next restaurant.

The next morning, just to make absolutely sure we were completely worn out from the rigours of the Inca Trail we decided to go on yet another walk, this time up Putukusi, which along with Huayna Picchu is one of the four sacred mountains that surround Machu Picchu. It was a very pleasant walk, for about half an hour, until we turned a corner and were faced with a sheer vertical face with a rather dodgy looking ladder going up it. Admittedly it was made of large branches and it seemed to be securely fixed to the rock face, even if it did appear to lean outwards at a few places and we could not see the top. We were determined to make it to the top, particularly Caius, who wanted to overcome his fear of heights (not the best place to start). After 120 rungs of intense concentration, and sweat, we reached the top. Caius found some solid ground away from the top rung and after the adrenalin levels had dropped we set off again. Around the next corner we were confronted with another ladder. It was not quite as long, but around the next corner was another and then another. This happened a few more times and finally we reached a path and a view of the rest of the route. It was steep but manageable and, better still, there were no more ladders.

Maybe it was our poor Spanish, but we were convinced that the tourist information officer in Aguas Calientes told us it was not scary and if we had been up Huayna Picchu we would not have a problem!

Earlier on in the walk, when he was clinging tightly to a ladder, Caius had said he was not going to stop until he could see Machu Picchu. It finally came into sight as we rounded the last corner and got a view over the other side of the mountain. From here Machu Picchu looked so small, but it was interesting to see it from a different angle and how extensive the terracing is around the buildings. From our vantage point we could easily make out all the geological fault lines that lie underneath the ridge that Machu Picchu is built on. There was a constant stream of buses snaking up and down the road, ferrying visitors from the recently arrived train from Cusco. We stripped off and lay our sweaty clothes out on the rocks to dry. Flying high above us was the rainbow coloured Andean flag. We were finally disturbed by a couple who had also made it to the top. Like most people, they had travelled from Cusco on the train and were using Aguas Calientes as a base to get to Machu Picchu. However, they had got all the way here (and paid the extortionate train fare), but were not prepared to pay $20 to go into the site as they thought it was too expensive. It seemed a bit like going to a posh Chinese restaurant and ordering Fish 'n' Chips.

For some reason going back down was not quite as scary as the climb up. Perhaps it was the thought that the quicker we got down, the quicker we would be back on 'firm' ground. It was certainly a relief when we finally made it to the bottom of the last rung..

Having been on the road for 50 days, that day marked the halfway point in our trip. With a jugo de naranja (orange juice) in hand, we contemplated how the holiday was going. So far, it was definitely worth everything. Time was flying by and the weeks disappearing rapidly. After just achieving one of our major goals we needed to consider what, and where, we were going next. It also reminded us that the day when we would have to go home would be upon us before we knew it. Such thoughts made us feel a bit home sick for the first time and so we decided to phone home. For a small fortune we bought a tarjeta de telefonicas (phone card). Apparently one card would allow us to make either a 40-minute call, or two 20-minute calls – perfect. Caius called his mum first and got the answer machine. Not only that, but the answer machine was so full he couldn't even leave a message. Great, that was half the card gone. Vicky managed to get through to her family, and for the next 20 minutes she listened to her mum fretting, telling her to be careful, why didn't we hire a car (you must be joking!), not to go to Colombia, don't buy drugs etc. Vicky put down the

146

receiver having not had a chance to tell her anything about our travels. Having spent only 30 seconds on the first phone call we reckoned there was plenty of money left on the card to call Caius' dad. At least someone answered this time, his stepsister Kate. She had just enough time to tell us that his dad had gone off to the beach for the day before the money ran out on the card. Unfortunately, 90% of the charge is used in the initial connection so spending 30 seconds on the phone costs just as much as if you stay on for 20 minutes.

The train back to Ollantaytambo was a particularly posh one, with soft, comfortable seats. Luckily we didn't have to pay extra for the ticket, as it was all included in our Inca Trail trip. Forking out a bit extra for a decent tour company definitely paid off. Given the low cost of transport in Peru in general, this train ride is probably the most expensive journey, flying excluded, in the country. With the knowledge that tourists will pay whatever is being charged just to get to Machu Picchu the train company can charge what the hell they like. Our single ticket from Aguas Calientes to Ollantaytambo (about 15 miles) would have cost $25 each – bargain. Windows in the ceiling meant we could watch the mountains slowly pass by as we trundled along the valley. The sun was just starting to set and the snow capped peaks, towering way above us, had a hint of red on them. It seemed more than two days previously that we had been walking in amongst the mountains and now we were leaving them, and Machu Picchu, behind. By the time we reached Ollantaytambo the sun had disappeared, only to be replaced by a beautiful full moon. The pink light on the mountains turned to a peaceful, eerily calm, glow.

The train station at Ollantaytambo was in total confusion and there was no one there to meet us, as promised. The conductor informed us that there was another stop further down the track where all the buses, that couldn't get through the narrow streets of Ollantaytambo, stopped to pick up passengers. Logically, we stayed on, but when the conductor shoved us off at the side of the road we realised we had made a mistake. Stuck in the middle of nowhere and with all the bus drivers denying any responsibility for three scruffy travellers (Bobby was also with us) we had no option but to walk the short distance back to the village. This confusion must happen all the time because a few minutes later a minibus came to our rescue and took us back to Ollantaytambo. When we hadn't shown up at the train station, they guessed what had happened and drove out to collect us. Back in Ollantaytambo, we hooked up with a larger bus to take us the last leg of our journey, back to Cusco. Unfortunately the driver had left the lights on and we ended up pushing the bus through the main square to bump start it.

The full moon hovered above the mountains, lighting up the valley around and ahead us. On the previous journeys along this part of the Sacred Valley we had not seen any of the peaks as they had all been shrouded in cloud. That night we could see for miles, the Vilcabamba and Salcantay mountain ranges looked tantalisingly close.

# Cusco to Arequipa

It was finally time to leave Cusco – time to leave the touts, the shoe shine boys, the harassing waiters, the beeping taxis, the postcard sellers, the tour agencies, the begging lady who smiled at us in the hope we would give her some money but used to thump Vicky on the leg when we walked past without obliging her.   Our feelings about Cusco were mixed.  On the one hand it is such a beautiful city and the Sacred Valley was wonderful, unfortunately these plus points were far outweighed by the commercialism of it all.   After spending more than 10 days in and around Cusco it was definitely time to go.  The elation of reaching Machu Picchu was still running through our blood, and we both felt a bit sad that this chapter of our journey was over.

A 12 hour bus journey, the longest so far, would transport us away from the tourist hot spot of Cusco, to Arequipa where we would be able to walk down the street, well at least across the road, without being hassled.

We sat in a contented silence on the bus, absorbing the scenery as it trundled by, passing through one village after another.  As we headed south towards the Altiplano the landscape became harsher and harsher, changing from wide cultivated river valleys to bleak, grassy plains.  Stretching from southern Peru and down through the centre of Bolivia, the Southern Altiplano is a particularly distinctive landscape.  The Altiplano is a much higher, wider and harsher environment than anywhere else in South America.  Herds of llamas and alpacas roamed amongst the grassy tussocks in search of food.  A common sight, these animals are highly suited to deal with the tough grasses, high altitudes and cold temperatures experienced on the Altiplano.

Up until this point our only encounter with these animals had only really been at Ingapirca in Ecuador and on Machu Picchu, and they were only really there for the benefit of the tourists, and their cameras. Our Machu Picchu guide, Lobo had explained the difference between llamas and alpacas, but unless they were stood side by side we personally couldn't tell which one was which. Comparing them, the alpacas are said to have shorter legs, more rounded bums, hairier faces and softer and fluffier fleece than llamas. To add to the confusion there are two other species of South American *Camelids*, the vicuna and guanaco. As the name suggests, *Camelids* are close relatives to the camel, but much smaller and lacking a hump. Their heads held high, they walk in a particularly weird way, swaying their long necks backwards and forwards.

Alpacas and llamas, are domesticated animals and are pretty widespread. They usually have colourful ribbons attached to their ears so it is quite easy to spot them from a distance. On the other hand, the likelihood of us seeing a vicuna from the bus was pretty slim, and the chance of seeing a guanaco was even slimmer. Existing only in the wild, they are both highly endangered species. Even during Incan times the vicuna were a highly prized animal, its fine wool reserved solely for the use by Emperor Inca himself.

With the knowledge that some of the best wool comes from the region between Cusco and Arequipa, and that the villages were all selling huge bundles of the stuff we guessed we were probably looking at alpacas out of the bus window (or were they llamas?).

Alpaca fibre is prized for its softness (equivalent to mohair and surpassed only by vicuna), uniform fineness and strength (it is three times stronger than sheep's wool). It became extremely popular during the 1920's and the production of alpaca fibre continues to contribute as a major economic resource in Peru. Although alpaca wool is favoured for clothing (it is much warmer and softer than llama wool), the coarser llama fibres are great for making ropes, sacking and blankets.

All we could think about when we saw these animals were the street vendors and stall holders shouting, "Alpaca joompa, joompa, joompa, Alpaca joompa". It was hard to believe that the wool from the alpaca comes in twenty-two officially recognized colours. Besides basic white and black, there are also a variety of beautiful shades of brown, grey, tan and fawn. All we had seen being sold were grey, grey or grey 'joompas'

Alpacas and llamas are reared not only for their wool, but for several thousand of years they have also been used as pack animals to transport goods as well as being an important food source. We had whoosed out on the guinea pig, but had given the alpaca and llama a try. Presented in the form of a steak or burger it is a far more inviting menu option than cuy, and must say it tasted pretty good - not dissimilar to bacon.

The journey to Arequipa was made particularly uncomfortable by a couple of young lads who fully reclined their seats right into our laps, providing us with a great view of the top of their heads. They seemed to take delight in making us as uncomfortable as possible. Rather than recline our seats and pass the discomfort onto the person behind us we found far greater satisfaction in wedging our knees so firmly into their backs that we could feel the vertebrae in their spines. Every now and again a good hard knee thrust, or a loud cough into their hair was the surest way to wake them up.

Instead of the usual 'lunch break' at a piss smelling café on the side of a busy road, the driver stopped in the middle of a small village. We were not allowed to get off, but a selected number of touts were let onto the bus. Disappointingly, only four or five touts were allowed on, and sitting in the comfort (or discomfort) of our seats we were offered bread rolls, water and fruit. All the other touts who had not been allowed to board the bus hung around outside, banging on the windows in an attempt to sell us more bread rolls, water and fruit.

One of the touts was a lady carrying a huge sack and an old card table. The table had been modified so that when she set-up, it fitted perfectly in the aisle. We watched with intrigue as she plonked the sack onto the table and opened it up to reveal a huge piece of cooked meat. Taking out a small butchers

151

cleaver she proceeded to hack off chunks of meat, wrap it up and sell it. She made her way down the bus, stopping every few seats to chop some more chunks off. As she wielded the axe down onto the table, there were bits of meat, gristle, blood and bone flying all over the place, including onto the passengers who just happened to be next to her. As she passed our seats we got a whiff of the wonderful smell emanating from the sack, and after a quick peak we managed to identify it as lamb. By the time we had decided that we were going to give it a taste, she had sold the lot and all she had left were a few dodgy looking scraggy ends.

Continuing the journey, we passed through Juliaca, an extremely desperate looking town. It was definitely the shabbiest town we had been to so far, and we could see why only half a page had been dedicated to it in our guidebook. Looking at the rows and rows of concrete houses we thought that half a page was quite generous. Apart from dust and traffic, every street seemed to be full of railway tracks, markets, shops and stalls. Unless we wanted to catch the train to Puno or buy a washing up bowl, Juliaca didn't really seem like the place to stay. The first thing we noticed as we drove into town was the graffiti scrawled, in red paint, on the wall of someone's house – 'BUSH AND BLAIR ARE TERRORISTS'. They may live in one of the grottiest towns in Peru, but at least the Juliacans have a good grasp of world politics.

Juliaca was the halfway point in our journey between Cusco and Arequipa. Beyond the town, the scenery became even bleaker, but even more beautiful as we drove into the middle of the Altiplano. Driving along a newly paved road we followed the route of the railway line, passing by lakes, mountains, a few piles of rocks, a couple of small villages, some llamas (or were they alpacas), and very little else.

For most of the journey we were over 4000m asl but we didn't dare drink too much water in case we needed the toilet. There wasn't one on the bus and the driver obviously had a bladder made of steel. He had kindly let us all out at Juliaca to use the facilities, but wasn't keen on stopping again. As the 10 hour journey turned into a 12 hour one (road works), mutiny brewed at the back of the bus. After much shouting, the driver had little choice but to stop and allow the passengers to go to the toilet. Nobody cared that we were stuck out in the middle of the Altiplano, exposed to the wind, with nowhere to shelter and not a grassy tussock in sight to squat behind.

We drove down into Arequipa just as the sun was beginning to set. The surrounding volcanic cones were illuminated all different shades of red, pink and purple. We forgot about our numb arses, backs, knees and necks for a few minutes and enjoyed the sight of the town lying below us in the valley, its buildings reflecting the last of the days sun rays.

# Arequipa

Theories suggest that Arequipa comes from the Quechua phrase "ari quepay" meaning "Yes, we will stay here", after the fourth Inca Emperor, Mayta Capac, decided to rest his troops after a long march from Cusco. After our long and uncomfortable bus ride from Cusco we thought we would do the same. Luckily we had booked a room in advance. It was the city's festival week (Arequipa Week) and we were arriving right in the middle of it.

In Ecuador we had managed to just turn up and find accommodation and transport, but as we headed into Peru we learnt early on that to get the hostel we wanted, it was worth booking in advance over the phone. These phone calls were particularly stressful and we had to do them as a joint effort. It usually required going for a coffee (or something stronger) beforehand to prepare our script and then toss a coin to see whose turn it was to make the phone call. Our set phrase would be said and then it usually went horribly wrong. The person at the other end of the phone would quite often say something to us and then disappear or hang up. If they disappeared, we would get excited at the thought that the person they had gone to get may speak a small amount of English. This was very rare and we would end up repeating our set phrase. If we did not understand what they were saying to us we had to pass the phone to one another in the hope that we could work out their reply. On numerous occasions we hung up and then have to call back once we had managed between us to decipher the information we had been told. It made us realise how important sign language is in a foreign country. We always managed to book a room but it wasn't the quickest of tasks. To top it all, when we arrived at the hostel, more often than not it was run by an English speaking European, often German.

On our first night in Arequipa we had homemade soup at the hostel, made right in front of us, accompanied with Pisco Sours. Pisco is a white grape brandy not dissimilar to Tequila that is generally made in Chile and not in Pisco, Peru, as the name suggests. Pisco Sours are readily available throughout most South American countries, but how it is mixed together really depends on the bar person. Our only previous experience of Pisco Sours was on a train from Exeter to Manchester where a friend, who had just returned from a trip to Chile, had kindly brought a bottle on the train in an attempt to make the journey a bit quicker – it worked. He mixed it with bitter lemon, which we just assumed was the way it was served in Chile. We had not been overly impressed and as a result, and even though it had been available everywhere in Peru, we had not bothered trying it again.

The cocktail being mixed together behind the bar looked completely different to the Pisco sours we had drunk back in the UK, so decided to give it a go. Crushed ice, lime, sugar, egg whites and copious amounts of Pisco where whisked up in blender. How come they can't make Tequila taste so good?

We soon realised why so many people had recommended that we visited Arequipa. Even though it is Peru's second largest city, with a population approaching 1 million, it had the feel of a town rather than a city. For us, it was the most attractive city we visited in Peru, not just because of it's architecture but it also has a very laid back feel to it (especially after hectic Cusco).

Arequipa is characterised by low, earthquake resistant, buildings constructed in the white, glistening, volcanic sillar rock, which gives the city its nickname 'La Ciudad Blanca' or 'White City'. The Plaza de Armas, with its fountain and gardens is one of the largest and finest central squares in South America. The Plaza is bordered on one side by the stylish white façade of the huge Cathedral (which is bizarrely painted pink inside) which looks more like a government building than a place of worship, and arcades topped with balconies on the other three sides. The balconies were beautifully adorned with greenery, lights and flags especially for the festival. Sitting majestically behind the Cathedral is the hazy conical volcanic peak of El Misti.

The active volcano of El Misti (5822m asl) is just one of three peaks which tower high above the city; the other two being the extinct Chachani (6075m asl) and the smaller peak of Pichu Pichu (5571m asl). El Misti acted as a good compass while walking around the city, its peak clearly visible at the end of most streets. Overlooking it from our hostel balcony whilst eating our breakfast certainly made the pan pipers, that had come to entertain us, more bearable

Arequipa is the best base for climbing El Misti. At 5822m it is the altitude that provides climbers with the biggest challenge, rather than its technical difficulty. We decided to give it a miss – we are not height junkies and judging by the amount of smog that collected around Arequipa at this time of year we were not expecting the view to be that great. There were a few people staying at the hostel wanting to climb it, including a couple of recently graduated teachers, who wanted to do it so they could say they had been up a volcano (they were geography teachers and did not want to disappoint their students). We made bets that they were full of shit and wouldn't make it. They didn't even manage to book a tour, opting for a trip into the Colca Canyon instead. By the time they came back they were too tired and seemed to have lost all interest in the climb.

One of our missions in Arequipa was to post our camera film back home. After being to the Galapagos and Machu Picchu we had managed to use about 12 rolls of film. With no great savings and relatively poor quality pictures, it all seemed too much hassle to have them developed in Peru. After a spate of stories involving stolen bags and cameras we decided it was time to post the film home. So we carefully packaged up the films, in two separate parcels just in case, using plenty of tape, writing the address on every possible surface. The counter assistant at the Post Office kindly told us that they were not acceptable and that we were not allowed to use tape, only glue to seal the packages. After buying some plain envelopes she instructed us to place our parcels into the envelopes and glue them down. She didn't seem at all bothered by the fact that we had not removed any tape at all from the parcels. They arrived safely in the UK two weeks later, unopened and undamaged – phew.

Arequipa is distinctive in many ways, including its food. We thought we would give some of the local culinary delights a try and headed out to one of the city's older suburbs. Our friendly taxi driver was keen to show us the sights, detouring us through the old narrow streets and past the luxurious mansions that surround the city centre. He was so chuffed with his 1 Sol (about 20p) tip that he insisted on taking a photo of us with El Misti in the background.

We found one of the recommended 'traditional' restaurants, which was half full up with locals. This was a good sign and the food that they were ordering looked really good. The owner was well prepared for gringos, but rather than translate the menu into English they provided a 'photo' menu instead. Unfortunately the food we ordered did not look half as nice as the other customer's food and nothing like it had done on the photos. Between us we had managed to order a plate full of boiled potatoes covered with diarrhoea, and some watery looking soup with a knuckle of unidentifiable meat in the middle. We failed with the food, but the tasty fruity chica to wash it down with had made up for it. We decided to stick to the homemade soup from the hostel for the rest of our stay.

The inhabitants of Arequipa have a reputation for being conceited or arrogant, especially towards other Peruvian regions. They are resentful and defensive of claims that other cities are of greater cultural importance. A strong and very real rivalry exists between them and the capital city of Lima. Politically, Arequipa is very rightwing and views itself as being very distinct from the rest of Peru.

As part of the festival, Arequipa was blessed with a visit from Peru's President and we arrived in the square just in time to witness his arrival. There were plenty of cheers, but there was even more "Boos" from much of the crowd. The chanting got louder and more aggressive. It was at this point we remembered that when a relative had been visiting the previous year there had been numerous riots involving tear gas and bombing of cars. We didn't really want to get involved in angry political demonstrations and on this thought we vacated the area as quickly as possible to hide in a café.

Roads were blocked off and people took to the streets during the morning of the start of the festival. Everyone was engrossed by a fat man wailing through a PA system. The locals could not get enough of him, but we couldn't get away quick enough. In the Plaza we watched various forms of street entertainment, one of which had roped in a tourist as part of his act. The entertainer was looking for another one to join in - we fled before he spotted us.

Many families took up position on fold away chairs, lining the streets ready for the procession, ensuring they would get the best view. We wandered around the bustling centre, which had an air of anticipation. The crowds swelled and got bigger and eventually the beat of drums could be heard, slowly getting louder. The streets were soon filled with music and colour.

At the back of the crowd, with a clear view over everyone's heads we watched the procession pass by for a couple of hours. Our sore feet couldn't take much more and we longed to sit down to watch the dancers and musicians. There was no way we were going to make it to the front of the crowds without being lynched, setting our sights on the balcony overlooking the square instead. Sitting high above us in the restaurants were what we assumed to be a select group of locals, mainly wealthy Arequipans who had probably booked their tables months in advance. There was no sign of any tourists and the likelihood that they were going to let two scruffy travellers join them was slim. The waitress at the restaurant told us we could not go up, having to settle for a seat downstairs instead. We must have looked totally rejected, because as we paid our bill, she changed her mind and said we could go up onto the balcony. This restaurant was at the other corner of the square to where the procession was taking place and we could only just see what was going on. There wasn't anything stopping us from walking along the terrace, so we made our way to the other end, taking up a seat directly above the festivities. We sat watching for hours, drinking beer and eating. It didn't take us long to become experts in the type of dance and music from different regions, the Arequipan anthem was definitely the best and most catchy, and it took us weeks to get the tune out of our heads. We seemed to be the only other tourists up there, but the locals were quite happy for us to be there. They were proud of their festival, and welcomed us because we were appreciating their efforts so much. At one point, an Arequipan sat across the table form us, leaned over and said, "this beats the Queen's Coronation, doesn't it?". It probably did.

A few costumes looked vaguely Scottish and we joked that it would be funny to see some Morris or Celidh dancing. It wasn't long until we heard the familiar drone of a set of bagpipes. The cheers that went up as he droned away suggested that he was going to survive at least a couple of tunes.

After about six hours watching troupes of dancers and musicians passing by, we asked how much longer the procession was going to last. "At least another six hours", the waitress told us. It had been a constant flow and we were amazed that there were enough people to keep it going another six hours. We managed to last another few hours before it got too cold to sit on the balcony any longer. We battled our way home through the crowds and fell asleep to the sound of the Arequipan tune strumming in our heads.

The following morning the town was quite subdued and the pan pipers who were supposed to serenade us during breakfast left early because they were too hung over.


Arequipa is also full of interesting museums, but the festival seemed more exciting and we only managed to visit a couple. The small Museo Santuarios Andinos (Museum of Andean Sanctuaries) has become world famous in the last 15 years, because of the 600 year old frozen body of Juanita, or the Ice Maiden. Her face, although slightly weathered over the last 500 years, is mysteriously beautiful. Analysis of her DNA has taught us a great deal about the Inca culture. Juanita was a beautiful teenage Inca girl who was discovered in near perfect condition on top of the Ampato Volcano (6,000m asl), 60km from Arequipa, her body preserved by the freezing temperatures on the peak for hundreds of years. Although other ice mummies have been found lower down the mountain and on other Andean peaks, Juanita remains the most important find. The Incas highly respected these mountains since the melt water from their snow-capped peaks form the headwaters of the mighty Amazon River, thousands of kilometres away. She was killed as a sacrificial offering to the mountain gods in an attempt to pacify them, and hopefully stop them erupting and spoiling local crops. Juanita set off on her final journey from Cusco, walking the gruelling distance to Ampato where she was given huge amounts of both coca and chichi. Along with the effects of altitude and cold she was barely conscious when a blow to the back of her head killed her.

# Condor spotting in The Colca Canyon

Apart from seeing the city the other reason why we had come to Arequipa was so that we could visit the Colca Canyon to view condors close up. We thought the Colca Canyon held the title as 'the deepest canyon in the world', at approximately 3400 metres deep, but the lesser-known Cotahuasi Canyon actually narrowly beats it. We enquired about a trip to Cotahuasi but were told it took two days to get there so thought we would settle with Colca, the worlds second deepest canyon. At its deepest point the Colca Canyon is still twice the depth of the Grand Canyon.

Most people 'do' the Colca Canyon with a tour group, but based on a number of recommendations we decided to go there under our own steam. The guided tours in to the Colca Canyon involved setting off from Arequipa at midnight, getting up at 6am the next day and even earlier on the third morning to walk up a path out of the canyon in the dark. There were far too many early mornings involved for us, and we had decided to 'sod that for a game of soldiers' and make our own way there. It turned out that the majority of the tours to the Colca Canyon used public transport anyway, so it was not as if we had missed out on a more comfortable bus.

The bus journey took us from an altitude of 2300m asl in Arequipa, up onto the Altiplano to 4800m asl and then finally descended back down to 3650m asl into the sleepy town of Chivay. The landscape from Arequipa to Chivay is a barren, semi-desert environment intersected by numerous eroded gullies. Herds of llamas and alpacas, could be seen in the distance, their brightly coloured ribbons flapping around their ears. The land supports little more than a few lumps of grass and, apart from a few houses, Chivay was the first settlement we encountered along the road from Arequipa.

Because Chivay is popular with tour groups we had booked a hotel room in advance. The owners were still surprised to see us. We took a room that had a great view, with windows on three sides. The sun poured in all day and it was like being in a greenhouse. As soon as the sun set the temperatures dropped rapidly, and at night we went to bed nearly fully clothed. We soon realised why this hotel had not been fully booked like all the others in the town. The bed that we thought was a double turned out to be no more than a large single - we fought all night for possession of the bedclothes, and the bed. The door to our bathroom had to be kept permanently shut because the smell that was being emitted from the toilet convinced us that something had died down there and was trying to come back to life. This was before either of us had even used it. Every time we flushed it the water got browner and the smell became worse. It got progressively smellier over the three days and became even more blocked every time we flushed it. We attempted to use the communal toilet, but it had the same problem. It is only really worth a mention because somehow we had managed to devote two pages of our diary to the stink.

The alarm was set for 3.55am. At least it was only going to be for one day, but it was the only way we would get to see the condors. By 4.30am, the bus station was a hive of activity. Market traders sat or slept next to sacks of fruit and vegetables, which they were going to be selling in a nearby town. Many had slept in the station for the night. The bus arrived late, as expected, and we took a two-hour journey to the Cruz del Condor. The first hour was in total darkness, but as the sun started to rise we got some really great views of hundreds of Incan terraces and steep drops down into the canyon below.

We were among the first people to arrive at the Cruz del Condor. The only others being local ladies who set up stalls on the roadside to sell tourist tat. Unfortunately a minibus load of loud arrogant French people turned up five minutes after we had. They started making a brew in the middle of the viewing area. It had not occurred to them that the more noise they made, the less of a

162

chance that the Condors would appear and the site warden had to keep telling them to be quiet.

Because the canyon is so deep (1200m at this point), the rising thermals are surprisingly strong and condors take advantage of them early in the morning to soar gracefully into the sky. You have to be there just at the right time to be able to see them, usually about 7 - 7.30am. They only hang around for an hour, sometimes less and we had already met a few people who had managed to miss them because their tour had been late. Eventually we spotted a condor, in the distance, fly out from the side of the cliff, flap its wings and return back from where it came. It appeared that they were just 'testing the waters' and the air had not warmed up enough for them to fly with minimal effort. It was obviously too much bother.

The Andean condor (Vultur gryphus) is a rare and endangered species. Its huge three-metre wingspan makes it the second largest bird in the world after the wandering albatross. We did not have to wait long before the whole family made an outing, four jet black adults and three dark brown juveniles.

It was brilliant watching these majestic birds, which we had wanted to see ever since watching Flight of the Condor on the TV in the mid 80's. This was a bit of a childhood dream coming true. We took plenty of photos expecting them to come out like all our other wildlife photos, a small pinprick in the far distance. Their size and closeness meant that they are easily identifiable, which is a real bonus and we managed to get some decent photos for a change.

By the time we left there were about 100 gringos clambering over the cliffs trying to get the best photo shot. Nicky and Caroline, the two girls we had met in Cusco who had been trying to get to the jungle were amongst them. Apparently their trip all went to plan, all their connections were on time, and the guide was where he said he would be. It sounded like they had seen much more wildlife than most people who had paid a small fortune for a jungle tour. Unfortunately, they had not brought their good luck with them on this trip and they had arrived too late at the Cruz del Condor and the condors had gone.

Walking back to the hotel a small girl grabbed our hands. She was about 6 or 7 and walked down the street with us, chatting away. We were so sceptical after Cusco, we were expecting her to ask for sweets or money, but like all people in this sleepy town, she was just being really friendly. She was about the only person to understand our Spanish and we managed to find our what she had been learning in school that day. When she got to her house, she waved us goodbye and ran inside.

After such an early start we were ready for a siesta and spent that afternoon in the nearby hot baths, wallowing in the 30°C water for many hours. Groups of tourists came and went, only having time for a quick dip before being hurried back onto their bus. The baths were so nice we did a return trip, early one morning. The ticket man was a bit surprised to see us, usually having to wait until the afternoon before the tourists turn up. We had the pool to ourselves and we agreed that our way of seeing the Canyon seemed much more favourable than taking an organised tour.

The following day we set off to explore the Colca Canyon a bit further and headed down the canyon for a walk along the valley. We kept getting accosted by locals, insistent on stopping for a chat. Not that we really understood what was being said to us anyway. A man went by on a donkey with his daughter sat in front of him. He said the usual pleasantries and the little girl shouted "Hola Gringos", which her father, and us, thought highly amusing. The term gringo, when used in South America, is not as insulting as it is in Spain.

There weren't many tourists around, and we had the roads and village squares to ourselves. Agricultural terraces dominated the lower canyon flanks, opening out around the meandering river to produce giant amphitheatres. We passed through a number of sleepy hamlets with quiet plazas and narrow dusty streets. Most of the villages have ornate white fronted churches, a legacy of prosperous silver mines in the 17th and 18th Centuries.

The Colca people have dwelt in the valley for more than 2,000 years, and have preserved many of their own ancient traditions. One of the survival skills of the ancient Colca people was their ability to store large amounts of grain for harder, and wetter, times ahead. The stores, known as 'colcas', gave name to the valley. Even under the Inca dominion, the locals kept themselves to themselves. It is said that the supreme Inca, Mayta Capac, married a princess from this region in order to formalise the conquest of the valley, but still struggled to influence the people. The Spanish were just as persistent, establishing all the villages along the valley in an attempt to centralise the population.

The sky was so blue it hurt to look at it, with no sign of a cloud for the whole day. The views along the dusty roads were amazing with snow capped volcanic peaks of Sabancaya and Ampato in the far distance. It had been on Ampato that the mummified body of Juanita had been found. Following an eruption in September 1995, hot ash, from Sabancayas, fell on the nearby Ampato, causing the glacier to melt slightly, and exposing her body.

Peru seemed geared up for tourists wanting to do organised tours, but we had come to the conclusion that, for most things, it was not really necessary. It was really easy to get caught up in this marketing trap, thinking that the only way to see anything was with a tour. It soon became apparent that the least enjoyable places we had visited were so heavily associated with tourism that they had been spoilt. There were loads of villages and small towns that were worth making the effort to visit by ourselves – wonderful places like Chivay, or the villages in the Sacred Valley. These places are still on the gringo trail but not everyone makes the effort to spend time there. By ignoring the guides and tour companies and going to these places, we had been able to appreciate that Peru has a lot more to offer than just shoe shine boys and postcard sellers.

# Poo-yes in Puno

Caius spent most of that night dashing, semi naked, down the corridors of the hostel to the toilet – we reckoned it must have been something to do with the hot pools at Chivay. Luckily we were back in Arequipa because the toilet in Chivay would never have coped. By morning Caius was totally useless and could not even pack his bag and lifting it was out of the question. "I want my mum" is all he kept saying. Why he wanted his mum is still unknown, she is definitely not the best person to nurse you through an illness. Her response usually extends as far as asking you if you have had a poo recently. This is her standard response whether it was for a cold, headache or cramp. Caius mostly definitely would have answered, "Yes", to her question.

The thought of catching a bus to Puno did not impress. A seven-hour bus journey was the last thing Caius needed. Images of our friend Matthew, who had a similar problem, making the driver stop the bus in the middle of nowhere and then squatting in full view of the entire bus filled him with fear. It was a struggle to get to the bus station and Vicky ended up carrying both rucksacks. He sat on the bus, motionless, willing his body not to let him down. It was a minor miracle that we did not have to make the driver do an emergency stop.

We made the sensible decision to pay a bit extra for a 'cama con bano' (bed with bathroom) as he did not fancy trudging to the toilet every five minutes in the middle of the night again. The consequences of 'restraining' himself came in Puno when he got the first opportunity to sit on a toilet. It was not a pretty site and Vicky left in search of fresh air.

Feeling better the next day we explored the lakeside town of Puno (with a few trips back to the hostel to use the facilities). To many South Americans

166

Lake Titicaca is a sacred and mythical place. Legend has it that the founders of the Inca Empire rose from the waters of the lake to create the civilisation. If they came out of these icy cold waters, then we reckoned they would have had to have been pretty tough.

A local tale tells how, when the Spanish arrived in Cusco, a group of Indians took a 2000kg gold chain belonging to Inca Huascar and dropped in into the depths of the lake. Unfortunately finding it may not be so easy, as it is the world's highest navigable lake, covering 10000 sq km, lying 3,810 metres above sea level, 80km at its widest and 280m at its deepest.

We too advantage of some decent computer facilities and spent several hours responding to e-mails. That would teach Vicky for writing to everyone the day before saying, "not heard from you for ages". It sounded like the summer in England was the best for years, bloody typical. Looking at the internet we saw headlines like "Railways buckle in heat" and "Hottest day in 40 years". We spared a brief thought, a very brief thought, for all the office workers, commuters, sweaty backs and smelly shoes. It wasn't so bad missing the great weather after all and the weather we had suited us just fine - endless clear, sunny days, with warm temperatures.

By looking at the quantity and quality of the restaurants, bars and cafés, we guessed Puno sees a lot of tourists. The actual town itself didn't have too much to offer, although it was a nice place to just wander around. The market, sprawling along the side of the railway, was the main focal point. We did not hang around too long though as the smelly fish and the sight of calf heads wasn't doing a lot for Caius' constitution.

Vicky Brewis & Caius Simmons

# Island Hopping in Lake Titicaca

A friend recommended we take a two-day trip out to a couple of islands on the lake, the Uros floating Islands and the 'solid' Amantani. A visit to the Uros floating islands appeared in every brochure or organised tour, so thought we better make the effort to go.

Down at the port we were harassed to stock up on refreshments and gifts for our tour. Sensibly we had already been to the market to get our provisions so we didn't need to pay the double 'gringo tax' that they were charging. As we sat on the boat waiting to leave we were treated to some traditional Peruvian music. The fact that he played the panpipes guaranteed he was not going to get any money from us.

The Uros Islands are made from many layers of tortora reeds collected from the lake, creating a platform on which people can live. The reeds are continually added to replace the rotting layers below. There are some 42 floating islands on Lake Titicaca, 16 of which are dedicated solely for visiting tourists. The other islands are for the Indian community that have supposedly lived on them for generations, building their islands, homes and boats from the abundant source of reeds that grow in the shallows of the lake. Approximately 3500 people populate these islands, continuing the tradition of fishing, providing trucha (trout) and pejerrey (kingfish) for the 'mainland'. Some of the fishermen still navigate the water channels through the reeds in their beautifully crafted, tortora reed 'canoes', some with huge figureheads forming an extension of the prow. However, most of the fishermen seem to use more modern motorboats.

The main buildings, like the school and church, are no longer built on the reed, and are constructed with modern materials which rest on stilts instead, moving up and down as the level of the lake changes.

From what we learned most of the inhabitants bugger off back to the mainland at night when all the tourists disappear. Most of them don't last out the rainy season either, preferring to spend it on solid ground.

We stepped of our boat onto one of the islands, trying to keep our balance on the spongy surface. We only managed to take a couple of steps before being accosted by a bunch of persistent souvenir sellers. The guidebooks were right, but the commercialism was far worse than we had imagined it to be. The islanders, justifiably, have capitalised heavily on the tourist excursions, making their money from all the tat they sell. Expressionless faced women sat behind piles of mobiles made from shells, miniature tortora reed boats and houses, those shell ashtrays that were really popular in the seventies, knitted finger puppets and the standard alpaca jumpers.

If we had collected all the different finger puppets we had seen for sale throughout Peru we would probably have had enough to give to an entire primary school. Ever since Cusco they had been shoved underneath our noses, usually as we walked along the street or by the more persistent sellers that used to stand at restaurant and shop windows waggling their puppets at you through the glass. Seeing the finger puppets on the islands was the icing on the cake for us and it made us realise that the Uros was no better than a tacky souvenir stall.

Once we walked away from the adult vendors, we were then subjected to the second barrage; throngs of children begging for sweets or selling postcards and small paintings they had made themselves. They were very enterprising, using the 'aah, aren't they sweet' approach to palm their stuff onto the tourists. We reckoned this was all part of their training to become a fully-fledged tout in the future. They only had one thing to learn – not to smile.

From a distance, the islands look idyllic - reed houses set in the middle of a lake, surrounded by a sky that is as blue as the water it floats on. Close up, it was all an image created for the tourists. We could not help but pick up on the rather false feeling of the Islands, with its small motorboats, solar panels and empty huts. It had been interesting to see how the islands are made, but we felt a sadness when we stepped back onto the boat to leave. Commercialism had really ruined the place and the islanders.

All the other passengers on the tour felt the same about the Uros, voicing their concern that they were no longer looking forward to their stay on Amantani if it was going to be more of the same

A group of locals met us at the small harbour at Amantani and we lined up to be allocated to a host family who would put us up for the night. It was just like being chosen for a sports team at school and, as usual, we were the last to be picked. The host families probably felt the same, with those that had not been allocated a tourist wandering off to sit on the harbour wall to wait for the next boat to arrive. In the long run they would not miss out because the whole island benefits from the home visits. Each family gets about two home stays a week, sometimes more during the high season. Rather than being paid every time they have a tourist to stay all the money is put in a pot and shared out equally among the host families. So if they do not get any tourists for a couple of days they would not loose out financially. This explained why we were not accosted when we landed and there had been no touting from the host families.

Ambrosio was going to be our host for the evening. We wondered if his surname was 'Rizzo'. He looked about 40 years old, but seeing as it was really difficult to put an age on some of the locals, he could have been anywhere between the age of 35 and 50. He was dressed in black felt trousers, a white shirt with a black waistcoat and a dirty brown Panama hat perched on top of his head.

Amantani is an island and home to about 4000 people, which are split into eight different communities all around the island. We were staying in just one of these communities and Ambrosio led us towards the settlement that spread out over the hillside. We were gasping for air as we made our way up the hill, trying to keep up with Ambrosio. He may be used to the altitude but we were about 4000m asl and we needed to stop for a rest every now and again. Looking behind us, back towards the harbour, we could have been mistaken for being by the coast. Our lungs told us otherwise. All the locals sauntered up the hill, Ambrosio nervously ripping a piece of grass apart, the women clicking away with their knitting needles.

The size of the dwellings surprised us, as they seemed bigger than most others we had seen in rural Peru. They all had bright green or orange painted toilet sheds outside and had obviously got some funding to do a "job" lot. Ambrosio's house was even bigger in comparison with the others in the village, with spectacular views over Lake Titicaca.

Arranged in a small courtyard the house consisted of storage rooms on the ground floor, with bedrooms on the upper level, accessed by a rickety staircase and a narrow balcony. We were shown to our room, which had the tiniest of doors. The doors are apparently made small on purpose to help keep the heat in during the cold months. The beds were made with reed mattress and are designed to stop draughts. It was going to be cold that night and for once we were pleased to see the beds were piled high with blankets.

A light switch on the wall took us by surprise, but we weren't shocked to discover the bulb didn't light up when we flicked the switch. There is electricity on the island, but is only available about twice a year during important celebrations when a community generator gets turned on.

On the advice of our tour agency we had bought a present to give to our host family. Looking at the candle stump on the bedside table we wished we had brought them a load of candles instead of a huge bag of oranges, apples and bananas. Fresh fruit and vegetables are difficult to get hold of on the island with the islanders relying on infrequent deliveries from Puno and tourists bringing them gifts. Just before we presented our bag of fruit to Ambrosio we spotted him in the garden peeling himself an orange. The tourists before us had obviously been as unimaginative with their choice of gift as we had. With a smile on his face he accepted the oranges all the same. At least we knew he liked them and they would all get eaten. A brand new paraffin lamp sat in one of the windows, a rarely used gift, because paraffin is so expensive. Apparently the host families get given so much rice and cooking oil that they hand it over to the local shop to be sold cheaply onto the other islanders.

Reaching right down to the lakeside, terraces straddled the hillside below the house. Agriculture obviously plays an important part in the island's self-sufficient economy, but stuck out in the middle of a lake they have little choice but to grow as much of their food as possible. For lunch we were cooked vegetable and quinoa soup, followed by fish, potatoes and orca - all grown or caught locally. Apart from quinoa, corn and potatoes, orca is about the only crop that can be grown successfully on the island. Given the problems of altitude and an unfavourable climate it takes over six months to grow a crop of orca. Its flavour is not dissimilar to a sweet potato, but seeing as it looks more like a big maggot, with a powdery texture it is hardly worth waiting six months for. Ambrosio went off to pick us some fresh peppermint so we could have a cup of tea. He reckoned it was just as good as cocoa to help with the effects of altitude.

The meal had been cooked by Ambrosio's wife and served by his daughter, Julia. The son was hiding out of the way. Most of the other tourists had their meals served either in their bedrooms, or they ate with the family in the kitchen. We reckoned Ambrosio's house was posh because we ate in a separate dining room (one of the store rooms). After we finished eating we took our dirty dishes through to the kitchen, a small tin roofed extension built outside of the main courtyard. How they managed to cook and live in the kitchen was beyond us. It was so small, with dirt floors with a small two ringed cooker in the corner.

Conversation with Ambrosio was quite stilted. He wasn't the chattiest of blokes and we couldn't even work out if he spoke very much Spanish anyway. The main language on the island is Quechan. Like us, he seemed to know a couple of phrases with which he could get by on. A few words were exchanged, but we reckoned it was the same few words he exchanged with all the other tourists that stayed with him.

Joining back up with the other passengers from the boat we walked up to one of the two hills that make up the island. At the top of the island are the remains of a pre-Inca stone temple dedicated to Pachatata, or Father Earth. There are plenty of buildings in honour of Pachamama, or Mother Earth whose religious figure is frequently encountered in much of the Andes, but there are fewer dedications to Pachatata. Father Earth tends to become more popular above 4000m asl, because of his associations with the weather and the natural elements.

One of the annual celebrations on the island involves a race to the two different temples on the island, Pachamama temple and the Pachatata temple. Surprisingly enough the runners who climb to the Pachatata temple are always the first ones back down to the bottom because their hill is much closer to the village. It's just as well really, because they believe they will be cursed with a bad crop and famine if Pachamama won.

The temple of Pachatata was a great place to watch the sunset over Lake Titicaca. It was a bit of a shame there were about 60 other tourists there. Tucked away in Ambrosio's house we had been completely oblivious to the fact that for most of the afternoon, boatloads of tourists had been landing at the harbour. The tourists are 'discreetly' spread amongst the whole island throughout the different communities and if we hadn't walked up to the temple we would have carried on in the belief that, apart from the other 10 passengers on our boat, we were the only tourists on the island.

Back down in the main square (concrete sports pitch) a band was strumming away. All the band members were being given handfuls of coca leaves, most likely their payment for the gig. To avoid disruption when they received their leaves, rather than stop play they just took off their panama hats and a pile of leaves were chucked in. The guitarist, pan piper or drummer would then replace his hat, leaves included, and continue playing. As soon as the dancing started all the tourists legged it to the back of the sports stand, leaving the locals to shuffle around the square on their own. As soon as it was dark enough a huge straw bonfire was lit and children, wearing particularly scary masks, skipped around the flames.

These 'fiestas' as the islanders referred to them are not important celebrations at all and are really just put on for the sake of the tourists. How they found the enthusiasm to play music and dance every night of the week was a credit to their 'tourist department'. They made it feel like it was an important event, happening only a couple of times a year. The fact that they hadn't bothered to start the generator gave the game away.

Luckily Ambrosio had given us each a hat to wear, so he could pick us out from the crowd of fleece jackets and alpaca jumpers. With a hat on our heads already, it also gave us a good excuse not to buy any of the hats that the women knit and sell on the path up to the temple. It must be said they were very good quality, but there are only so many hats you can wear at any one time. The typical Peruvian hats are the same as the typical Ecuadorian (and Bolivian) hats – woolly, with earflaps. The flaps are not necessarily designed to keep your ears warm, but to keep the wind from battering your face, covering the cheekbones to stop them from being burnt and cracked. Ambrosio spotted us across the square and came to rescue us from the dancing to take us home for more food.

In the knowledge that we would have to dress up in traditional costumes to go to the main 'fiesta', we tried to hide away in our rooms. Our friend who had recommended the trip to us had warned us about this part of the evening, but there was no escaping the fact that we had to don the clothing and go dancing. Julia dragged us out and made Caius put a large grey poncho over his head. Of course he had to wear his hat as well, but compared to what Vicky had to wear he got away very lightly. Vicky, however, had to wear two bulky skirts, a white blouse, a very wide belt and a black shawl. Julia didn't give her the chance to take off any of her clothes, and together with a t-shirt, a long sleeved top, a jumper and fleece coat she looked particularly bundled up and uncomfortable. Just to make it even harder to breathe, a large belt was tied tightly around her waist like a corset. The skirt she was wearing was not really designed for tall westerners and looked more like a miniskirt on her. This probably wouldn't have been so bad if it wasn't for the fact that she still had her trousers and walking boots on.

Julia, on the other hand, looked delightful in her pretty blouse and swaying green skirt. Ambrosio and his wife obviously liked dancing as much as we did, leaving Julia to accompany us to the village hall to where the 'fiesta' was taking place. Seeing all the other tourists bundled up in the costumes made us feel marginally better, but there was no escaping the fact we all looked totally ridiculous. We were then subjected to an evening of dancing to pan pipe music. Lining up in pairs we shuffled backwards and forwards, with the occasional twirl. This traditional dancing wasn't difficult, but it wasn't very inspiring either. After a few hours all the tourists started feigning tiredness as an excuse to escape the torture. Julia guided us home in the dark, and then to the hall to dance the night away with all her mates. They made it feel like the 'fiesta' was put on especially for us, but it was really just an excuse to have a bit of a party every night.

Looking out from our balcony we gazed at the stars until we were too cold to stay outside any longer. With no streetlights, or a glow from house windows the night sky was amazing. Whether it had anything to do with being 4km closer to them than usual, but it did feel like we could almost touch them.

Having not gone to bed until the early hours of the morning, Julia looked particularly rough and bleary eyed when she served us breakfast. Before we left Caius made the family line up for a typical gringo photo. They must be used to it but still looked embarrassed, with Ambrosio's wife hiding behind him in an attempt to avoid the camera. It was our first photo we had managed to take without feeling like we were being invasive. We said our farewells and Ambrosio took us back to the boat. It amazed us how the whole island had gone to such an extent to entertain a relatively small number of gringos. They had certainly succeeded in making the visit a memorable one. Based on what we had seen on the Uros islands, Amantani could have easily gone down the same commercial route but they had organised it in such a way that it is discreet and doesn't feel too touristy.

Vicky Brewis & Caius Simmons

Our next stop was the island of Taquile, where the locals are famous for using age-old weaving techniques and wear colourful traditional clothes. From what we could work out, Taquile used to operate a similar system to Amantani, whereby host families have tourists to stay overnight, but it seemed like they don't really bother too much anymore. The island is home to about 3500 residents. It was evident from the lack of warmth from the locals that they don't really like outsiders. They are eager to stick to traditional values and aren't keen on people from the mainland coming in and disrupting their culture. The only drawback it seems is the high number of recorded disabilities associated with inbreeding.

There are a number of ancient Inca traditions and laws that the people on Taquile like to observe. For example when a couple meet they first must live with each other for two years to make sure they are happy with their decision before getting married. If they have children within this time, they must wed. Within the two years, they may split up at any time, holding no grudges. However, if they are still together after two years, they must get married, and never divorce. It sounded like a sensible idea to us.

Even though Amantani is only a short boat journey away, the people of Taquile speak a completely different language. The Amantani's first language is Quechan, whilst on Taquile they speak Aymarian. Their clothing, especially the men's traditional dress, was also very different. The men on Amanatani stick to black and white cloth, with various shades of Panama hats. On Taquile the men wore long, floppy woollen caps, like nightcaps, embroidered waistcoats and braided sashes around their waists. The different styles of hat tells you whether a man is married or in a relationship and if they are single, or whether they are looking for someone. The hats are all woven by the men and can take several months to make. We reckoned that they should introduce the same system in nightclubs to avoid the hassle of trying to pull, or save the embarrassment caused by cracking onto someone who is already "taken".

On the boat back to Puno we got talking to a German couple who were on a whistle stop tour of South America. They had 'done' Ecuador, made it into Peru cramming in Lima, the Inca Trail, Arequipa and Lake Titicaca - an amazing feat in two weeks. When we asked if all their holidays were the same, they said "yes" and proudly told us all about their trip to Asia. It was another three-week tour where they went to nine different countries, spending most of their time in an airport from the sounds of it.

# Bolivia

(not to scale)

# Across the Border

The big Bolivian official at the border was not very impressed that Caius had filled in his immigration forms in red ink. He was even less amused when he realised that Caius had lent the pen to half of the other passengers on the bus. He mumbled a load of grief, warning him "not to do it again" and indicated that he might have to fill in the forms again. This was almost as petty as American immigration, reminding us of the time when we had been sent to the back of the queue because we had used the 'wrong colour blue ink' on our forms. The Bolivian immigration officer was not so picky and stamped the form regardless of the pen colour.

We had finally arrived in Bolivia.

The currency in Bolivia is imaginatively called Bolivian Bolivianos, the official abbreviated term being "BOB". Both of us are too young to remember the old shilling, but it still made us feel 'at home' to refer to the currency in Bolivia as BOB.

We tried not to look guilty as we handed over our dollar notes in exchange for some BOBs. The notes had been in our pockets since Cusco, when a hotel owner palmed them off onto us. It was not until we tried to pay for our hostel in Arequipa that we found out that no one would accept them because they were slightly scuffed and one of them had a tiny rip in it. Apparently the banks would not change them, Lima being the only city that could cope with dirty notes. After our experiences in Ecuador this came as a bit of a surprise to us, the Ecuadorians would accept anything. We felt really guilty, like we were trying to get rid of fake notes. We were expecting them to be rejected by the

179

woman at the money exchange but after checking with her colleague, the cashier handed over some Bolivian notes and coins across the counter.

# Copacabana Beach

The nearest town to the border crossing is Copacabana. As we arrived at the town boundary an official climbed on to the bus, muttered a couple of words and started collecting money from everyone. This was a local tax that anyone entering Copacabana had to pay, or so he claimed. It turned out he was collecting for the Bolivian Gravediggers Foundation, a cunning disguise for a Gringo Tax. He even had the cheek to give us a ticket to prove we had paid it.

We were getting off at Copacabana but the bus was continuing onto La Paz, and it would be another hour or so before it left. Well, that is what we thought our bus driver told us. The information he was actually giving us was that, being in Bolivia we were in a new time zone and needed to put our watches forward an hour. It wasn't until later on in the day when we asked someone the time did we finally realise that we were an hour behind everyone else in Bolivia. It explained why all the restaurants had stopped serving lunch so early.

The "places to stay" list that Charlie had given us on the Galapagos was looking pretty limp and tatty by now, but we had distinctly remembered the hostel they had recommended in Copacabana – *Hostal La Cupula*. As good travellers do, we had passed on this recommendation to the 'whistle stop' German couple we had met on the Amantani boat. They told us they still had not decided where they were going to stay, so we passed on the directions anyway. The bus journey from Puno had been the first time during their travels they had let their bags be put in the hold (they had sat with their rucksacks on their knees for all their other journeys). It looked like they were going to be some time before they got themselves organised. They were still struggling to unlock the wire mesh they had secured around their rucksacks as we headed off up the hill to the hostel.

Just as we reached the hostel gateway a blond haired man, carrying a rucksack covered in a wire security mesh, overtook us at high speed. He squeezed past us, reaching the door just before we got there and gave a triumphant "whoop". He had been a bit ambitious running at this altitude (3800m asl) and was too out of breath to speak to the hotel receptionist to try and book a room.

As long as we still got a room we were not that bothered, but we thought it had been a bit mean of them seeing as the hostel had not even been listed in their guidebook. In their hurry to choose the best available room, they hadn't realised that the room they had picked was right next to the busy kitchen and communal room. Our room was directly above theirs, so we made sure we clomped around on the wooden floor making as much noise as possible.

The main reason the hostel had been recommended was because the beds were so comfortable and we were supplied with big fluffy, light duvets. It was worth the money just for these and certainly deserved our award for the 'Best Hostel' of the trip. We were able to snuggle down, keep warm and breathe all at the same time. Blankets are not nearly so comfortable and the only way to keep warm is to pile on more, which then means you can't really move around or breathe properly because they are so heavy. It maybe that some of the mattresses we slept on could have been ridden with lice, but woollen blankets are also very itchy. Blankets are certainly no substitute for a nice soft, cotton duvet cover (and a decent nights sleep).

The cultural differences when we crossed the border were once again very apparent. Even though we were only a couple of kilometres from Peru it felt completely different. The best thing was that nobody appeared to hassle you in the way they did in Peru. We were able to walk down the main street without being pestered by shop owners and stallholders. Rather than walking slowly by and trying to get a glimpse of what they sold, we were able to stop and look more closely at the merchandise. Not that we were planning on buying anything, anyway. Restaurant owners would let you look at the menus without telling us how great their food was. The roads were quiet, with only the occasional bus. The passing taxis were not hooting their horns every other second. Taxi drivers stood leaning on their battered cars, chatting with their mates, not worrying about the passing trade that they might be missing out on. We sat in the square warming ourselves in the hot sunshine and even though our shoes were due for a clean there were no boys ready and willing to shine them. We were enjoying this new country and we had only seen a couple of streets.

The only down side seemed to be the beer. A new country usually meant we would get some different beer. The regional beers in Peru had all been good so far, even if they did all taste pretty much the same. The local tipple in Copacabana was Pacena (from La Paz) and was particularly rough with a nasty salty aftertaste. We hoped it wasn't a 'taste' of things to come, as enjoying a beer every evening had become a regular occurrence and the thought of missing out on it was a bit worrying.

The town is the original Copacabana and not the Brazilian beach resort that the name is better known for. Copacabana does have a beach, but the waves lapping up against it are from Lake Titicaca and not the Atlantic. The likelihood of finding bikini clad girls or men posing in their pouches were going to be slim, but the abundance of new hotels overlooking the lake gave an impression of a popular holiday resort. It was hard to believe it, but thousands of Catholic pilgrims descend on the town a couple of times a year to attend festivals that pay homage to the Virgen de Copacabana, Bolivia's patron saint. Copacabana Beach (Brazil) adopted the name when an image of the Virgen de Copacabana was taken to Rio de Janeiro in the 19th century.

We popped into the Cathedral to see the image of the Virgin Mary and were a bit surprised to discover she had a brown face. The fact she is often referred to as the Dark Virgin of the Lake should have been an indication of her colouring, but as we are so used to religious icons represented as white

Europeans, it hadn't been quite what we were expecting. A number of miracles supposedly occurred not long after her first appearance, but sensing our scepticism we doubted she would manage to make the beer less salty, or the buses more comfortable on our behalf.

The impressive white domed Cathedral dominates the main square in the village. Outside there are stalls selling flags, banners, streamers, rosettes, fake money, sweets, fake jewellery and an amazing array of all kinds of tat. These are sold to decorate buses, cars and trucks that come here to be blessed by the priest with holy water. This ritual is not just restricted to festival time, every Sunday the square is full of vehicles adorned with this paraphernalia and people hoping to be granted all the things they desire – abundant harvests, good health and a bit longer out of the old banger. Unfortunately it was now Monday and we had missed the weekly celebrations. There were a couple of tour buses parked up outside the Cathedral with a few token streamers attached to them. Judging by the number of pensioners hobbling around town, we reckoned the buses were Bolivias answer to Wallace Arnold. Part of the blessing, known as ch'alla, involves the priest dousing the vehicle with alcohol. The drivers were enjoying a quick drink with the leftovers before they carried on with their tour. This blessing has a lot to answer for, as the drivers are under the impression they can drive the mountain roads like complete loonies and not have an accident. Judging by the amount of beer they were downing, they needed more than a blessing from a priest to keep them safe during their travels.

Long before the Spanish appeared and imposed Catholicism on the population, Copacabana was already an important religious site for the Incas. At one stage the entire Copacabana peninsula was a dedicated religious area and there are still a number of Inca ruins scattered around the village. Standing on the hillside, overlooking Copacabana, we tried to imagine what the significance of a couple of carved stones and some holes in a rocky crag were. If we had been there on the morning of June 21 (winter solstice and also the first day of the Aymara New Year), we would have realised that the sunlight shines through these holes, lighting up a stone lintel that is suspended between two rocky outcrops. It seemed that the Spanish had the same problem as us working out the importance of these rocks. Not realising the astronomical appeal of this site they mistook the lintel for gallows and named it Horca del Inca (Gallows of the Incas).

Throughout history Copacabana has always been the most important destination for pilgrims in the southern Andes. Their destination was not actually Copacabana itself but a couple of Islands, the Isla del Sol and Isla de la Luna, on Lake Titicaca. It is thought that even as early as 500AD the Tiwanaku's made their way to these islands to visit religious shrines and perform rituals. By the early 16th Century the Incas regarded it as the most important and sacred site in their Empire. Thousands of Incas would have travelled here under the belief that Viracocha, the creator god, had risen from the waters of the lake and standing on a rock on the Isla del Sol had beckoned for the sun and moon. A clever marketing ploy by the Inca rulers, who also claimed Viracocha had created Manco Capac and Mama Ocllo (the founding fathers of the Incas). Inca literally means "peoples of the sun" and by associating themselves with the sun's birthplace, the Lake, it would only add credence to them.

Following the old Inca trail along the coast to Yampupata sounded very romantic, walking the 17km to get there didn't. Catching a boat from Copacabana to the Isla del Sol was by far the easiest option and we planned to walk around the Island instead. We had chosen to travel with a firm recommended by the hostel, thinking it would be good to give our money to a smaller company. Sitting on the shoreline, waiting for our boat to turn up, we watched the tourist boats fill up with passengers. We waited, and we waited. We watched other boats come and go and there was still no sign of ours. After what seemed like most of the morning (30 minutes to be precise) a lady came out of a small shed and informed us that the boat we were waiting for had left the day before with a large group of tourists and would not be back until the following day. Luckily we managed to squeeze on the tourist boat just before it left. No wonder they have the monopoly over other boat operators in the village.

The boat ride across was great, admiring the beautiful coastline from the top deck. The water was the same colour as the sky; bright blue and we sat plying on the sun cream.

The main village on Isla del Sol is Yumani and it is situated at the top of a steep hill overlooking Lake Titicaca. The Incas had kindly built a stairway to take us to the top, but it didn't seem to make the climb any easier. We had to stop every so often to catch our breaths. When we did stop the strategically placed touts thought we had stopped to buy some of their wares. After our experience of shop owners in Copacabana we reckoned that these traders were from Peru and not Bolivia, as they were being very insistent we should buy an alpaca 'joompa', or a hideous finger puppet. We were really smug with ourselves on the way back down the following day when we found a path that avoided all the touts.

After booking into a hostel we decided that if we wanted to make it around the island in one day we would have to set off straight away. It took us ages to even get out of the village, with its maze of paths and dead ends. We kept finding ourselves outside someone's front door, or a water pump and at one stage we were standing outside an outdoor toilet with no footpath in sight. Finally we passed the initiative test and headed northwards along the coast. The hillsides were covered in agricultural terraces and even though they were pretty dry at this time of year they are relatively productive. Insulated by Lake Titicaca, temperatures on the Island tend not to fall as much as those on the mainland and as a result it benefits from a much warmer climate.

As we approached the small town of Challa we could see groups of villagers hanging around a bit of boggy wasteland. There were about 100 of them altogether, spread out in groups of four or five. We couldn't work out what they were up to, but we ruled out a welcoming committee for the two gringos making their way down the hill towards their village. Given the name

186

of the settlement (same as *ch'alla*) we wondered if they were waiting for a priest to turn up and, in the absence of any cars, bless their llamas with beer. We walked on without too many stares and even though we were desperate to know what they were doing we didn't dare ask in case they said they were the lynch mob.

There were plenty of distractions along the way and we had ample opportunities to stop and rest. We popped into a local museum that was full of traditional clothing (mostly big feathery hats and ponchos), and were shown around by a very enthusiastic youth. We had stupidly told him that we knew a bit of Spanish, but unfortunately our understanding of Spanish and his idea of how much we knew were about the same – not a lot. We smiled and nodded as often as possible, while trying to read the English information boards without him noticing too much. When he finished he just walked off, not even asking for a tip. This place was strange.

We had to keep reminding ourselves that we were at nearly 4000m asl, in the centre of Bolivia and that the shore we were standing on was Lake Titicaca. If it wasn't for the fact that we got out of breath so easily and that there were cows drinking the water from the shore we could have easily convinced ourselves we were standing on a beach by the sea (cows would not be drinking salty water).

At the most northerly village, Challapampa, a villager stopped and started rabbiting away to us. As usual we didn't really have a clue what he was saying to us and he soon wandered off when he realised his efforts were a lost cause. We had managed to pick up a few key words from his conversation and after comparing notes we worked out he was the curator of the museum that we had wanted to visit. He had been telling us that he had just closed for lunch but if we wanted we could take the key and let ourselves in. We spun around to chase after him, but he was gone.

We had planned to stop at the main archaeological site, the sacred rock Titkala, where Viracocha would have stood and created the sun and the moon. We think we may have seen it, but we weren't entirely convinced it was the correct rock. The rock we thought it may have been turned out to be a picnic table constructed from local stone. We then proceeded to walk right past the hallowed stone without realising it was even there. There were no tourists around to ask, the last of which had departed long ago on the boat back to Copacabana. We did find some ruins and we convinced ourselves that this is where Mr Inca came to sacrifice fair maidens. The views were stunning and with the entire site to ourselves it was magically peaceful.

The walk back to our hostel was along the spine of the island and by the time we got back we were shattered. We had seen a few people on the way back including a group of about 40 villagers, working together, making repairs to the footpath. We also met a young girl dressed in traditional costume dragging an alpaca behind. For some reason she wanted us to take a photo of her and pay her for the privilege. We didn't oblige her and she seemed more grateful for the drink of water we gave her instead. She was probably even more tired than we were, standing on her feet all day trying her best to smile at passing tourists.

The round trip had taken over seven hours so naturally we treated ourselves to a beer, while watching the sunset. We didn't care that it was a salty Pacena – it was cold and refreshing.

We were accosted by another young girl trying to sell us an alpaca jumper. "No, gracias". She was obviously bored, and just said "alpaca" again and again. She got an equally bored sounding reply of "No, gracias" from us. This carried on for a while. We then told her, "No, me gusto alpaca" (I don't like alpaca). Seemingly, she thought this reply was amusing and we got a smile out of her before she went off to hassle some other tourists.

We stood on our hostel balcony, gazing at the stars. In daylight we had panoramic views of Lake Titicaca, Isla del Luna and the distant Cordillera Real – it was magnificent. When it got dark, our view changed to thousands of stars, sparkling above us. It was particularly clear that night, and we noted in our diaries that Mars looked "particularly orange and massive".

The boat that we booked turned up but then headed off in a totally different direction than planned. We had to barter for another return ticket with different company, which were mysteriously, but not surprisingly, more expensive than it had been on the outward journey. We managed to get a discount as long as we didn't tell any of the other passengers. There was obviously a good 'beer fund' scam the ticket collector had going.

Copacabana is also famous for something else. It is the home to the Bolivian Navy, the headquarters of which are situated on the edge of the lake. Since gaining its independence in 1825, the Republic of Bolivia has lost nearly half of its territory, including its Pacific Ocean coast to Chile in 1879. Bolivia has since remained landlocked, much to the embarrassment of Queen Victoria, who once ordered a Royal Navy fleet to bombard its capital. The Navy only exists as a token to remind the rest of the world that Bolivia once had a coastline. As we cruised into port we passed by the headquarters and watched a couple of sailors struggling to control a canoe. They were being watched by a colleague, who sat in his pedalo, on dry land. It was almost too cruel to take a photo.

Bolivia was back on-line again after a day without the internet and we were able to e-mail everyone to remind them that it was a Monday morning, and to wish them a pleasant day at work. There are three Internet cafés in Copacabana, and all three are extortionately priced. It turned out that there used to be only one café offering Internet services and could charge whatever he liked. Then along came the other two new Internet businesses, charging much-reduced prices. The established company put their prices down to near nothing, threatening to put the new places out of business. They had no option but to set their prices extortionately high. We tried haggling but the boy seemed to understand their overpricing no more than we did.

# Mars Attacks

The following night, Mars was the closest to Earth for 26,000 years and Copacabana was one of the best locations in the world to see it. The biggest and smartest hotel in the town was fully booked out with NASA scientists, who had made the trip especially to witness this event.

At 4.00pm we could see some clouds forming on the horizon, by 5.00pm the wind had picked up and by dusk we were in a full storm, with heavy rain, hail and snow showers, thunder and lightning. The storm carried on right through the night until dawn, when the clouds parted and the sun reappeared. So much for being the best place to see Mars. By the time we surfaced from our cosy slumber, the sun was shining and Copacabana was covered in a dusting of snow.

It reminded us of when there was a total eclipse of the sun in England. Caius' family happened to live close to the line of totality in Cornwall and it was billed as one of the best places in the country to see the eclipse. As the eclipse started, it clouded over and during totality the heavens opened and rain fell in torrents for the four minutes of total dark. As it got lighter, the rain stopped, and when the sun and moon separated, so did the clouds.

# The Worlds Highest Capital City?

The road to La Paz took us along the shore of Lake Titicaca. It was a bit of a surprise when we all had to disembark and cross an inlet by a small taxi boat. The Israeli's on the bus were not overly impressed because we had to pay extra (all of about 20p) to get across. We were pleased we had not stayed on the bus as it was loaded onto a particularly rickety, unstable looking barge and taken across the choppy waters. The harbour was full of similar rotting, sinking vessels and the barge that was transporting our bus looked like it would be joining them very soon. Despite the intense swaying and rocking the bus was being subjected to, the rucksacks miraculously stayed on the top and made it the opposite shore in one piece.

We tried to ignore the fact that our little taxi boat wasn't in great condition either. We spent the five minute journey working out where they could have possibly stored the lifejackets, and which of the other passengers we would have to trample over if we needed to get out in a hurry. It was with some relief when our feet touched solid ground and we boarded the bus to carry on with the journey. We just hoped that our bus driver hadn't stopped off at Copacabana Cathedral for a blessing that morning.

As we drove towards La Paz the temperature steadily dropped. The mountains looked menacing in front of stormy skies and the dusty plain was covered in mini tornadoes carrying dust and dead grass upwards. Small mud farm buildings were spread across the plain and farmers wearily worked in the fields. We did not envy them. In the distance we saw a large crowd of people - a protest perhaps. As we got closer we realised they were building a house. All the local community had got together and were there to help assemble the new dwelling. Men were crawling all over the roof, some were carrying rocks or adobe blocks, while others helped with the carpentry and another group building the walls. Groups of women were hanging around chatting, helping or cooking big vats of steaming soup. It would be great if we could build houses like this in the U.K. It looked so idyllic and great fun as well.

La Paz is located spectacularly in a canyon, which has been gorged out of the surrounding Altiplano. At a height of 3500m asl, it makes it the highest capital city in the world. Technically, the capital of Bolivia is Sucre as this is where the Supreme Court still resides and is therefore the legal capital and seat of judiciary. In effect, La Paz is the capital of Bolivia; being the seat of the Government and Congress and is the main political and commercial centre for the country.

In terms of history La Paz is a relatively new city and was established to link Cusco and Potosí by the Spanish in 1548. Its 'favourable' location, with easy access to vital resources, was the main reasons for the growth of the city and it now has a population of just over one million. The city merges seamlessly with the urban centre of El Alto, which sits high above the deep valley on the Altiplano. El Alto was recently declared a city in its own right and adds almost another million people to the population of the La Paz region.

Anyone flying into La Paz would in fact arrive in El Alto, which has become famous for being the highest airport in the world. There can be serious consequences of landing at an altitude of over 4000m asl, the main one being altitude sickness. Many people we met were suffering from severe headaches, vomiting and they were really struggling to walk around without getting out of breath. We didn't imagine that many people considered this when they booked their tickets. The other problem with landing at La Paz is that, due to the reduced air resistance at this altitude, the plane has to speed up to land. The runway is reported to be nearly five miles long, to give it plenty of time to stop. We heard many different phrases describing the landing; the most popular seemed to be, "never again".

Agricultural reform, issued as a result of a National Revolution in 1952, resulted in a radical change in land ownership in the countryside. Indigenous peasants organised into communities were given back the control of hacienda lands, and workers, now released from the grasp of wealthy landowners, headed for the city. El Altos main population consists of Aymara migrants. A local lady told us that their migration is usually not permanent and many of the families still keep a country residence, only coming to the city to trade in the markets. Therefore a high proportion of El Alto residents are temporary, using their house for short periods at a time, perhaps a couple of months each year. The homes are never left empty, with some families sharing a house or renting out rooms and beds for people in search of temporary work. El Alto has nothing for the tourist (it is not even listed in the guidebook's index), and we had got a good feel for the place driving through it - lots of poverty and miles of very run down, poor looking dwellings. We decided to give it a miss.

After consulting the list Charlie had given to us on the Galápagos we had made the decision to visit the jungle from Bolivia, rather than Peru or Ecuador. We had our hearts set on an eco-lodge and needed to start considering some sort of anti-malaria protection before we booked anything. Having heard a string of horror stories about the side effects larium (one of the most common anti-malarial), and following weeks of deliberation and research, we decided to take Doxycylin. We thought we would be relatively safe with an antibiotic.

Unfortunately, one thing we overlooked was that Caius had never had a need to take antibiotics before and his body didn't appear to react well to the strong dosage. After reading the instruction leaflet that came with the pills we realised he was experiencing most of the side effects listed under the 'stop taking these if you get any of these' section.

One more tablet and another morning of feeling like shit was enough for us to make the decision that we would give a trip to the jungle a miss. It was not worth the hassle, especially as he probably would have spent the entire time feeling ill. He would also have to continue taking the tablets for three weeks after the trip. The tour company who were trying to sell us the trip explained that we did not need to worry about malaria as it didn't exist in this part of the Amazon. We did not really fancy the risk.

We found ourselves in a position where we would be arriving in Santiago almost 10 days earlier than planned. Our rough itinerary had been to go to the jungle and then spend a couple of days each in the towns in the southern half of the country. After a morning of deliberation, we decided to add Sorata to our list of places to visit and by spending a day or two extra in each of the towns we would time our arrival in Chile to perfection. We were both bitterly disappointed about not being able to go to the jungle, but it meant we no longer had to rush from town to town and we would also have extra money to spend on better accommodation and food.

# The Worlds Most Dangerous Road

One of the primary tourist attractions from La Paz is to travel down 'The most dangerous road in the world'. Our guidebook suggested that the safest way to attack this road, which has vertical drops of up to 1000m, is on a mountain bike, thus earning a tacky T-shirt. We wondered who would be the safest travellers using the road - the cyclists probably as the poor buses and lorries would have to swerve to overtake the cyclist. It was not the going down we were worried about, it was the coming back up. Being Bolivia's main link with the Amazon basin and Brazil, it is a busy road and it is the volume of traffic that makes it so dangerous. The Bolivian government had just completed a new relief road so that there would be a one-way system on the worst stretch. Unfortunately they did not build the bridges strong enough to handle lorries, buses or mini-buses. Seeing as they are the only vehicles that really use the road that doesn't leave very much other traffic that could safely drive along the new road!!

One of our fellow passengers on our Galápagos tour told us about his experience of travelling along the road. Noel had caught the bus from Rurrenabaque in the Amazon basin up to La Paz. The journey should have taken no more than 20 hours in total. It was the beginning of the wet season, and it had been raining continually for three days. The dirt road was flooded in places, churned up and slippery. It took 36 hours to reach Coroico, the beginning of the 'Most Dangerous Road in the World'. The driver sat chomping away on coca leaves and, apart from occasional toilet stops, had not left his seat for a day and a half. Half way up the road there was a waterfall pouring down onto the road, making it impassable. Because the bus driver wanted to make up some lost time, he forced himself up the single-track road, with a 500-metre sheer drop on one side, past all the other waiting vehicles, to the front of the queue. It had finally stopped raining, but the water level across the road was at waist height (the driver had been in to the middle to check). The waters started to abate and when the driver was satisfied that the water level was low enough (now only half way up his thigh) he wanted to get going. Noel had got off the bus, refusing to go across. Fortunately, the bus made it safely to the other side. Unfortunately, Noel was left stranded. The bus driver was urging him to hurry and he had no option but to cling onto the side of the next vehicle coming across (the lorry driver would not let him into the cab in case they got washed over, to a certain death). The entire journey, with the same driver, had taken 44 hours. Noel swore he would never travel on the road again, even in the dry season.

The views are supposed to be spectacular, if it is not misty, dark or raining. We had met several travellers who had known people who had been killed on this road - one a French cyclist and a group of six Israelis who went over the edge in their bus. Approximately 400 people die on this road every year and 36 people went over the edge only two weeks previously. By our reckoning there was another fatal accident due very soon. We would like to say we went down and it was the most amazing thing we had ever done, instead we chickened out. Do we regret not going? Not in the slightest and we wouldn't have worn the T-shirts anyway.

The pavements of La Paz were full of street vendors and shoeshine boys. The street vendors stood or sat side by side, hunched over tables and rugs displaying their goods for sale. Stacked in neat pyramids were piles of soaps, biscuits, pan scrubbers, fleeces, dish clothes, fake leather jackets, plastic sandals and CD's. Old wizened men and women shuffled their way along the side of the road pushing small cartloads of peanuts or popcorn (well it looked a bit like very big puffed popcorn, but tasted more like cardboard).

The shoeshine boys filled in the gaps along the pavement. Most wore sinister looking dark balaclavas, which was a little disconcerting. Apparently, there is a bit of a stigma attached to shining shoes and rather than let their friends recognise them doing such a menial job, they preferred to cover their faces.

Along with the familiar sight of the street stalls and shoeshine boys, we noticed a new addition to the regulars on the street scene – mobile phone hawkers. Young men (and women) carrying mobile phones attached to their belts with thin chains roamed the streets offering the use of their phone. Phone prices are so high in Bolivia, especially rental charges, that most families do not have their own phone line, relying on mobile services instead. These touts act as mobile phone boxes and the chains are to stop them from being pinched (the phones that is).

As we sat and ate supper we watched a huge demonstration going on in the streets in front of the restaurant. We weren't really sure what it was about at first, but the effigies and puppets of George Bush told us the mood was not very friendly towards the Americans and the Western world.

La Paz is famous for its demonstrations and riots, and as more and more people joined the crowds the atmosphere became tenser. One of the buildings in the old square was peppered with bullet holes and we prayed they had not been a recent occurrence. There were talks of a revolt kicking off around the country over the export of natural gas. We didn't wait around long enough to find out exactly what it was all about and instead sneaked along the back streets to the hostel and the safety of our bedroom. The demonstration turned out to be relatively peaceful, with only a few minor scuffles being reported.

La Paz definitely felt like a city to us – it was big and it smelled, not dissimilar to London really. Hundreds of taxis filled the streets and the roads were clogged up behind traffic lights at every junction. There was a definite business area, with large banks and modern high-rise buildings full of offices, and businessmen strolling the streets with black briefcases and mobile phones. And of course there was the fair share of MacDonald's and Starbucks to ensure that Bolivia is being propelled into the Western world.

There is some lovely architecture in La Paz, especially around the older squares and there were plenty of museums to keep us occupied. If you strayed out of these areas, it was a completely different story and a row of beautifully restored colonial buildings quickly turned into a row of boarded up houses sprayed with graffiti. As with most of the cities around the world an effort is made to keep the centre 'clean' and La Paz was no exception.

# Witches' Market

Mercado de Hechiceria or the Witches' Market has become world famous, providing the tourist with an insight into the world of Aymara mysticism and herbal medicine. The busy stalls line the roadside, with very colourful and strange items for sale. Most disturbing are the dried Llama foetuses, hung up by the dozen by their front shrivelled legs. Well over 90% of Bolivian families have a dried llama foetus thrown under the foundations of their house for luck and protection. We watched as the 'witches' made up brightly coloured paper plates for their customers with weird and wonderful things, like dried frogs with cigarettes in their mouths (for good luck and prosperity), armadillo shells, dried flowers and gross looking luminous sweets. The whole ceremony of buying and selling was taken very seriously, with advice been given on what were the best charms, food and alcohol, depending on the occasion. Compared to all the other stalls in the streets, the 'witches' were doing a roaring trade. Owning a witch stall seemed to propel the vendor to the upper end of the scale in the pecking order of market traders, commanding a lot of respect from passers by.

The witches market was a prime area to take a photograph, and tourists would happily snap away, without taking any care to respect the privacy of the stallholders. We thought we had better get permission before we took a photo as we didn't want a nasty curse being put on us, or our films. We went around asking at the stalls, but we kept getting a very abrupt "No". One old man, who was divvying up some noxious looking liquid into plastic bottle, was particularly rude to us. They must get sick of tourists taking photos of them. Eventually, to our relief, we found a nice lady who was more than happy for us to take a

Vicky Brewis & Caius Simmons

photograph of her goods.  She was too busy chatting away to a shop owner on the other side of the road, which also meant she would not be in the picture.

# White Gold

We took a visit to the excellent Museo de la Coca, a small museum crammed into a couple of small rooms giving a very comprehensive overview and history of the coca plant. *Erythroxylum coca is a* tropical shrub, of the family Erythroxylaceae and is commonly found growing wild in Ecuador, Peru and Bolivia. Its small green leaf which, when dried, is not too dissimilar to a small bay leaf. It is also the raw material for the drug cocaine.

Although processing the coca leaf to produce cocaine is a relatively modern concept, the Andean people have used the leaf for thousands of years for medicinal, cultural and religious purposes. Archaeologists say that coca was first cultivated in the Andes as long ago as 3000BC. Bolivia has been growing the coca plant for centuries, but it was not until the Incas came along that it was grown in any great quantity.

You can buy dried coca leaves in any market and is usually sold from huge bins, tubs or bags. There is plenty of demand, with at least three million Bolivians, or 80% of the adult population regularly practice coca 'acuillico' or chewing. Strictly speaking, the leaves aren't actually chewed. Instead, the dried coca leaf is moistened with saliva, gently sucked and the 'invigorating' juices swallowed.

There are many theories about how to get the best results from chewing your leaves. Stripping the leaf of its stalk with you teeth and then putting the remaining leaf between the gum and cheek seemed a popular method. When the cheek is full a piece of lime-rich material, such as limestone, cereal grain or burnt seashell is added to help separate out the alkaloid properties. The lime also gets the saliva glands going.

It tastes pretty gross, but we persisted with it because there are supposedly a number of benefits to chewing coca leaves. It is meant to give you more energy and it has been said that Inca runners would chew coca leaves, helping them to travel up to 250km a day to deliver their messages. During the colonial period, Quecha and Aymara Indian labourers in the silver mines consumed coca to protect them against the effects of high altitude, stave off hunger, tiredness and the cold. It did appear to help when we were at high altitude, but rather than chew the leaves we found coca tea, *mate de coca* (leaves infused in hot water), to be more enjoyable.

According to scientists chewing coca leaves is not dangerous or addictive. It just makes your teeth green and your breath smell like you had been eating silage instead. Years of chewing the leaves had obviously taken its toll on most of the population, who all seemed to have either a mouthful of fillings or no teeth at all. Communication problems are also a possible side effect. This is, not due to any serious chemical reaction, but just trying to talk with a gob full of leaves while your mouth is semi-anaesthetised. Dribbling can also be a problem for the novice chewer. Back at home we found we could achieve a similar effect by dabbing clove oil on our lips.

Culturally, chewing coca leaves is very important especially for the indigenous people, many of whom call it the *hoja sagrada*, or sacred leaf. The government recognise its importance within society and allows the cultivation of 12,000 hectares of coca for cultural and medicinal uses, such as coca chewing.

Outside of the Andean belt coca was really unheard of until the mid 1800s when Angelo Mariani, a chemist in Paris, produced a wine made from the leaf. The success of this wine inspired other drinks companies, such as Coca Cola, to adopt this leaf for its 'medical benefits'. Even though cocaine was taken out of Coca Cola in 1908, the company still imports coca leaf. In 1995 the company, apparently, bought 200 tons. Maybe it was used for the staff Christmas bonus rather than for 'flavouring'.

It was well known that chewing the leaves resulted in the numbing of the mouth, but it took until 1860 before anyone finally managed to isolate the active property of the leaves - the alkaloid, cocaine. Cocaine soon became important medically after it was used, during an eye operation in 1884, as a local anaesthetic. Its clinical application was mainly as a general painkiller, and it uses were fairly widespread; dentistry, minor operations, asthma, mountain-sickness, sea-sickness, morning sickness during pregnancy and cramps, to name a few. It also became popular in psychiatry and as a substitute for morphine.

Cocaine is also a highly addictive drug and it slowly became more popular, not just medically, but also socially. Among the first famous users were Sigmund Freud, who called it a "magical substance", and the fictional detective, Sherlock Holmes. Robert Louis Stephenson wrote Dr Jekyll and Mr Hyde during a week of binging on the drug. Other famous users of coca-based products included Queen Victoria and Winston Churchill.

To a Cornishman, china clay is known as white gold. In Bolivia, white gold is cocaine. Bolivia's economy is one of the poorest in the Americas, ranking ahead of only Haiti, with 75% of Bolivians living below the poverty line. But it does have one of the world's most commercial cash crops right on its doorstep. For thousands of poor people growing and harvesting coca it puts food on their tables, clothes on their backs and a roof over their heads - something that they feel the government has not been able to provide for them. Unfortunately, it also provides the thousands of drug users the cocaine they need to satisfy their addiction.

The demand for coca leaves has become another means by which richer countries control the lives of those in the developing world. However, trying to curtail the expansion of the coca industry is to enter into a political minefield.

Very simply, on one side is the mighty US who is trying to stop the cultivation of coca by encouraging eradication programs in return for money to build new schools and hospitals. On the other side are the local farmers, *campesinos,* who consider coca growing as part of their culture and a necessity if they are to survive. They will do anything to defend their chance to grow the crop and the forceful eradication programmes have had little success. They are usually met with unhappy and violent demonstrations by angry campesinos.

The Bolivian government provides some money for farmers that substitute their crops from coca to coffee, rice or maize but the figures still don't add up for them. Agricultural prices are state controlled and the indigenous population find it difficult to make a decent living from their crops. Growing coca is far too lucrative for them, when sold into the drugs industry. For example, a farmer may be paid $350 a year for producing 2,500 kilos of coffee per one hectare of land. 600 kilos of coca leaves can be grown in the same area of land, for which they will get a legal price of $3,000. Understandably they don't care what happens further down the drug chain.

In order to produce cocaine you need coca leaves, and lots of them. It takes 300kg of coca leaves to produce 1kg of cocaine. Luckily for the Bolivian coca growers the plant is native to the country and it is extremely easy to grow. The coca bush reaches heights of about 2.5 metres, it is extremely resilient, requires minimum maintenance and each bush can produce four harvests every year for several decades. With demand for cocaine increasing at a rapid pace, the Bolivian farmers are prepared to take risks and grow a few plants. Estimates show that coca cultivation in Bolivia is growing annually at a rate of between 20-25%. Bolivia is now the world's third largest producer of the coca leaf (after Peru and Colombia).

The search for land to grow coca creates a more serious problem - farmers are extending their agricultural lands to establish new coca fields at the expense of forests. It has been estimated that 15,000 hectares of virgin forest in the Chapare region have been cleared to grow coca. This not only causes the loss of flora and fauna habitats, but also increases soil erosion. Historical and traditional methods used for growing coca have not been regarded as harmful to the land or the environment, but many of the new farmers are inexperienced in subtropical agricultural methods. It is estimated that about 90% of farmers are using pesticides to improve their production, with obvious knock-on effects through the whole ecosystem. High quantities of toxic chemicals, from agriculture and from processing the coca, are being dumped into rivers and onto the land. The full environmental picture cannot be realised because of the dangers involving collecting data.

The big money made from the drug does not go to the growers, but to the people who work in the 'kitchens', usually deep within the Amazon jungle. The coca leaves are dissolved in paraffin and hydrochloric acid, in large oil drums. With heat, the dissolved substance hardens, and is called 'pasta'. The pasta then leaves Peru or Bolivia and makes its way aboard Amazon riverboats or unmarked light aircraft for the big time laboratories in Colombia, where it is washed in ether or acetone to produce $C_{17}H_{21}NO_4$. So where do these processing chemicals come from - chemical companies, such as Shell Oil and Exxon import them, with estimated sales of many millions. This white, crystalline alkaloid, under the co-ordination of big time drugs barons, is then shipped at whatever price and means possible to the US.

Most of the cocaine refined from Bolivian coca leaf is consumed in the United State. A 1994 survey by the US General Accounting Office suggested that in the previous year around one million US citizens snort cocaine at least once a week. Current usage estimates are broadly similar. Even though 75% of the world's cocaine comes from Colombia (est. 2002) much of the original coca originates in either Bolivia or Peru. After Colombia, Bolivia is the second largest producer of cocaine.

As we walked around the museum, we gradually filled our faces with free coca leaves. It seemed such a simple action, but after visiting the museum it made us realise how important the coca leaf contributes, and continues to play in the social and economic environment in Bolivia.

# Unfriendly Locals in Sorata

Our guidebook talked about a "peaceful and enchanting town" a few hours away and Sorata sounded like the ideal place to chill out for a few days. At only 2695m asl with a sub-tropical climate it couldn't get any 'chillier' than it was in La Paz.

This was our first real experience of catching a bus in Bolivia and we were unsure of the protocol. The bus companies in Bolivia either operated from a terminal (usually the long distance buses) or from their own depot. It just so happened the bus depot for buses going to Sorata are located miles out of town on the back road to El Alto, but we hadn't realised this when we got into the taxi. After driving around for 30 minutes we were starting to get concerned that we had asked him to take us to Sorata and not to the bus depot. It was a bit of relief when we spotted a bus with a sign stuck in the front window saying Sorata on it.

At least we didn't have to worry about our bags being pinched, as the driver piled sacks and boxes on top of them and covered them with a tarpaulin. Perhaps they were expecting it to rain. Once we started driving along the road it soon became apparent why the bags were protected. Dust spewed up from behind the bus covering the sheet in a thick layer of dust.

We bought our first *salteña* from a street vendor who had insisted it was "sin carne". He was right - it was filled with poultry and not meat. It reminded us of Caius's aunt once saying, "you are a vegetarian, but you eat beef don't you?" A *salteña* is not dissimilar to a Cornish pasty, but only smaller. The filling is usually chopped beef or chicken in spicy tomato gravy. If you are lucky you also get a bit of boiled egg or an olive. There is a certain art to eating them so as not to end up with hot sauce running down your hands, between your fingers and finally down the sleeve of your coat.

Throughout Peru we had only really been on long distance bus trips. We were back on a 'locals' bus and this meant the obligatory hour to get out of the city. A middle-aged bloke sat next to us and pointed out sights of interest along the way. For once we understood what he was saying to us – he told us in English. An ancient farmer behind us leant over and asked in perfect English "Can you tell me what time it is now, please?" It was like being back at home again.

Our journey took us through a couple of small towns to the north of Lake Titicaca. The guidebook had strongly advised that we did not get off along the way. The local population were particularly volatile towards tourists as well as white Bolivian nationals. Considering how friendly the other passengers had been towards us it was difficult to believe that it could be hostile.

The last section of the road down to Sorata was a bit of a white-knuckle ride along a very narrow dirt track, with a sheer crumbling rock face rising upwards on one side and a never-ending cliff down the other. The only problem was that you couldn't help but look out of the window because the views down the valley were so spectacular. A girl we later met in Sorata said the road was comparable to the 'most dangerous road in the world', but with less traffic, a bit shorter, and not as "butt clenching".

We dropped almost 1750m to a more comfortable altitude of 2695m asl. Warm sunshine streamed through the windows and lush green vegetation lined the roadside - the first greenery we had seen in weeks.

A two-year old girl was sat on the seat across the aisle from us. Perhaps it was the white skin, blond hair, or the blue eyes, or Caius wiggling his ears at her, but she was very intrigued by us. When she wasn't staring at us, she was either clamped to her mother's breast or sat on the floor of the bus sucking on oranges. After about three hours, the oranges must have made their way down through her system, curdling the milk in her stomach nicely. A stench started to surround her, drifting upwards towards our nostrils.

Vicky Brewis & Caius Simmons

Her mother decided that, rather than wait until the bus stopped, it was necessary for her to change the nappy before we arrived in Sorata. We both nearly gagged from the smell, and it was enough to bring tears to our eyes. As we passed through the main square the nappy was ripped off and slung out of the window onto the street. It was not the most opportune moment, but then leaflets on *'How to Dispose of your Rubbish'* don't seem to have reached all of South America yet. A very happy dog proudly pranced down the street with the nappy firmly gripped in its teeth.

The touts were waiting for us when we go off the bus, with flyers being shoved in our hands from all directions. It appeared that the Europeans who had decided not to live in Vilcabamba in Ecuador had settled here instead. Most of the accommodation was run either by Germans, Germans or Germans. We opted for a French-Canadian run establishment, which, until recently had also been run by some Germans.

Our hotel, a huge old mansion, was called Casa Gunther and as the name suggests is named after the German family who lived here in the 19th century. During this period Sorata was full of merchants, especially Germans, trading in quinine, coca and rubber.

Unfortunately, the building had seen better days and the huge old rooms were starting to look a bit neglected. The walls, being over a metre thick, were unlikely to crumble, but it did not stop the paint from peeling off them. Most of the rooms looked like they had not been changed since the Gunther family had lived here, including the bathrooms. The previous German owners had tried to keep the place well maintained even building a couple of newer rooms and a bathing pool, but the rooms were now looking dilapidated and the pool was more like a garden pond than a hot tub we could relax in.

The hotel had a large group of Irish walkers booked in and the only cheap room available was a large musty room, with sagging "banana" beds (where your feet and head rest considerably higher than the rest of your body), hidden away in a dark corner of the old house. One of the main draws to the place is the fabulous lush garden and the only thing we could see out of the tall

208

windows was a courtyard used for washing clothes. The money we had saved by not going to the jungle was just about to come in useful and we were able to afford to upgrade and stay in one of the newer rooms. It was definitely worth the extra couple of quid to be able to sit on our balcony and watch hummingbirds dart between flowers in the garden.

The town centre was peculiar. All the locals stood and stared at us, and although we did not feel unwelcome they were not particularly friendly. Even though they must have seen hundreds of tourists they couldn't help but gawp at us. Maybe we looked like Germans?

It did not take us long to discover Pete's Place - a great café / restaurant run by a Brit, surprisingly enough called Pete. Pete had moved from London and had married a Bolivian, and was making a killing with European and American tourists in Sorata. He knew exactly what to serve; a mixture of traditional Bolivian and British food, at good prices. A typical menu consisted of the popular Andean quinoa soup, followed by homemade salteñas with mashed potato, and for pudding chocolate brownies or apple crumble. This was all washed down with hot chocolate made with proper cocoa powder. There were no omelettes or chicken and rice to be seen.

Flipping through the books and maps Pete provided we learnt that, until recently, Bolivia was one of the most racist countries in the world. This is hard to believe given the diversity of the population, but the racism extends internally rather than externally as we expected. Over 55% of the population are either Aymara or Quechua in ethnic origin, the remainder being mestizo (mixed white and Amerindian ancestry) or white. The official government language remains Spanish, but over half of the 8.6 million residents of Bolivia speak an indigenous language, principally Quechua (the language of the Inca Empire) or Aymarian. There are also over 30 other languages spoken in smaller regions. The racism is primarily directed towards the mestizo and the whites, but is also prevalent between the indigenous populations. If they were racist towards each other, we certainly didn't stand a chance of getting a smile out of any them.

It was not just the pleasant climate that attracts European expatriates but also the regions popularity for walking. Sorata is a good base for doing long treks in the surrounding mountains of the Cordillera Real, but we had just come here to relax. Pete's message board displayed a warning about llama herders robbing trekkers at gun point, relieving them of not just money and other valuables, but also most of the clothes they were wearing, including their boots. We didn't fancy loosing our boots, so instead we headed down the road to check out the San Pedro caves a few miles out of town.

Walking out of town early in the morning we got a great view of the snow capped peaks of Illampu (6363m). By midday the mountaintop would be obscured and engulfed by swirling clouds. Powerful rivers have eroded down through the hillside producing multicoloured valleys, with shades of red, blue, green and yellow, contrasting with the bright blue skies above. Everything on the Altiplano had looked 'washed out', but without the harsh bright light the landscape and colours surrounding Sorata appeared more defined. It made a nice change to be able to distinguish between a house and the land around it, rather than it all merging together into a brown dusty haze.

The San Pedro grotto is only really worth the visit if you are interested in bats, or, caves. As our two young guides (the owners children) led us down through the cave we could hear the bats tweeting and fluttering above our heads. We shone our torches up to see them more clearly; later to find out it was really bad for the bats and their habitat. Oops, so much for our knowledgeable guides stopping us. The further down we went the sound of the generator, which was used to power a series of lights strung across the side of the cave, became fainter and fainter. The air became hotter and more humid, beads of sweat started to run down our faces. On reaching a small lake at the bottom the lights ran out and unless we hired a small inflatable boat (for an extortionate amount of money – well at least £1.50) we could go no further.

Back outside, in the cool clear air, we enjoyed a refreshing orange. A flock of green parrots headed down the valley towards the Amazon basin. We didn't seem to have missed much from our jungle trip – humid conditions,

210

tropical birds, nocturnal mammals and fresh fruit. One bonus was that there were no swarms of biting insects. Maybe the trip in the inflatable boat would have made the experience complete.

There was no electricity when we went to put a light on that evening. Six o'clock was a little early to go to bed and the lack of power scuppered our plans to watch *The Mummy* on video in the hostel lounge. We headed to Pete's Place in search of light. Pete was well prepared for the loss of power, with candles already lit and on the tables. He explained that these blackouts were a common occurrence and they were well stocked up with gas for cooking with.

The square was pretty deserted the following morning, with all the shops and stalls closed up. This was particularly unusual and even after a heavy night of celebrations during festival time the traders always seemed to manage to open up shop, never missing the opportunity to make a sale. Sorata was still without electricity and they were taking advantage of the fact that they didn't have any power. Perhaps it was their way of getting rid of the tourists, because we decided to cut our trip short and headed back to La Paz.

A few days later Sorata was on the Foreign Office website on their 'Places to Avoid', being listed somewhere between Afghanistan and Iraq. The Bolivian President was in the process of signing a deal with the US that would allow natural gas to be exported through a new pipeline from the Bolivian jungle. Bolivia has South America's second-biggest reserve of natural gas. It is estimated that Bolivia has a trade deficit of between $300 and $500 million, so by exporting cheap gas to the US and Mexico it would be a good way of balancing the books. Surprisingly enough the Bolivians were not to happy, especially the rural population who had become tired of being left to sink further into poverty while their government give away all the country's resources at their expense. To rub mud in their faces the gas was to be exported through Chile, via a port that was in fact part of Bolivian territory until Chile seized Bolivia's coastline in their 1879-83 wars. To make matters even worse, US-backed attempts to eradicate coca growing in the central Chapare region as part of Washington's 'War on Drugs' enraged the coca-growing peasants, fuelling the protests even further. There were weeks of strikes and street protests, which saw the killing of dozens of people.

At one stage during the protests scores of tourists were held hostage near Sorata and many more were stranded due to roadblocks. Some Peruvian tourists and protesters were killed during clashes with the army and police along the road from Lake Titicaca and La Paz. We were glad to have left the area when we did.

All border crossings in this area had been closed from Peru and the only way to get into Bolivia was through Chile, entering Bolivia from the south. We had friends and met scores of people who had been stuck in La Paz for a week or more. Just as we returned from South America there was a small paragraph in the press reporting that the US-educated (and friend of George W Bush), President Sanchez de Lozada had eventually resigned and the deal with America had not gone through. Carlos Mesa was appointed president after his predecessor was forced into exile, fleeing to Florida. Coincidently Florida's Senator is Jed Bush, George Bush's brother.

Back in La Paz, we bumped into Andreas (the tall Sicilian we met in Ecuador). It was his last night in South America, so we met for supper and took him out for a few farewell drinks. He was missing a Sicilian festival at his hometown that evening, so we had a couple more to celebrate that as well. The weather started getting really cold, with a bitter wind whistling down the streets, mixed in with snow and sleet. We felt a bit envious that he would soon be sitting on a beach enjoying some sunshine.

Andreas started to tell us about his robbery. The scam was well documented in our guidebook so we finished off the tale for him. A man had run past Andreas, dropping a package at his feet, but not realising, he just carried on running. Andreas picked up the package and tried to chase after the man but he had gone. He was left with a brown envelope containing a wad of dollar notes. Another man also saw what had happened and suggested to

Andreas that they should split the money. They walked into a dark alleyway and counted out the notes. The person who had dropped the package then turned up on the scene accusing them both of stealing his money. When they handed it back to him he insisted some of it was missing. Andreas had to get out his wallet to prove he was only carrying a few dollars. Without knowing what was going on the two men shuffled the envelopes and quickly disappeared, leaving Andreas holding an empty brown envelope and an empty wallet. The two men were obviously working together. Andreas could only laugh and blame himself for being dishonest and shrugged off the fact he had lost $95 (1000 BOB). He was leaving the next day and had bought all the hats and blankets he needed to take home.

We made it to the Terminal Terrestre to catch an early-ish bus for Cochabamba, which surprisingly left on time for a change (8.30am). The bus drove out of the Terminal, around the corner, parked up for 10 minutes and then drove back into the Terminal again, parking in exactly the same place as we had been before. Suddenly the 8.30 am service had become the 9.00am departure to Cochabamba – a good scam we thought. Luckily they remembered to load our bags on the second time, but the bus did not leave on time and it took another hour before we finally drove out of La Paz.

*Death on the Nile*, staring Peter Ustinov and David Niven, was put on the video machine. The added bonus was it was in English. Phrases such as, "Hurrah", "Jolly good", and, "What a bounder" making it sound totally ludicrous. The young kids on the bus seemed highly disappointed that the film didn't involve vast amounts of shooting, swearing, gore and blood. We were just about to find out 'who dunnit' when an Indian lady next to us took an interest in our map of Bolivia and started chatting to us.

She spoke a in a mixture of English and Spanish and we taught each other loads of new words, which was great. She was 45 and had two sons (aged 17 and 16), which meant she would have been nearly 30 when she had her first son. Compared to most of the young mothers we had seen, this seemed quite old to have had children in Bolivia. With a house in both La Paz and Cochabamba, she regularly travelled between the two cities "on business". As the owner of one of the Witches stalls in La Paz she had to go to Cochabamba to stock up on llama foetuses and 'ingredients'. We didn't dare ask what was so special that she needed to go all the way to Cochabamba.

We offered our newfound friend some of our peanuts. This is something we would have probably done if we had got chatting to someone on a train in the UK. She accepted some but warned us never to encourage begging. She regarded Bolivia as a 'sad place', but we couldn't work out if she was referring to the people or the countryside. Having been to America herself, her hope was that her sons would have the opportunity to travel there someday and make their fortune. Looking out of the window at the bleak landscape we could see why she wanted more for her sons' future. Making a living in this kind of environment would have made anyone sad.

# Daylight Robbery

The area of Cochabamba 'shot' onto the worldwide stage in 1967 when, in the village of La Higuera, freedom fighter Ernesto "Che" Guevara was executed. The village is actually a couple of hundred miles away from Cochabamba, but it just so happens to be located on the border of the Cochabamba administrative region.

*The Motorcycle Diaries* (based on Guevara's book and has also been made into a film) tells the story of how the middle classed Argentinean medical student took a nine-month motorcycle trip through South America in 1952. Guevara's epic journey introduced him to the poverty and inequality of the South America people, and became the catalyst to him joining Fidel Castro's Communist guerrillas in Mexico. Having helped to overthrow the corrupt Batista regime in Cuba in 1959, Guevara was rewarded with a place in Castro's government. In 1961 he led the defence against the US-sponsored Bay of Pigs invasion, and shortly after left to fight North-American imperialism in Africa and to export the revolution to the rest of Latin America.

On October 9th 1967, while Guevara was leading an uprising against the Bolivian government, he was captured and executed by the Bolivian army. His death ensured his elevation from romantic freedom fighter to heroic martyr, dying for the revolutionary cause. His iconic image was further strengthened by his reported last words to his executioner were "shoot, coward, you're only going to kill one man". For 30 years the exact location of his body remained a mystery. In 1997 his remains were exhumed and returned to Cuba.

Cuban photographer, Alberto Korda, took the photo of the handsome, bearded, beret-wearing left-wing radical in 1960. This image has become one of the most famous photographs, appearing on millions of T-shirts, badges, key rings and posters. After the Mona Lisa, it is the second most reproduced picture in the world, but Korda has never made a penny in royalties from it. His family recently sued Smirnoff for $50,000 because they made a vodka advert using the image and they believed they should have gained permission. The money was donated to Cuban Medical Research.

Cochabamba is an urban sprawl - lots of villages all backed up against each other, with neat, tidy suburbs, mixed in with large industrial estates and processing plants. The city itself gave a very mixed message. Judging by the number of 4WD and flash cars being driven around there was obviously money to be made in the area, generated mainly from agriculture, and probably a healthy drug trade as well. In contrast, the poverty was very noticeable, with far more beggars on the streets than we had seen anywhere else so far.

Compared to the harsh environment of the altiplano we had just driven down from the valleys surrounding Cochabamba are extremely fertile. At an altitude of only 2600m asl it also enjoys a very favourable climate. Its warm weather and good soils means that all sorts of produce can be grown in abundance. As a result it attracts a large number of people who migrate to the area in search of work. Unfortunately, there is just not enough money to go around to support the growing number of families who have come to Cochabamba in the hope of making a decent living.

Cochabamba is the main city in the region, attracting many people from the surrounding villages who stock up on supplies and sell their wares at its numerous markets.

The main indoor market, *La Cancha* (Quechan for walled enclosure) was split into sections, each area selling the same product or service. There were 20 or more stalls selling toys, another 20 with plastic shoes, followed by 20 selling cakes, sewing services or suits, and all the fruit and vegetables you could ever want. You name it, it was there and each stall was pretty much identical to the one next door, the same type of cakes and the same plastic shoes. The market over spilled onto the neighbouring streets, which were packed with smaller stalls that sold nothing really specific – dishcloths, hammers, sewing kits, cellotape, sweets, biscuits and, of course, plastic shoes.

There was no intention of us buying anything, but it was interesting to wander around nosing at all the different stalls. We had seen plenty of tourist markets, but this was definitely the largest 'locals' market we had encountered so far. Everybody, anyone and everyone seemed to be there and the fact that the market was held everyday was a fascinating concept. In an attempt to discourage begging the Bolivian government offer incentives, like tax reductions, to help people set up their own stall. We felt the success of the scheme could be its own undoing, as there did appear to be a glut of traders. How any of them made a decent living was beyond us - there are only so many plastic shoes, or suits, a person can sell in a month. It didn't seem to be helping the begging situation much either, especially in Cochabamba.

We decided to pay tribute to Las Heroinas de la Coronilla by visiting a monument dedicated to the local women folk who tried to protect the city from attacking Spanish troops during a rebellion against the government in 1812. All the men were fighting elsewhere in the country, leaving the women to protect their homes by themselves. They were unsuccessful in their attempt but are honoured with a load of statues for their gallant effort.

Just as we approached the monument, a man walking down the steps confronted us. The fact that he was pointing a gun at us made us think he was not just out for a morning stroll through the park. The words, "OH SHIT" came to mind, and also to Vicky's lips. We did not know if the gun was real, it looked like he might have bought it at one of the market stalls, but we didn't really fancy finding out if it worked properly.

With our hands in the air we were made to stand close to the wall so we were out of sight from anyone who might be standing at the top of the monument. After sticking his gun in the back of his trousers he started rummaging through our pockets. The only things he managed to find were our Swiss army penknives, which, after investigating what they were kindly gave them back to us. After finding nothing of value in our pockets he started getting a bit flustered and decided to pull a knife on us. Looking at the condition the blade was in we reckoned he probably should have kept our penknives. The rusty blade looked like it had been lying in the back of his tool drawer for many years, but we were unsure whether he had made the effort to sharpen it recently.

Our main concern was how erratically he was waving the knife in front of our faces. He seemed extremely nervous, even more than we were. He blurted something in Spanish, but we couldn't understand a word he was trying to say to us. We thought that it was probably not the best time to use the phrase we had recently learnt, "Más despacio, por favor" (Could you speak more slowly, please?). Our reply of, "No tenermos dollares" (We have no dollars), worried him further and he became more and more anxious because he still hadn't found anything.

Based on the state he was getting into we decided that he might do something rash, so we showed him the side pockets in our trousers. Given the fact that he was the mugger, and supposedly knew what he was doing, he had somehow managed to miss them on his first body search. We thought the zips might have given away the fact that there may be other pockets. It made us wonder if he had done this kind of robbery before. When he tucked his knife away in his pocket so he could search for valuables, we noticed he had another knife in his belt. It looked just as rusty as the other one.

Gleefully he took out our wallets, but his delight quickly turned to pure disappointment when he looked inside to find about 100 BOB (worth about £10) and a £10 note. Did he really think we were that stupid to carry huge amounts of cash on us? He obviously didn't know that the majority of travellers used ATM's and only take out small amounts of cash each time from the bank. Along with a small amount of cash, Vicky's purse also contained the Sucre note which the banker had given us in Alausí, Ecuador. She was not very impressed by him taking this, but he just saw it as another note. The fact that it was obsolete and only worth about 0.05p was irrelevant to him. He waved the rusty knife at her when she started to protest.

He didn't really have much of an opportunity to search our pockets properly as a jogger came around the corner and disturbed us. Luckily for us he had only had time to look in one of our trouser side pockets. The other one had a camera in it. He also hadn't noticed that there were other hidden pockets within the side zipped pockets, or that we were wearing money belts.

The gun appeared again and, after a bit of a stand off between the jogger and our robber, the jogger ran away shouting "Policía!" as loud as he could.

Thinking that all tourists are loaded with cash, the robber was determined he was going to find some more money on us. We kept telling him we didn't have any. He had chosen the wrong people to rob this time and was going to be out of luck. He decided we must have it all stashed in our rucksack, but was disappointed to find only a pair of binoculars, a bottle of water, sun tan cream and a Bolivian guidebook. At one stage during his search he had his back turned to us, with his gun and knives tucked away in his belt. Turning to Vicky, Caius said, "Shall I have him?" She sensibly told him, "No, it's not worth it". He was only about 5 feet 8 inches tall and we could have easily overpowered him.

The robber finally decided that his time was up. He had not found any more valuables and the jogger might have managed to alert the police. He waved the gun at us and told us to keep quiet and made his get away through the thick vegetation.

We looked at each other and said, "We've just been robbed". Visiting the monument was no longer very appealing so we headed back into town to try and report the robbery to the police. Five armed policemen (not policeman with five arms) came running up the hill towards us, quickly followed by the jogger who had disturbed our robbery. We pointed them in the right direction, but they were two or three minutes too late and the robber had already disappeared. We were quite relieved - the last thing we wanted was bloodshed.

Luckily for us the jogger spoke English. He told us he was a little bit annoyed with himself because he usually carried a gun with him when he went running. We were pleased he did not have it that day, as we think he would not have hesitated to use it on the robber. Based on his knowledge on guns, which seemed to be pretty good, he reckoned that the gun the robber was carrying was real. He told us that police had been patrolling the park recently because there had been a few reported 'incidents'. Most of the guidebooks or hostels warned us of any dodgy areas, but there had been nothing to suggest that the park could be unsafe.

We gave a *Crimestoppers* reconstruction to the police and they came to the same conclusion as us – the robber was an amateur and it was probably his first 'job'. He had definitely been more nervous than us and he didn't really have a clue where to find our belongings. The police were impressed that we had taken precautions to conceal our money and passports. We were very proud of the M&S trousers we had bought - the main feature that had sold them to us was the fact they had plenty of hidden and secret pockets. All our friends had laughed at us when we showed them off before we left. Although money belts are quite uncomfortable and sweaty, at least they saved us from having our passports and more money being taken.

Another walker had witnessed our robber speed away on the back of a motorbike. His accomplice had been waiting for him around the corner on the 'getaway vehicle'. Assessing the event later we agreed that we could have easily 'had him' but we were glad we had not attempted anything. With his friend loitering in the bushes behind us it could have easily turned nasty. Either we could have both got hurt with his gun or knife, or we might have ended up injuring him more than we intended. The last thing we wanted was a severely injured robber on our hands, trying to explain ourselves to the Bolivian Police.

Back at the Police Station the officers were very nice to us but they were not interested in taking our details or completing a statement. We asked about a report for insurance purposes and we were told we would have to go to another station if we wanted to do this. The jogger kindly took us to a Police Depot at the other side of town. The yard was full of new recruits having gun training and they all looked at us blankly when we explained our request. They sent us down the road to another office. The jogger was starting to get a bit despondent but took us anyway. Inside the office were two policemen sat opposite each other behind large desks. Looking at their portly figures we guessed that the only activity that ever went on in the office was making tea, and eating cakes and biscuits. They were not interested in the slightest about writing a report on the incident. The typewriters on their desks were obviously just for show. As they wiped the sweat running down their foreheads, they informed us that we would have to go back to the original Police Station. We had been sent to the 'jobs worth' department of the Bolivian police force.

Bolivia has one of the lowest crime records in the world. This is partly due to the fact that they have very few laws. Therefore, there are no laws to be broken. The other reason, which we had just been made clear to us, was that if they don't report the crime then it couldn't be included in the crime statistics.

We agreed with the jogger that we were banging our heads against a brick wall. He told us that crime, especially theft, in Cochabamba was on the increase. It was a bit of a surprise when he told us that it was not just tourist, cars and houses that were targeted, but also kidnapping children. His parting words to us were, "don't stay here, go somewhere else".

We didn't have any option but to stay in Cochabamba for an extra day as the only next available bus to Sucre was the following evening.

The robbery had shaken us a bit and we decided to give a visit to some local Inca ruins and village market a miss. The region around Cochabamba is famous for producing Chica, and we had been hoping to visit one of the many villages on market day to sample the local beverage. Our enthusiasm for the drink had diminished and agreed we didn't actually like it that much anyway. As long as we stayed close to the town centre, or where there was going to be plenty of people we felt relatively happy. After the jogger's comments about the town we were not entirely convinced of how safe we really were though.

You cannot help miss the huge statue of Christ when you arrive in Cochabamba, which sits on top of a small hill overlooking the city. This is the

Cristo de la Concordia and at 34m high it is apparently bigger than the famous JC statue in Rio de Janiero. Its location is not as dramatic or impressive as the Rio statue, but as the biggest monument in South America we really had to make the effort to visit it.

Our adrenalin levels were still a bit high after our mugging and we managed to freak out two other British people, Josh and Ali, who were also staying at the hostel. We agreed to all go together to pay our homage to JC. The 'safety in numbers' approach was enough to make us relax and after walking and chatting with them our confidence slowly returned. Understandably, we opted out on the walk up the hill to the base of the monument, going for the cable car up to the top instead. The monument we had walked up to that morning looked tiny from the top and we sat for a while, enjoying the panoramic views, trying to forget what had happened to us.

At the bottom we treated ourselves to a cup of freshly squeezed orange juice bought from one of the many street vendors. The vendors have small carts, full of oranges, with a squeezing device clamped to the side. On request they would squeeze you a fresh cup of orange juice, usually into a plastic cup, but if you are going to hang around for a chat they offered a proper glass. We had seen the vendors before, usually on the busy main streets or in the markets, but for some reason we had never really given it a go. After our first cup there was no stopping us and we couldn't resist having another, and another.

We headed to the other side of town, on our own. Every time we found ourselves on a street with no other people around we would speed up and keep checking behind us. We do the same when we walk along deserted streets in some British cities, being more conscious of our surroundings, where you are on the lookout for anything unusual. Being mugged is usually just a case of being in the wrong place at the wrong time and for us this just happened to be in Cochabamba.

In the early 1900's the fifth richest person in the world was Simon Patino ("the King of Tin"), who had been raised in a village close to Cochabamba. We visited his massive house, Palacio de los Portales that had been built specifically for him, even though he actually never got to live there. The house was fabulously furnished and decorated with riches from across the world, with no expense spared; marble fireplaces, fine wooden floors, statues and paintings that had all been made on commission. It was also surrounded by a beautiful garden. By the time the palace was completed, Simon had become so rich and powerful that he was no longer in the favour of the Bolivian government and spent much of his time abroad. His family claimed that the altitude was too bad for his health and therefore could not live in Cochabamba. There had been no need to ever restore anything in the house because it had never really been used, including a brand new snooker table. The only person ever to have stayed there was Charles de Gaul, who supposedly complained because the beds were too short.

On the whole Cochabamba was a pleasant town to visit and there was plenty to see and do even though it is relatively unvisited by foreign tourists. Apart from a quick visit to the excellent local Archaeology museum we spent the rest of our time sitting around the many leafy squares, drinking freshly squeezed orange juice. There were also some very good restaurants and cafés and at least we could almost guarantee not being robbed if we were sat inside them.

We found a little French café, whose owner had been to France for two days about 20 years ago. She had loved it so much she had decided to buy the café when it came up for sale and served excellent coffee and crepes. She had a deal with a coffee grower who blended the beans especially for her. It was so strong that it took us almost 30 minutes to stop sweating after our espresso and cappuccino.

We finished off our visit to Cochabamba with a meal at an Argentinean restaurant. This was obviously where the wealthier inhabitants of Cochabamba went for lunch, as it was full of rich old ladies and their daughters, and smart looking business men. If we had been eating in a restaurant somewhere in

Europe it would have cost us a fortune. Vicky treated herself, opting for a shoulder of lamb. She got what she asked for, a whole shoulder of lamb (and nothing else), cooked to perfection. The Argentineans are very keen on eating meat, with the only real vegetarian option being tomato soup, presented in the smallest of bowls, which was luckily accompanied by a basket of fresh warm decent bread.

We could have quite easily spent another day in Cochabamba eating and drinking, but that was all there was to keep us there and thought we better leave while we had a sweet taste in our mouths. It was time to move on and we left that evening on the night bus to Sucre.

# The Cocaine Bus

When we had bought our bus tickets to Sucre the company had a glossy poster of a very nice looking bus on display behind the counter. They had told us it was not a 'bus cama' (a bus with big comfortable reclining seats which sometimes reclined so much that they made a bed), but there was plenty of legroom and it would be very comfortable.

Not surprisingly, when we turned up at the station, our bus looked crap. It looked like we were going to have to wait until our next journey to get a comfortable bus. The inside was even more disheartening, with small lumpy seats cramped together and to top it all there was no toilet and, even worse, there was no TV. This was a bad start.

The bus pulled out of the station half an hour late (nothing unusual about that) and after only 10 minutes of driving we pulled into a greasy spoon on the outskirts of town. It appeared that the bus driver and his assistants were the only ones that had not found time to eat. We all hung around outside, waiting for 40 minutes, while the driver had his supper. As usual the whole area stank of piss and the toilets were a dirtier version of the toilet in the film *Trainspotting*. We both came out gagging. These toilets gained the lowest possible mark on the Debbie and Lucy's (who we met on the Inca Trail) toilet experience scoring system. Luckily it was dark and we couldn't see what we were standing in. Even the locals were appalled and we could hear them complaining bitterly, in Quechan, about the state of the toilets.

The scenery between Cochabamba and Sucre is supposed to be stunning, but unfortunately no buses run during daylight hours. Luckily a full moon lit up the landscape and we managed to get a few glimpses of lush rolling hills and pretty wooded river valleys silhouetted by the moonlight. In reality there was probably not a blade of grass in sight and the trees were probably covered in layers of dust. The moonlight made it look far more romantic.

The seats in front were reclined right onto our laps and the passengers behind sat with their knees digging into our spines. We managed not to dig our knees into the people in front, so the people behind were obviously doing it on purpose. After several hours of aborted sleep attempts we were woken when the bus decided to stop in the middle of nowhere. We thought perhaps the driver had needed a sleep, soon realising we were very mistaken and it was in fact because the bus had overheated and his assistants had gone off hunting for water from the nearby stream.

By about 3am our brains were resigned to the fact that it was never going to get any more comfortable and we managed to doze off. Woken by the rising sun shining through the windows we found ourselves driving along a large dry river gorge. The main road had collapsed and a diversion took us right up the middle of the valley. By the time the rains arrived the valley would be full of water tumbling down at vast speed. We were very glad it was the dry season.

In an attempt to get more sleep Caius wrapped his coat around his head, blocking out any light and fell back to sleep again.

We had stopped at a routine checkpoint on the outskirts of Sucre. Caius was only just waking up and having just taken his coat of his head was trying to adjust to the bright sunshine that poured through the window. Caius mistook a Policeman waiting to see his documentation for a tout trying to sell us Empinadas. "No gracias", didn't seem to get rid of him and earned Caius a sharp jab in his side. As Caius' eyes adjusted, he noticed this 'tout' had a huge gun and decided not to argue, and fumbled sleepily with his money belt for his passport.

Random bag searches were occurring, with individuals being escorted off the bus and made to point out their luggage from the hold underneath. A female officer looking in the overhead racks at the back of the bus shouted something. Turning around we could see she was holding up a brown package about the

226

same size and shape of a football. Everyone on the bus turned around, went "Ooooh" in a big chorus, while trying not to laugh. We think what they were saying translated to, "Who's been a naughty boy then?"

The police all disappeared off the bus clutching the package, a very worried bus driver in tow. It was obvious we were not going anywhere for a while so everyone piled off the bus. As we were only about 5km from Sucre some of the passengers jumped into waiting taxis and sped off – including, it appeared, the owner of the bag they had found the parcel in.

After a while a couple of ladies explained that the mysterious package contained 3kg of high quality cocaine. The police stood around scratching their heads wondering where the owner of the parcel had gone, and the bus driver was looking particularly worried. He had obviously had to fork out quite a bit of beer money as bribes to keep him in a job.

Some officials arrived from Sucre, along with a photographer, to record the incident. They even did a reconstruction of how the policewoman found the parcel at the back of the bus. Unfortunately we didn't get a chance to go, "Ooooh" again. We hoped the story would get into the papers. If there were photos, and you looked close enough, you would have been able to see two gringos in the background waving out of the bus window.

When we arrived in Sucre we were only about an hour late, which was not too bad considering the morning's events. It certainly helped us to forget about the uncomfortable journey we had endured.

Vicky Brewis & Caius Simmons

# Sweet Sucre

Bolivia is named after the Venezuelan independence fighter Simon Bolivar "the Liberator" and was formally established as a Republic in 1825 after three centuries of Spanish rule. Sucre was named after Simon Bolivars most powerful and influential general, Antonio Jose de Sucre, who subsequently became Bolivia's first president.

Armando (bit of a nut, ha ha), our taxi driver gave us all the facts we wanted to know, and more, about Sucre. The only real snippet of interesting information we managed to grasp was that it has a population of about 75,000, which considering it is the administrative capital of Bolivia isn't very big at all. He also informed us that the annual fiesta was just about to start and we had arrived at the perfect time to witness a week of dancing and music.

Charlie had specifically recommended the Grand Hotel to us but, unfortunately, it was fully booked. Armando rubbed his hands in glee and with BOB signs flashing before his eyes he took us to a hotel he "personally recommended". The cost of accommodation in Sucre is generally higher than other parts of Bolivia as they get so many tourists visiting, but the quality is also marginally better. The hotel Armando took us happened to be the most expensive looking hotel we had seen for ages and we really wanted to go elsewhere. Armando was determined he was going to get his commission so booked us in with a special discount which included breakfast. We agreed to stay for one night only and reserved a room at the much nicer looking Grand for the following evening.

228

The next morning we were served possibly the most terrible breakfast we had eaten for at least a couple of weeks. Consisting of very stale bread rolls and revolting coffee that resembled black treacle we didn't even manage to finish it. Under the impression that our breakfast was included in our room rate, we were annoyed to be charged for it when we checked out. Our 'special room rate' was working out more expensive than the advertised normal room rate (which included breakfast) and there was no way we were going to pay the extra. From studying our receipt, the hotel receptionist had written our exclusions onto our registration form after we had signed it. It surprised us how much of the language we suddenly mustered up and managed to stand our ground for about 15 minutes, arguing in Spanish. A couple of Bolivian tourists joined in, helping to support our argument. In the end we paid what we wanted and just walked out. If the police couldn't catch a drugs smuggler who had walked right past them, or file a robbery report, then they were not going to worry too much about a couple of gringos not paying for two bread rolls and a coffee. Armando would just have to lose out in his commission.

Whilst checking-in to the Grand Hotel we made sure it included breakfast – it did. We had a room overlooking a central courtyard full of tropical plants, banana trees and fountains. Apparently Che Guevara had once stayed in the room next door. More important than this the room had Cable TV with a couple of English speaking channels. It was a real bonus to be able to catch up with the news (they hadn't found any weapons of mass destruction in Iraq) and slob out in front of a film.

Sucre is a beautiful city with a very cosmopolitan feel to it. The city sits in the eastern lowlands at an agreeable altitude of about 2700m asl. In comparison to Cochabamba the streets in Sucre felt safe, the people were friendly and it is clean and tidy. Sucre was given UNESCO World Heritage status in 1991 and all the colonial buildings are freshly painted white. According to Armando they are repainted every year. Sucre appears to be a relatively rich city, benefiting from the wealth it acquired during the colonial period when the Spanish favoured the city as a centre for the exploitation of nearby silver deposits. To the outsider there are no real signs of extreme poverty, with very few beggars on the street. We very easily passed the time of day wandering around exploring buildings, courtyards and gardens, and eating food in pleasant cafés and drinking in trendy bars.

Our guidebook, rightly recommended, that we visit the textile museum. It gave a full history and an account of the textiles of the local communities. A project was set up in the 1970's to get the locals weaving again because traditions were rapidly being forgotten. There are two main communities involved in the project, the Jalq'a (who make black and red weavings dominated by scary looking animals) and the Tarabuceño (which are white and black, with rainbow like stripes running discretely through them). The weavings usually depict a story, usually representing what has happened in the local community during the last year. One such event is the tradition of 'pulling the goat'. We didn't actually manage to discover what it involved, but it sounded painful, especially for the goat.

One of the main tourist attractions in Sucre is taking a ride on the Dino-Truck. It is particularly popular, not just with foreign tourists, but also with the many Bolivians who come to visit their capital.

As we sat waiting in the café for our truck, Josh and Ali (who we scared with our robbing story in Cochabamba) walked in. They had just arrived on an overnight bus from Oruro and looked terrible - obviously no bus cama for them either. After we told them about our bus experience and the cocaine trafficking incident, they probably wished they had never bumped into us in Cochabamba. Within the space of two days we had been robbed and witnessed a drugs bust – we certainly didn't seem to be attracting too much luck. They didn't fancy waiting to find out what the third incident we were going to get embroiled in and sensibly gave the Dino Truck a miss for another day.

The Dino Truck was a bright yellow truck with wooden benches fitted inside to sit on. The fact that we all stood out like sore thumbs anyway, with our pale skins, rucksacks, walking shoes and cameras, meant we really didn't need

230

any more help attracting attention to ourselves. Sitting on the Dino Truck felt like we had been herded together and paraded through the city just to show the locals which tourists were visiting Sucre that week.

We were driven to a quarry about 5km out of the centre, not far from the police checkpoint where the drugs bust had been. The quarry is currently being used to extract limestone for the production of cement. In 1994 the workers unearthed the world's biggest collection of dinosaur footprints. The miners geological knowledge was a little limited, to say the least, and they were a bit confused to have found them on a 100 metre high wall, which is on a vertical incline of about 70 degrees.

Looking at the dry, dusty landscape around us, it was hard to believe that this region was probably once an estuary, surrounded by lush vegetation. The dinosaurs tramping across the mud flats in search of food would have left their footprints impressed in the soft ground some 65 million years ago. Formation of the Andes caused uplift and displacement of the ground, tilting it to create almost vertical faces. Almost 5500 perfectly preserved dinosaur footprints, from an estimated 150 different types of dinosaurs, are scattered across the cliff face.

Unfortunately the quarry owners are still mining out the bottom of this spectacular and fascinating cliff. There are already signs that the cliff is being put under the strain. The large stress fractures are an indication that it will soon collapse, probably after a spell of wet weather - taking with it these amazing prints. There are talks of trying to stabilise the cliff face with mesh, glass or a large umbrella structure at the top to stop the water, but the measures that need to be taken to protect it would be extremely expensive and they cannot guarantee they would work. The company has to stop quarrying in a few years time anyway, but this will probably be a couple of years too late and 65,000,000 years of history will be gone forever. It is not economical for the company to stop quarrying sooner – the quarry makes about $10m a year from cement production and only $20,000 from tourists and palaeontologists visiting the footprints.

We arrived in Sucre at the beginning of a week's celebration, marking the city's annual religious fiesta in honour of the Virgin of Guadalupe. One of the strangest part of the celebrations was when the Bishop of Sucre blessed hundreds of vehicles in front of the Cathedral. We gathered it is a fairly common tradition in Bolivia especially during religious celebrations and even though we had seen a couple of buses being blessed in Copacabana it was nothing in comparison to the number of vehicles we saw in Sucre.

The cars were completely covered with brightly woven rugs and blankets. The drivers hung their heads out of the window in order to see where they were going. The rugs act as a tabletop, with various items laid out on it - silverware, dolls, huge fluffy toys (like the ones you can win at fairs), plates of food, and one car had a carry cot strapped to the bonnet with a baby inside. The tradition of 'pulling the goat' was obviously still relevant and a live goat made an appearance on the top of someone's car. It was probably not going to be alive for much longer.

It was apparent that the drivers believed that the more stuff they had on the car, the more luck they were going to be blessed with over the coming year. That was if they managed not to crash the car before they got to the front of the cathedral. The city centre was in total chaos with cars stretching for about a mile down the street. Around the square the vehicles were all lined up, two or three a breast across the road. To make sure they were as close to the front of the queue as possible the 'blind' drivers jostled for position, beeping the horns as they pushed their way through.

The square was heaving with police and army protecting all the silver and paintings that had been brought outside for a makeshift alter. After a particularly long Catholic service, the vehicles are blessed with holy water and then beer poured on top. The car, its driver and their family would now be safe, prosperous and fertile until the following year when they would all queue up again for the next blessing.

The drivers then parked up, finishing off the rest of the beer. Most of the alcohol had already been consumed before they even reached the Bishop, but they all managed to find a few more bottles stashed away in the boot to have a couple more swigs before driving home.

This ceremony was just the beginning of the festivities and later that day there was a procession of dancing troupes and musicians going through town. It seemed very odd to us that none of the dancers had costumes. After all we had heard about the flamboyant traditional dresses we were a little disappointed to see that they were wearing jeans and t-shirts instead. And where were the semi-clad women Caius had been promised. It transpired that it was a practice, with the real procession, costumes and all, happening later in the week. Even without the costumes the practice procession was pretty impressive, with dancers and bands still strutting their stuff well into the night.

# Tarabuco

Whilst travelling you build up a 'guard' to try and protect yourself and your belongings. Most of the time it is simple things, like wrapping your rucksack handles around your feet when you are sat in a restaurant, or ensuring you don't have any belongings in your pockets if you are seated nearest the aisle on the bus, or that the easily accessible rucksack pockets are full of dirty washing only. Following the robbery we had built up our defences and become slightly paranoid, double checking everything.

A trip to the small market town of Tarabuco was an ideal way to gently ease ourselves back into travelling mode. Popular for its Sunday market, Tarabuco is one of Bolivia's biggest tourist traps. It makes a good day trip from Sucre and we also thought it would give us a chance to buy some of the weavings the region has become famous for.

After our escapades over the previous few days, we opted for a special tourist bus to take us to the market. It felt like we were cheating in some way, but we really needed to boost our confidence a bit more before we ventured out on our own again. Because the bus was full of tourists we felt we could relax a bit more. Admittedly, the journey felt a bit like we were on a 'package holiday', especially when four musicians started busking at the front of the bus.

The market is just as popular with tourists as it is with the locals, who travel from miles around to stock up on food and other necessities. The village is a great place to wander around, browse or just sit and observe the locals going about their everyday business.

We sat and observed the tourists buying traditional weavings, hats, gloves and musical instruments, while the locals were stocking up on jeans, trainers, batteries and plastic washing up bowls. It seemed odd that they were buying casual clothing when all of them were wearing their traditional costumes.

The men all wore brown ponchos with coloured rainbow stripes woven in. Many wore a rigid black hat, (called *monteras*) which are styled on conquistador helmets. A few had battered tin miners helmets, complete with headlamps. The women were just as conspicuous, with their pretty black shirts trimmed with sequins and lacy blouses. Their hats, known as *jugullos* looked totally impractical and silly. We couldn't figure out what had possessed them to wear an upside down paint tin on their heads, which they had painted black, attached flaps to the back and covered in sequins. This was obviously their 'Sunday Best', worn, not just for the tourists, but also to display their distinct cultural identity.

We were desperate to take a photo, but finding a discrete opportunity was difficult. We had to content ourselves with a few random pictures taken down the street, across the square, or out of the bus window and just hoped we managed to capture some of the stalls, ponchos and hats in the shot.

Stalls lining the streets were piled high with weavings, ponchos, capes, blankets, hats, scarves and musical instruments. There were so many colours, yet the market couldn't really be described as colourful. The dyes used are derived from vegetable matter from the likes of coca leaves and cochineal resulting in subtle, muted tones rather than vibrant colours, a bit like the personalities of the locals.

There were so many things to choose from and, unlike the stalls in Otavalo and Pisac, we could browse among the stalls without the owners harassing us to buy something. Because they didn't nag us, we weren't put off from venturing into the small shops, or take a closer look at the weavings laid out on the pavement. Bolivian stallholders had a much better approach to tourists and as a result they probably sold more than their Ecuadorian and Peruvian counterparts. We certainly bought more stuff than we intended to.

Although there were many shops, with all their goods spilling out onto the pavement, there were also smaller stalls displaying only a handful of goods.

It was from one of these traders we bought a *chuspa* (a small bag for carrying coca leaves). The lady only had a couple of small bags and a few belts for sale, all weaved by hand in the distinctive Tarabuceño style. The quality was as good as we had seen in the textile museum in Sucre. It was beautifully woven and she explained to us, in a language we did not understand, all about the different customs and traditions depicted on it. Her excitement was contagious and she was so proud of it, it was difficult to tell if she really wanted to sell it to us. Either that or she had developed a particularly good sales technique. We couldn't even consider bartering down the price, and left the stall with a bag which is little use to us as we have no coca leaves to carry around.

The best present we bought were a couple of rattles made out of Alpaca toenails, stringed together into bunches. They are designed for wearing on the wrist or ankle, and depending on the size of the nails different musical notes can be played. The thought of wearing the horny toenails was pretty gross, especially as they also had hair still attached to them.

When the market started packing up at 1pm there was a mass exodus of people, the tourists climbing onto their buses and the locals piling on to the back of trucks and lorries. It was a strange sight to see the locals altogether, especially with their military like headgear which, together with their matching multicoloured ponchos, they looked like they were preparing to be taken into battle.

On our last day in Sucre we headed to a *Mirador* that Josh and Ali had recommended to us. We were rewarded, at the top of the hill, with a café selling delicious 'world famous' iced Cappuccinos and good views over the city. We sat, fully relaxed, with the warmth of the sun on our faces overlooking the rooftops. We felt sad to leave Sucre, and that's coming from people who don't even like cities. Our next stop, we felt, was going to be completely different.

# Mining in Potosí

We were right in our presumption. Our bus journey took us up through the mountain passes above Sucre and then onto a cold and barren plateau. Potosí, the highest city in the world (4300m asl) appeared out of nowhere right in the middle of the sparse landscape. We could understand why the Spanish had settled in Sucre - a warm climate and low altitude – but Potosí is basically cold, bleak and exposed. Immediately we felt the change in temperature and altitude, and even the short walk from the taxi to the hostel doorway was a struggle.

The hostel was not very welcoming, but from what we had seen and read it was about as good as it was going to get. People were huddled together in the corner of the small courtyard in an attempt to catch the last rays of the weak afternoon sun. Inside, the room was no warmer and we stood pretending to smoke, with plumes of white 'smoke' emitting from our mouths and nostrils.

The beds had been designed by someone very short, either that or by a very astute businessperson who saw that they could get more money by making the rooms en-suite, at the expense of longer beds. The beds were about a foot too short and somehow they had managed to find sheets that were even smaller. Our hopes for a good nights sleep diminished even further when we realised that we had not been provided with six blankets as we first thought, but only two, folded over three times. After Sucre, this was a real shock.

Today, two-thirds of Bolivians live below the poverty line. This has not always been the case, and in fact, between 1545 and 1660 the country was one of the richest in the world. This was largely due to the vast amounts of silver

237

extracted from the silver mines in Potosí, where an estimated 16,000 tons of silver was shipped to Spain during this period. This wealth, however, was squandered funding the Spanish Inquisition (nobody expected that!) and Catholic Crusades such as the rather unsuccessful Spanish Armada against England (hoorah).

The city looked just as we imagined a Bolivian mining town to look like - desolate, rundown and covered in dust. The only thing that was missing was the tumbleweed. The difference between Potosí and Sucre seemed immense.

Potosí's past wealth is still evident, with its old colonial town houses, numerous elaborate churches and doorways, and the impressive square. It was obvious that the money has long dried up, its buildings not having seen a lick of paint for a number of decades.

The spectacular Cerro Rico (Rich Mountain) dominates the city and we marvelled at it magnificence as we strolled, shivering, around the windy streets of the centre. Cerro Rico is a perfectly shaped conical mountain, towering above the impressive buildings in the city centre, and the poor and shabby looking *barrios mitayos* area where the mineworkers live. It is because of this mountain that Potosí has become so famous. From a distance it looks like a normal mountain, but inside it resembles that of a honeycomb, with thousands of miles of tunnels dug through it.

Many people we had met during our trip had recommended a mine tour to us, most of them telling us that it was one of the best things that they had done in Bolivia, although it was an experience they would never want to repeat. This intrigue was enough to sign us up for the tour, which at $10 each was expensive by Bolivian standards. After we had read the disclaimers on our contract we wished, on this occasion, that they had not been kind enough to translate it into English.

Along with ten other nervous looking gringos we boarded an old yellow school bus, cramming ourselves onto seats that had been made for very small school children. We were driven around a few blocks of narrow streets until the bus pulled up outside a house hidden deep in the maze of shacks, crumbling houses, and churches.

Crowding into the small backyard of the house, we were allocated suitable clothing and equipment to change into. These consisted of a rather fetching plastic overcoat, yellow plastic trousers, steel toe capped Wellington boots and a hardhat that was complete with an electric lamp. It was good to see that they were conforming to all the Health and Safety regulations. We definitely looked the part. The clothing was clean, and we agreed that this was good news, as it implied we wouldn't be crawling around in the mud too much.

Suitably dressed in our mining gear, our bus took us to a part of town known as the Miners Market, where the workers buy all their provisions they need for their day down the mine. Supplies mainly consist of dynamite, lamps, coca leaves, cigarettes, water and alcohol. Our guide suggested we buy some presents to take to the miners who would be showing us around, so we purchased some dynamite sticks, fizzy drinks and a huge bag of coca leaves. We were glad it was not Friday, the day the miners indulge themselves with a little tipple, which at 96% proof is a bit like mentholated spirits rather than single malt. Seeing as a litre only cost about £1 it is good value, even for paint stripper. The miners usually share a litre bottle between two. That seemed pretty hardcore to us, especially at 8 o'clock in the morning.

One of the main items for sale at the market is coca leaves, lots of coca leaves. Throughout the day, whilst working down the mines, the miners don't eat anything except for coca leaves. A miner can chomp his way through 30g of coca leaves every day - roughly equivalent to a small carrier bag full. The workers eat a large meal first thing in the morning, usually a couple of platefuls of food each and then on their way up to work they fill their mouths with coca. Before they arrive at the mines they will have used half of their bag of leaves. At lunchtime, when they stop for a 30-minute break, they spit out the leaves they have chewed all morning and then fill their mouths with the remaining half bag of coca.

Coca is such an important element in a miner's life, as it suppresses hunger and helps them cope with the altitude and heavy manual work. The Spanish initially banned coca because the church saw it as a symbol of their 'pagan cult', claiming it was evil. However it was part of their everyday lives and without it they became poor workers and even poorer miners. Production levels fell so dramatically that they had no option but to allow the miners to chew the leaves again. In fact it was the church who actually cultivated the plant and regulated the distribution of leaves to the miners.

We filled our mouths with coca leaves. Our cheeks, stretched to capacity, stuck out like gerbils. Compared to our guides we had used only a small amount, but they seemed to manage to find space to stuff a few more leaves into their mouths. By the time we had reached the mine entrance, our teeth had gone green and black dribble marks were evident on the side of our slightly numbed mouths. Admittedly we didn't really feel the effects of the altitude (4400m asl), probably because we were too busy concentrating on chewing and trying not to drool all down our front.

Conditions in the mines have changed little since operations started there over 500 years ago. They have claimed an incredible eight million lives, mostly from accidents and silicosis (a deadly lung disease caused by inhaling silicon dust). The mortality rate is a lot lower than in the past, but the life expectancy of a miner is still only 10 and 15 years once they start working underground.

The Spanish basically imposed forced labour on the inhabitants of their newly discovered territory, drafting in men from as far away as Cusco. Each year, approximately 15,000 men were brought to Potosí to work in the mines, less than 5,000 returned home.

Just to get an idea of what we were letting ourselves in for we asked our guides if any tourists had ever lost their lives during a tour. Only one in the last 20 years, we were reliably informed, and that was because he leant too far over a shaft to try and get a photo. The shaft just happened to be very big and very deep.

The mine entrance was about seven feet round; with rails (for trucks) leading horizontally into its black yawning mouth. Brick lined in places, this part of the mine is one of the original tunnels dating back to the colonial times. The numbers of workers who had passed through this entrance over the last 500 years was difficult to comprehend.

After about 50 feet into the mine, the tunnel narrowed and lowered to about five feet high and a couple of feet wide. It quickly became claustrophobic; the coca leaves kept us going. Our guidebook stated that 1 in 10 visitors get scared at this point and turn back. They were right; we were soon down to nine in our group.

After about 10 minutes (it could have been five or 20 minutes – our concept of time quickly disappeared) from the entrance, we arrived at an underground museum. Greeting us at the doorway was a statue of El Tio (Uncle). Depicted as the devil, complete with horns and forked tail, the miners pay homage to the figure with offerings of coca leaves and alcohol. In return they are blessed with a safe day at work and hopefully plenty of rich deposits. The Spanish had not managed to rid the mines of this pagan symbol. The large smile on his face was probably because of the bottle of beer he was holding, but he was definitely pleased about something because he had also been portrayed with a particularly large erection. We secretly gave him some of our coca leaves; we had a feeling we would need something (or someone) to guide us safely through the mines.

The museum was pretty basic, but it was interesting to see how similar the equipment was to those used by Cornish tin miners before they shut down in the 1980's. Our guide later told us that most of the modern equipment on show in the museum was just for display and is very rarely used. They are just too expensive to run and maintain, and instead most drilling, lifting and transportation is done by hand – the same primitive manual methods used since Colonial times.

We were given one final opportunity to turn back before we headed even further into the mountain. Apprehensively, we all declined the offer. As we passed the limit of where fresh air could be pumped to, the conditions immediately changed - the temperature rose, humidity rocketed and the air was full of dust, gas and dynamite fumes. Every now and again we had heard the deep boom of dynamite being blasted in other sections of the mine. Small pieces of rock fell, with a large ping, on our hard hats.

The guides led us through a small opening at the side of the main path. Leading to a small passage only a couple of feet wide, we clambered down the few crude and slimy steps on our bums, hands and knees. It continued steeply downwards for about 60 feet, occasionally edging our way past black gaping holes. These vertical shafts looked like they could be very deep and we decided not to attempt to take any photos down them.

By the time we reached the bottom of the passage, the group was silenced. Joining onto another tunnel in this new level we shuffled along slowly, crouched over to prevent our heads banging on the roof.

The valuable minerals are only found in rich 'lodes' running like veins through the mountain. The tunnels link the numerous veins, but to save time, money and digging they are made only big enough for a man to squeeze through. Very few wooden supports are used to shore up the tunnels, partly because the rock is generally fairly stable, but mainly because it is too expensive to buy. Conditions are therefore very cramped in the mines and we were constantly trying to avoid hitting the sides and top of the tunnel in case we dislodged loose rock and mud.

The mountain still contains the highest concentrations of silver in the world, but since the early 19th Century, when surface deposits dwindled, it has become more and more difficult to extract. The ore that is extracted nowadays is made up of silver, zinc, lead and tin, and very rarely do the miners find a vein with decent concentrations of silver in it.

The mine is run as a cooperative. Groups of miners work together, sometimes with as many as 30 or 40 in each team, but sometimes there may only be five or six. Quite often the team consists of family members, with fathers, sons, brothers, uncles and cousins working alongside each other. Each team mines their own vein which they have had to find themselves. No plans of the mine seemed to exist and the miners rely on their own knowledge and experience, which has often been passed down through generations, to help them discover new veins. There is no guarantee that the ore they mine will be any good, but if it is poor quality then they are paid less, or not at all, by the cooperative. The miners dig in the hope of discovering a vein containing high-grade ore rich in silver and zinc.

The average wage for a miner working 48 hours week is 400 Bolivianos per month, which is roughly equivalent to about £70 or $100. The amount they are paid depends solely on the quality of the ore mined, with any profits made divided equally among the workers. The fewer men in the group, the greater slice of profits they receive. On the other hand, more men in the team means more ore can be extracted, but less returns. The average Bolivian professional, such as a teacher, takes home a similar salary, so miners are comparatively rich - but what a price they pay. They also have to buy all their own tools, drinks, coca leaves, dynamite and headlamps, which doesn't leave them a lot to pay for housing, food and clothing for their family.

We came across a couple of miners filling large hard pails with ore, which were then being winched up to the level above. From there the ore is tipped into one tonne trucks and wheeled, by hand, out of the mine. The two miners had to bag and winch up about 40 tonnes of ore a day. They relied on getting regular deliveries of ore from the rest of their team. While our guide explained the process, four young lads arrived pushing a large two tonne truck overflowing with rock - two of the lads were only 14 years old. Of the 7000 miners working in Cerro Rico, 1000 are children aged 14 or younger. Unceremoniously, they dumped the ore onto the ground and disappeared back into the black to collect more.

Cerro Ricco is riddled with thousands of tunnels, shafts, passageways and dead ends – a maze that we could easily get lost in. We were reassured with the knowledge that our guides were ex-miners who knew their way around the dark labyrinth. Many of the guides, including ours, still work in the mines during the quiet tourist season. It is their only way to earn a decent living. They led us confidently through the maze, with us following closely behind.

Scrambling our way down through smaller and smaller passageways we eventually reached a section where the tunnel opened out into a small cave like area. We still couldn't stand up straight, but it felt less claustrophobic and we were able to relax for a short while. Some of the miners were taking advantage of the extra room and had stopped for their lunch break. Small heaps of soggy chewed coca leaves lay on the ground and the miners were in the process of stuffing their mouths with fresh leaves. A couple of them were puffing away on cigarettes - we are about 4350m asl, deep inside the mine with no fresh air, hardly any oxygen, surrounded by dynamite, and they were smoking. We felt really out of place intruding on their well-earned break. They didn't seem to mind too much, especially when we gave them a bottle of orangeade and a packet of cigarettes to share.

Beyond the 'dining-area' the rocks closed in again and we were back in another small tunnel. Miners dodged past us carrying sacks full of rock on their backs. One miner had somehow managed to find the space to stop for a pee, washing his hands in his own urine as he did so. Water is too heavy to carry and would be used for drinking long before it was wasted for washing. The tunnel got lower and lower and we had to resort to crawling on our hands and knees for about 30 feet.

The heat was intense and sweat poured off our foreheads. The plastic coats and trousers didn't help matters. Apparently, the high concentration of arsenic in the rocks reacting with oxygen helps to increase temperatures. Our key-ring thermometer showed a temperature of nearly 40°C. Vicky had the added problem of her glasses, which kept fogging up. With sweat dripping into our eyes it was tempting to rub them, but the guides warned us not to because our hands would probably be covered in arsenic. The surfaces of the walls were coated in a thick crust of mineral deposits, many of which are harmful. No wonder the miners did not want to eat anything when they are down the mines.

Leading off from the small tunnel was a low horizontal shaft, just big enough for one person to squeeze through. We had to take turns to go through the tunnel, as space at the other end was too small for all of us. The shaft went back about 20 feet and after shuffling along on our bellies we found a lone miner beating a horizontal hole into a vein of ore using a long drill. Once the holes are long and deep enough they are packed with dynamite, which is then detonated. The driller had just enough space to swing his hammer and sweat sprayed off his bare back every time he struck the drill. The heat was unbearable and it was a relief to crawl back out to let the next person go through.

After the dynamite has been blasted, and the dust has settled, the displaced rock is extracted by hand using picks and is then carried, in makeshift rucksacks made of Hessian or plastic, upwards to the next main level. The two tonne trucks are filled and then wheeled off by the four teenagers we met earlier. It was such a labour intensive, and physical, process. We were worn out just walking along, never mind having to carry a sack full of rock, or push a heavy truck.

The journey up through the tunnels and passageways was easier said than done. Gasping for air and desperate to get back out into the open, we scrambled our way up as quickly as we could manage. Back at the main tunnel, near the museum, we rested, panting uncontrollably for at least five minutes. The 10-minute walk back to the mine entrance seemed to take an eternity.

The feeling of relief to be out in the open air was immense - not only the need for light and air, but to be alive. We certainly didn't envy the miners who worked there under Spanish rule, where four-month shifts without seeing daylight were the norm. Two hours had been more than enough.

As we got accustomed to the brightness of the outside world again, our guide demonstrated how dynamite is used, setting up the detonator and lighting the wick. He paid a sarcastic tribute to George Bush and Tony Blair, probably more significant than he realised – it was September 11th.

It was an experience never to be forgotten. We were caked in mud and soaking wet with sweat. Our necks were aching and our legs wobbling from squatting and crawling around.

Our guidebook quoted someone called Bartolome Arzans de Orsua, who in 1703 summed up his visit quite well. *"There are those who, having entered only out of curiosity to see that horrible labyrinth, have come out totally robbed of colour, grinding their teeth and unable to pronounce a word; they have not know even how to ponder it nor make reference to the horrors that are there."*

Everyone was affected physically and emotionally by this cruel and disturbing glimpse of underground life, and sat in thoughtful silence on the bus back to town. We returned our clothes to be cleaned, ready for the next group of unwary tourists. It was certainly the most unforgettable $10 we had ever spent.

Apart from the mine tour, Potosí was memorable for three other things. Firstly, was the smell of urine. The majority of street corners, doorways and gutters had been used as a toilet and there was an overwhelming stench of piss everywhere we went.

Secondly, was the lack of decent food. Potosí is definitely not the place to visit if you are after culinary food. It was here that Vicky ate her grossest meal throughout the entire trip. Supposedly a Brazil nut sauce on pasta, it was more like porridge on spaghetti, all congealed together. On stepping outside the restaurant, the fresh air (mixed with the smell of piss) made her gag, but she courageously fought back the urge to throw up on the street.

Lastly, is the image of a young shoeshine boy, sat on his box of brushes, shivering and crying. It was dark, the wind was severely bitter and it was freezing. Tears were streaking down his dirty face. He was about eight years old and it broke our hearts to see him like this. We stood and watched as a tear fell off his cheek and splashed on his trousers. What could we do? This was the second time this had happened to us, the other had been in Sucre only a couple of days previously. Was it a scam? He was still there an hour later – the same dark alley, still crying. We felt awful. We had been told not to encourage

246

begging, so we bought him a big bag of chips instead. We thought they would at least warm up his legs, if nothing else. It was a stark reminder of how difficult life is in Bolivia.

Vicky Brewis & Caius Simmons

# Wine and Steak in Tarija

We left Potosí, and the smell of urine, just as the sun was setting. The last rays of light reflected of Cerro Rico, making it look even redder. Trucks and miners were still crawling, like ants, all over the mountain, snaking their way up and down the multitude of roads that are cut into its slopes. All traces of vegetation have been scraped away, replaced with mine entrances, roads, piles of slag, redundant shafts and corrugated shacks.

Around the other side, it was as if we were looking at a completely different mountain. The scenery was a complete contrast and Cerro Rico was transformed from a scoured hillside, to a landscape dotted with low scrub and grazing llamas. From this other perspective you would not be aware that there were men, and boys, sweating away deep within the centre of the mountain. Only a small section has been touched by mining activity, where a couple of roads have sneaked their way onto the lower slopes. We wondered how long it would be before the entire mountain is dug away?

Twelve hours later, after a very lumpy, bumpy and particularly uncomfortable bus journey we arrived in the small city of Tarija. The bus company hadn't quite grasped the concept that 5:15am was not the most convenient time to arrive. It was still dark for a start. The markets were not even open and it was still too early for any of the local buses to start operating. The bus station was full of passengers hanging around waiting for it to get light. Our only consolation was the fact that it would be the last night bus we would have to endure and we left the bus station in the knowledge that the next bus we would catch would not arrive at such an unsociable hour.

Throughout history, Argentina has been keen to absorb the rich Tarija region into its country. However, when Bolivia became an independent republic in 1825, the Tarijeños opted to become part of Bolivia, instead of Argentina. The region around Tarija is very isolated from the rest of Bolivia and is heavily influenced by Argentinean customs and traditions, retaining a very distinct culture.

The main reason why we had put Tarija on our travel itinerary was because a friend, who had done some geography research in the region, recommended it to us. It didn't take us long to work out why it was worth a detour off the main 'gringo trail'. The town sits at a very agreeable altitude of 1924 metres asl, with a very Mediterranean feel to it in terms of its architecture, climate and colour. Even the grass in the main square was green - a novel sight after spending months travelling through the dry, barren landscape of the Altiplano.

Sitting in the square, with the warm sun on our faces, we spent hours watching life go by. It was a great way to pass the time of day in Tarija and also appeared to be the favoured pastime for the townsfolk as well. Without even having to move from our seat in the sun, we were able to get a shoeshine, drink endless cups of freshly squeezed orange juice and buy cake.

When we didn't fancy sitting in the square, there were also plenty of decent restaurants and cafés that we could while away a couple of hours drinking coffee, beer and eating salteñas. All the eating places were very busy and full of people, and obviously did not exist for the tourists alone. In fact there were no foreign tourists to be seen anywhere. The quality of the food and wine in Tarija turned out to be a welcome treat. Influences from Argentina were evident and the menus were generally not ideal for vegetarians, mostly limited to large perfectly cooked steaks that melted in the mouth. Vicky was in her element, while Caius stuck with a standard South American omelette.

There appeared to be a larger proportion of wealthier looking residents wandering around the town, many in checked shirts, leather boots and with cowboy hats. It intrigued us how such a remote city made all its money – it certainly wasn't tourism, and the farms didn't appear that extensive. The natural gas industry had attracted some of the wealth, but money was apparently made through the illegal import and export of contraband across the Argentinean border. Until the recent collapse of the Argentine economy many Tarijeños travelled to Argentina to work. With better pay, and a favourable exchange rate, a lot of money could be made. Recent improvements in the financial situation in Argentina have meant that travelling and trading over the border to work is a lucrative option again. Legal or not, Tarijeños had money to spend.

We arrived just in time for a small festival. The main streets were lined with stalls selling chica or food, and banners were strung between buildings. People crowded onto the pavements all through the town centre and around the square. A procession was obviously about to start, so we joined the throngs and waited for the music and dancers to begin. Everyone started to cheer when a Toyota Landcruiser, complete with loud speakers and commentary passed by. We decided we were missing something vital, as we couldn't see the attraction in a 4WD blaring out tinny radio music.

After hanging around for a short while, we realised it was not a procession at all that we were watching, but a bike race. The cheers had been for the lead cyclist, who was just about to cross the finish line – we had managed to miss him. Competitive cycling is not generally a sport associated with Bolivia, but it was all very professional, and the majority of the bikes were racing bikes, with skinny tyres. It must have been a very uncomfortable ride, as there are only a few kilometres of paved road around the Tarija area. All the other roads are bumpy dirt tracks.

We had to wait a couple more days before the proper festival took place, this time with no cyclists. It was not Tarija's main festival, but was a fairly important celebration in honour of its patron saint, San Roque, who supposedly rid the area of leprosy. South Americans take their religious celebrations very seriously, however small and this one was no exception.

It is one of the largest all male processions in South America, with 1500 local men taking part. Known as Chuncho dancers, they dress up in a particularly bizarre costume - black shoes, head dresses which covered the head and face completely, huge feathered turbans, heart shaped bags and tan tights. Images of the Klu Klux Klan came to mind, only more colourful.

With a line of men on either side of the road, they walked in silence through the streets. The only sound was a beating drum and a whistle to signal the 'dancers' to twang their clacker. This was done in unison and was particularly sinister.

We were keen to see some of the local countryside and finally forked out some money to go on a couple of tours in the area. Standing in our hostel reception at 4am, feeling groggy and half asleep, we started to regret booking a walk on a local Inca Trail. We still hadn't recovered fully from arriving in Tarija at the unsociable time the previous day. It was also very cold and dark, and to top it all the hostel owners had locked us in, despite them promising they would leave a key out for us. It took us 20 minutes of doorbell ringing before someone finally materialised. We may have felt rough, but we definitely did not look as awful as she did. We had obviously woken her from a comatose, alcohol induced sleep, following their festival celebrations and we were pleased we were moving hostels and would not see her again.

We felt heartened when a clean, shiny, almost new, red, 4WD jeep turned up on time to pick us up. Together with our guide, driver and Liz, another day-tripper, we headed out of town. Liz claimed she was from Scotland, but the lack of any accent told us otherwise. It turned out she was actually from Guernsey, and just happened to go to University in Edinburgh. Not quite the same as being Scottish, but we let it pass without further comment.

The start of our walk was at the Sama Reserve, a protected park a couple of hours drive from Tarija. Our first stop was to get breakfast. It was good to know our driver and guide had their priorities right. Not surprisingly, the café owner had not opened up yet - it was only 5:30 am. This did not stop our guide hammering on the door to get him out of bed. He looked pretty sleepy, but not as bad as our hostel owner had done. Within five minutes he was in the kitchen and we were sat around the table enjoying a mug of mate de coca. We were pleased to see he had put some trousers on before he started making us fried egg sandwiches.

The road to the Sama Reserve was the same one we had travelled along when we came from Potosí. The first journey had been in the dark, but this time it was starting to get light and we could clearly see the road ahead of us. Unfortunately we could also see the very steep drop at the side of the road. Well, it was more of a track than a road. The driver explained that it was easier to drive in the dark because you could usually tell if a vehicle was approaching as they normally had their lights on. Large quantities of dust envelope the vehicles, making it extremely difficult to see the road and anything coming towards you. Having lights on didn't really make a difference in the daylight and the driver was just hoping he wouldn't meet any vehicles coming the other way. It was scary enough in a small 4WD and we tried not to think about large buses driving around the hairpin bends as they sped down the hillside.

The road took us back onto the Altiplano, and into the Sama Reserve. We soon realised why the Park Warden was surprised to see us. His last visitors had been two weeks previously and we guessed that not many tourists came up this way very often. We fed his domesticated Vicuna with some of our coca leaves, in the hope that we might be able to get a photo of it. This was a bit optimistic as she thought the camera was food and kept trying to eat it as well.

It was still another hour's drive before we could actually start walking. The landscape around us, like most of the altiplano, was barren. There was some wildlife though, and we passed a lake full of flamingos, and other birds, that looked like a black and white pelican, strutting around regally. We commented that it was very 'rural' and Liz reckoned we must be townies. Rural Britain and rural Bolivia are worlds apart. Caius was brought up in a house that most people would call remote – no mains electricity or water, or inside toilet and to get there you have to leave the car and walk the last bit up to the house.

Houses in the Sama Reserve were no different, apart from the fact that the people who live here do not have the luxury of owning a car, or even being near a bus route. They are at least an hour's drive, or a half days walk from the nearest settlement. The Sama Reserve, and most of Bolivia, is remote, more remote than anywhere we had been.

The driver stopped at one of the few mud houses that dotted the hillside. The family was a friend of the driver and he had stopped to deliver some gifts to them, mainly sweets for the children. The family was involved in a programme to try and increase the number of llamas in the reserve and to encourage traditional herding methods. From the wool, they made coarse llama blankets and material that is then made into trousers and other clothing.

All the woollen goods they made were to order, so we couldn't really buy anything, which we were quite pleased about. We did not have any room in our rucksacks for a huge wool blanket and the thought of wearing wool trousers made us unbearably itchy. Our driver had not stopped here for our benefit and we did not impose on the family. The kids were all wrapped up, their shiny pink cheeks poking out from a bundle of hats and scarves. Not quite knowing what to make of us, they stared at us from a distance. It was difficult to try and absorb their surroundings without staring back.

Their adobe house did not look like it would shelter them much from the persistent cold wind and the warm blankets were probably the best way to keep warm. There were no trees in sight, so a hearty fire (other than for cooking) would have been out of the question. At least they had plenty of llama droppings to burn instead.

After we left the house, the state of the track got gradually worse and worse. Judging by the amount of shrugging and pointing that was going on in the front seats we guessed the driver and guide didn't really know where they were going. Eventually they decided to abandon the truck and start walking. We walked to the top of the pass together, where we parted company with Liz and the driver. She had only really come for the ride and was going back through the Park to see some more of the wildlife.

Vicky Brewis & Caius Simmons

The view from the top of the pass was stunning. We were back at 4000m+ asl and we're pleased that most of the walk was downhill. The Inca trail dropped below us into a large open valley surrounded by sunburnt hills. Apparently the path was used to transport gold in its heyday, but is now rarely walked. Only some of the granite paving had eroded away and was generally in excellent condition. The path followed along the side of the hillside, and then descended down into the valley below.

A small detour took us to a large carved rock. This was the local calendar and at certain times of the lunar cycle, with a lot of imagination, you could apparently work out which month it was.

Our guide spoke no English, but we were able to converse for the whole day without too much problem. We spoke a lot about the geography, geology and archaeology of the region; luckily all the words are similar in both languages.

Our elevenses break was at the schoolyard at the bottom of the valley. It was a Sunday, so there were no kids around. There was also not a house to be seen and we were intrigued to know where all the pupils came from. This school apparently had 17 pupils; just enough to be able to use the football pitch around the corner and plenty for the choir in the church next-door.

We asked our guide if Chagas beetles or vinchuca (also known as the 'assassin bug') was still a big problem in this particular part of the valley. In rural areas it is estimated to have infected as much as 90% of the population. The beetle crawls out of the adobe walls and thatched roofs at night to feed on human lips, injecting a horrible poison. If bitten you will then die a horrible death, your blood coagulating until it clogs your heart up. It is guaranteed to kill you, but could take as long as 20 years before you finally die. Our guide explained that many of the local villages in the Tarija district have had grants to try and eradicate them. All the houses are fumigated, they get new tiled roofs and the walls rendered and painted. We had noticed a few properties that looked particularly clean and new, but it obviously hadn't quite made it this far up the valley.

254

The only person we met along the way was the local shop owner. His shed was full of huge bags of pasta, rice and flour, and cans of tomatoes. The blackboard behind the counter (his table) was the local 'slate', listing how much each family owed. Once again, we wondered who his customers were, as we hadn't seen any houses since we left the schoolhouse. The shop owner was extremely proud of his new drying racks for camomile, which he picked himself. He sold his crop to a local co-operative that mixed it with a few coca or peppermint leaves and made them into tea bags. He did not seem too bothered that between us, and our guide, we managed to clear his shelves of all his boxes of teabags.

Our guide put on his shorts in anticipation that we would have to wade through the river to get to the other side of the gorge. When we reached the bank to cross over, the river was only a trickle and we did not even have to take off our boots and socks. It had been an exceptionally dry summer, and the rains that usually came in January and February had not been as intense as usual that year. Many of the crops and fruit trees in the valley were starting to suffer and some of the local farmers had started to water their plants to stop them wilting. We were told that Tarija had been experiencing random water cuts because the local reservoir, one of the biggest in Bolivia, was so low.

Lunch was eaten at the top of the final pass. The views were amazing, overlooking Tarija, many miles away. Mountain Cara Caras (a bird of prey) soared overhead. We tried to educate our guide about Paddington Bear when our mascot made an appearance for some photos. He seemed interested, but we think the story was lost in the translation.

The walk down to the Tarija valley from the top of the pass took us from a height of about 3500m asl to 2000m asl, over a distance of only a few kilometres. It was a relentless down, down, down - and our knees were aching by the time we reached the bottom.

We sat in silence while we recovered. It was a silence like nothing else, all we could hear was the ringing in our ears, which just got louder and louder. Not a breathe of wind, the rustle of leaves, no birds signing, or even insects buzzing. The quiet was so peaceful and relaxing, and even the guide appeared to be affected by the deafening silence.

While waiting for our driver to come and collect us we relaxed in the garden owned by one of the Park Wardens. It was a great end to a magical day. It was possible that we could have arranged the trip ourselves, but it would have been a real headache to sort out. Without any public transport we would not have been able to make it to the start of the walk, never mind finding the trail. We would never have bought any camomile teabags and we would have had to walk for another few hours before we could even consider finding some transport back to town. Instead, we sat talking in the sunshine and eating jelly.

By the time the truck arrived we were all exhausted, and even our guide had fallen asleep. The coca leaves he had been shoving into his mouth all day had done little to suppress his tiredness and his teeth were still chomping while he slept.

The tour agency was horrified to see us back so early and thought something had gone horribly wrong with their plans. It was just that we had managed to walk the trail quicker than any other tourists had done so before. Our feet certainly felt like we had walked it in record speed and, that evening, we treated ourselves to a good bottle of wine.

In the morning, our legs were aching, but thought we better walk to the bus station to sort out our transport to Tupiza. We had been looking forward to finally travel by day and traipsed around all the companies advertising buses that ran 'en el dia' (in the day), but with no luck. It turned out they had stopped the day bus about a year previously, so we would have to endure one more night bus. Public transport was a great way to travel around, but it always takes an age to sort out, and by now, after nearly three months, we were beginning to get a bit tired of it – especially when all we got to see was the back of a bus seat.

A visit to Tarija is incomplete without the obligatory vineyard and fossil tour. Tarija has gained a reputation as being home to the highest vineyards in the world. Since colonial times, when Franciscan monks first started growing the vines, the industry has steadily grown. Today, over two million litres of

256

wine each year are produced in the wineries, or bodegas as they are called, in the valley surrounding Tarija. This is enough to fulfil demand within Bolivia, but strong competition and cheap exports from Chile and Argentina makes it difficult for them to break into the international market.

We had already sampled a few glasses of homemade wine, port and singani from a doorway in the town, and had been pleasantly surprised. Three glasses later we had felt a bit merry and decided to invest in a couple of bottles. Singani is an evil tasting, white-grape brandy of about 40% proof. It is very similar to any of the distilled firewater that you can get elsewhere in the world. The locals know it as Chufflay, supposedly named after the British mining engineers who used to 'shoo flies' away from the tops of their glasses. Why flies would want to drink this horrid stuff is beyond us.

Our 'tour guide' was an American lady, Valerie, who was stereotypically dressed in white pumps, jeans that were too tight and a tucked in T-Shirt, and she also had a strong southern American whiny accent. First impressions didn't convince us, but she was really nice and was as pleased to speak English as we were. We asked all the questions we had been desperate to know the answers to – jobs, money, transport, price of petrol (30p per litre), schools, food, hobbies and everyday life stuff that Bolivians do. She was delighted when we told her that you could get a five-day weather forecast for Tarija on the BBC website. In fact, you could get a forecast for most towns in Bolivia, except for Sucre, the capital.

Our first stop was the fossil area which was located in the middle of some Spaghetti Western style badlands. Sedimentary layers of volcanic ash, sands and clays have covered, fossilised and preserved a variety of Pleistocene megafauna. Everywhere we walked we had to step over bits of Andean elephant tusks, armadillo shells, horse teeth and huge quantities of vertebrae bones. Flooding has heavily eroded all these sections, but research further up the valleys has revealed undisturbed and more complete skeletons.

We then headed to Bodegas y Vinedos de La Concepcion, a vineyard with a reputation for high quality fine wines. Many of the bodegas are a bit funny about letting people visit their plants but the owner here was quite happy to let our guide take us around - Valerie had done so many tours she knew the script off by heart. The processing plant was not too different to those in Europe, but because of high costs some of the processes are still done manually. All the labels are stuck onto the bottles by hand. Seeing them all stacked up, we reckoned it was going to take quite a lot of Pritt.

We were more interested in the sampling and they were busy bottling Chablis, which we were given the first taste of. Even though the wine is made from the Chablis grape, the French wine producers are trying to claim it is specific to Northern Burgundy. This would mean they would have to rename it – Concepcion does not really have the same status, or ring, as Chablis.

The owner told us that the first person to taste a wine would determine whether it would be successful or not. If it was a flop, it would be our fault – luckily, it tasted great – crisp and dry. We also tried the red reserve wine, not as nice, but drinkable all the same. We were glad we had not been the first to try it. The Singani was particularly strong and nicer than the homemade stuff we had tried in the doorway in Tarija. This was quickly followed by the barrel aged Singani, which tasted more brandy like. At $27 a bottle, we decided to give it a miss, buying a couple of cheaper bottles of wine instead to add to our collection.

Staggering out into the fresh air we were pleased we had eaten a big lunch. Valerie was also feeling, and looking, a bit pissed too. This was worrying, especially as she stumbled getting into the jeep and dropped her keys trying to get them in the ignition. We had to stop at the next shop to buy some biscuits for her in an attempt to soak up some of the excess alcohol.

The next wine tasting place was a lady's house that made wine for the local market. The cellar room was housed in a huge old barn and was full of barrels and huge demijohns. We tried three different types, sweet red, dry red and dry white, all very nice and far superior to our attempts at homemade wine. A few locals turned up with empty coke bottles, stopping for a quick drink and a chat, while their bottles were filled up with their favourite tipple.

The barn walls were covered in winemaking paraphernalia – old photos, bottles and labels, and the owner explained that her bodega was particularly popular with Bolivian holidaymakers. She sold all sorts of tat and gave us the option to have the wine we bought in a normal bottle or in a gross one decorated in authentic straw holders. We felt quite hammered, but managed to suppress our giggles at the near pornographic photos she sold of young scantily clad girls stamping on grapes. She had plans to expand the 'visitor centre' and had just been into town to try and buy a couple of mannequins that she planned to dress in traditional costumes. This was a woman who had sussed her market out and was prepared to milk it as much as she could possibly get away with.

Valerie had luckily sobered up a bit by the time we left and she decided to take the scenic route home, because she was "having such a ball". She got lost and had to turn back when we came to a dead end. While turning the jeep around we got stuck - it turned out she had the handbrake on full. The alcohol had not improved her driving.

As darkness fell, we were still a good hour from Tarija, and our bus was due to leave in two hours. We eventually found the normal road back, but on the way up a hill our jeep just died. There was no power at all - the jeep was not going any further. We were in the middle of nowhere, it was now very dark and Valerie had forgotten to charge her mobile phone up. After consulting a local farmer we dumped the jeep in his farm entrance and decided to walk towards Tarija in the hope we could hitch a ride.

Swaying up the road we headed towards town. After all the liquid we had been drinking Valerie and Vicky were desperate for a 'bano natural'. Just as they dropped their trousers a tractor kicked into action ahead of us and the lights flashed on. The poor driver must have had a shock of a lifetime, with two luminous white arses revealed by his headlights. He probably had, like us, a good laugh about it afterwards with his friends down the pub.

Luckily we were picked up by an off duty caminetta driver, who was intrigued why three foreigners were walking in the wilderness in the pitch dark. He got us back to town with only a few minutes to spare before our bus left. We

259

left Tarija, after a very enjoyable visit, pissed and laden with six bottles of wine and a bottle of singani.

Thinking we had been the only two tourists in the town, we were pleasantly surprised to see two other Westerners on the bus - Charles and Catherine. They had been on the wine tour that morning and it freaked them out a bit when we knew their names before they had even introduced themselves. We had seen their names in the visitor book at the last bodega.

Tarija had not been on Charles and Catherine's list of places to visit in Bolivia, but due to the number and severity of roadblocks they had been unable to leave La Paz by bus. They had been stuck there for over a week waiting for the strikes to finish, but in the end their only escape was by plane.

With their strongly French accented English we automatically assumed that their command of the English language was not great, so we made sure we spoke slowly and clearly to them. If necessary we could have spoken a little louder, just to make sure that they had understood us. It turned out that they had been living in New York for seven years and their English was excellent, complete with swear words and slang, but they had luckily managed to retain a fantastic French accent. Why can't the English accent be so sexy?

They were particularly annoyed to learn that they had been caught out by the random ticket pricing charged by the bus companies and had paid more than we had for our seats. It was some consolation to learn that the lady behind us had paid even less than we had.

As suspected the bus was not a bus cama, but an extra short bus with even less seats on it than normal. We wedged ourselves into the usual cramped bus seats, but we were too comatose to realise that it was particularly uncomfortable, and very bumpy. After a great night's sleep we were rudely awoken at 4.45 in the morning when the bus pulled into Tupiza. It was still pitch black and again we cursed the bus company. Why couldn't we have left later and arrived at a sensible time?

A notice in the hotel advised us that anyone arriving before 6.00am had to pay for that night's accommodation. This was a great scam as all the buses arriving in Tupiza do so before 6.00am; they must hate it when the buses are late. We ignored this completely and the night porter was too sleepy to notice that we had written down 6.30am as our arrival time.

Vicky Brewis & Caius Simmons

# Being Butch Cassidy and the
# Sundance Kid

Tupiza can be described as more of a village, rather than a town. A lovely, sleepy, isolated settlement, it sits in the middle of the harsh desert landscape of Cordillera de Chichas, and like many other parts of Bolivia, agriculture and tourism have replaced mining as the main activity in the area. The beautiful red mountains surrounding the village dominate the view at the end of every street.

The 'walk around town to get our bearings' would have taken less than 10 minutes if we hadn't bumped into Josh and Ali in the main square. We had said our farewells to Josh and Ali in Sucre almost a week previously. Thinking that was the last we would ever see of them, it was great to meet up with some familiar faces.

That evening, we opened a few of the bottles of wine we had acquired in Tarija. With a couple of drinks inside him, Josh decided to tell us the real reason why they stayed so long in Sucre – we had just thought they wanted to enjoy the fiesta and hang around with their friends who had shown up. It turned out that Josh needed to pay a visit to the doctors because he was having trouble sitting down, which in itself is not very amusing. The funny part was, that, when he tried to explain to the doctor about his problem, which he was a little bit embarrassed about, the doctor just burst out laughing. Rather than saying "Soy embarasada" (I am embarrassed), Josh had said "Soy embarasado". For everyone with little understanding of Spanish, Josh had told the doctor he was pregnant.

We had come to check out Tupiza for a reason, namely Robert LeRoy Parker and Harry Alonso Longabaugh, more famously known as Butch Cassidy and the Sundance Kid. Outlawed from the western United States for a series of bank and train robberies throughout the 1880's and 1890's they fled from America and finally arrived in Tupiza in 1908. They had heard about the Aramayo mining company based nearby and thought they could make their fortune hijacking convoys of mules carrying the miners payroll. Word got out quickly about who the culprits were and scores of angry unpaid miners scoured the hills and valleys for the two white robbers.

A four man military patrol spotted the outlaws 100km northwest of Tupiza in the village of San Vincente. Following a short gunfight, Sundance was supposedly injured. Rather than be captured, Butch apparently shot his wounded partner dead before turning the gun on himself. It was nothing like the huge shoot out, with the hundreds of Bolivian soldiers, that is portrayed in the film. The two bodies, buried in unmarked graves, were exhumed in 1991 where forensic tests showed they weren't actually Butch or Sundance. Had these been the correct graves or had they managed to escape? One theory suggests they did get away and moved to Europe, where they underwent facelifts to disguise themselves.

For such a small place, there was a particularly wide range of activities to keep us occupied, most of which involved jeeps, horses or mountain bikes. Before we knew it we found ourselves booked onto a jeep tour and a two-day horse ride. We think we must have been drunk when we agreed with Charles and Catherine to do the latter.

The owner of the hotel and tour agency mistook Charles for being Israeli because he haggled so much to get the best deals. It seems that the Israelis have got themselves a bad reputation in South America, bartering down to such low prices it is almost insulting. They may be able to get away with it in Australia and New Zealand, but in a country so poor as Bolivia, where the prices are minimal anyway it is not worth haggling too low. Needless to say, Charles only managed to save us about 50p each.

The jeep tour gave us a good feel for the surrounding landscape. The closest we had come to seeing something similar was the badlands in Southern Spain, only this seemed about 10 times bigger and far more colourful. Charles and Catherine compared it with the Grand Canyon, but smaller. Whatever it was like, it was pretty amazing and after a couple of hours gazing at views of red, green and blue hills we were almost looking forward to our horse ride. If nothing else, at least the scenery would be fantastic.

After our four-hour horse ride in Vilcabamba (Ecuador) we had been undecided whether we would be able endure a two-day trek. However, this is how Butch Cassidy and the Sundance Kid had done it and the only way we were going to really appreciate the countryside would be on horseback.

When we booked the trek we insisted that we go down to the stables to check out the horses. After the condition of the horses we had ridden in Ecuador, we wanted to make sure that they were going to be up to carrying us for two whole days. Seeing that they were well-fed and sturdy looking put our minds at rest. We made sure we chose the biggest, most placid looking horses and we were reassured by the stable boys that they were "muy tranquile".

It appeared that they had fed them overnight on Coca leaves, or perhaps very strong coffee, because when we turned up the following day to start the ride they were all wired up, wide eyed and raring to go. They were most definitely not 'muy tranquile'.

Charles had an image of himself as a bit of a cowboy in the Wild West, and his multicoloured horse was aptly called Apache. The only things he had forgotten to bring with him were the cowboy hat and a lasso.

Caius' horse, Tobacco, insisted that it was going to be in front of all the other horses and every time anyone tried to overtake he would steer himself in front of the others to cut them off. To make sure there was a safe distance behind him, he had a habit of farting to ward of any challengers. Vicky's horse, Negra was quite happy being at the back, and hated anyone behind her, kicking any horse that got too close. This was basically the line up for the next two days – Caius at the front, Vicky right at the very back.

The scenery was fantastic from the start, and we were soon riding through pretty wild countryside. The first stretch of open road was enough to get the horses excited and we were soon cantering, which was particularly scary as most of us had only been on a horse three or four times before. Not wearing any helmets was also a bit disconcerting.

It did not take us long to realise that we had absolutely no control over the horses, they all had a mind of their own. If they wanted to canter they would, no matter how much we pulled in on the reins. Saying "whoa" did not work and our guides told us to try saying "shush" instead. It took us while to work out that it had to be pronounced with a certain accent for it to work, or maybe our guides had been winding us up.

There were some great rocks and cliffs, and the colours were amazing. We passed through Peurta del Diablo (Devils Door), a big rock split down the middle, which you could ride under. We took a break at the Canon del Inca where huge tall cliffs were eroded into fascinating red formations.

Getting back on the horses after our rest was not quite so great and our bums were beginning to feel a bit tender after the short break. The feeling was soon forgotten as the horses took off on a canter and then sped up to a gallop. They also had another gear, faster than a gallop, which was even more terrifying, jostling you uncontrollably until your feet almost slid out the front of the stirrups. The sudden change in pace made you lean back and we realised why it was only one handed riding – the other arm was there to help you balance yourself in the saddle. By lunchtime we were walking like real cowboys, bow legged.

The horses, having had a decent rest and a drink regained their energy and as soon as we were back on the saddle, they took off at full speed cantering through the river. There were cries of agony while we hurtled along. Tobacco decided he would start bucking for no apparent reason, but luckily Caius had watched a few rodeo programs on the TV, and managed to cling on. This was turning out to be a pretty advanced lesson, the fastest he had ever done before was a trot and that was on a lead.

We joined another girl, Geraldine and her guide, which meant that the horses had to re-stamp their authority. The jostling started again and a few hairy moments to show who was boss. Tobacco, an old guide horse, was obviously tiring. He became weary of Apaches endless energy, and soon resigned himself to being second in the pack. The horses were gradually more and more weary, and at one stage Negra went down on her knees, stumbled back up and carried on like nothing had happened. Fortunately we were only walking at the time.

Eventually we arrived at our destination, a village called Quiriza. Sitting down all day should not be exhausting but we were feeling as tired as the horses were. We helped to unsaddle our nags and fed them carrots. It was satisfying watching them have an invigorating roll around in the dust and straw, and images of a nice relaxing bath to ease our aching joints dominated our thoughts. A dream is all it would ever be.

Our host family we were staying with were out, so our guides broke in through the window and let us all in. The house looked really posh from the outside (for this part of Bolivia). Inside it was simple, with minimal furniture and basic facilities. Charles asked if he could have a shower. The guides just giggled and smiled at him. So there was no running water or toilet, but we did have a bed, which was a bonus. Geraldine, who was with a different tour agency stayed with a family in the village, sharing half the house with a load of chickens and sheep.

A dorm room was our accommodation for the night. Just as the tour agency had promised us, all the bedding was provided. Charles and Catherine looked disgusted at the state of the sheets and we could only make a guess at when they were last cleaned. They didn't smell dirty, but seeing as we stank of horses it was irrelevant. Catherine and Charles were jealous of our sleeping bag liners and annoyed because they had left their sleeping bags in Tupiza. It certainly wasn't the worst bed we had slept in.

Our hosts were a young couple with two small children. They didn't appear to be your typical farming family that we had seen elsewhere in Bolivia. For a start they had a tractor, the first we had seen in months. They also owned a 4WD jeep, had mains electricity and they owned a huge TV for the kids to play games on. We had obviously landed on our feet.

Smelling like we had been rolling around in horse shit all day, we headed into the village on the back of the 4WD, the house dog chasing us along the road. It was festival night and our host informed us that we were invited to go along with them to join in the celebrations. She actually told us that the only reason why she wanted us to go was to see how Westerners danced.

Stared at by the entire male population in the village, all sneering "*gringo*" and "*amigas*" at us, we walked the gauntlet through the school playground to get to the main hall. This was defiantly not the friendliest of welcomes; it felt like we had been projected into a Western movie, Charles and Caius envisaged either a full scale brawl or shoot out to resolve the problem.

The hall where they were hosting the festival party was very big and very well lit by loads of bright strip lights. Hundreds of small chairs had been placed around the edge of the room and a few locals were watching the 'festivities'. At one end of the hall was a stage hosting a DJ rapping along to pan pipe music. Huge speakers blasted out the tunes, and disco lights flashed rhythmically across the room. There was a line of 'young ones' shuffling in a line in the middle of the 'dance floor'. Memories of school and youth club discos came to forefronts of our mind. We were wishing we had stayed in for the night.

Just as we thought it couldn't get any worse, our host called over the Director of the school for us to meet. We had brought with us a bag of pens that someone had palmed off onto us in Puno and we suggested to our hosts they could pass them onto the local school on our behalf. They insisted we took them to the festival with us and we thought we would have the opportunity to sneak them into the school letterbox unnoticed. At this stage, we hadn't realised the festival was being held in the school. Our hosts thought it would be nice if we could 'present' the pens to the school personally. How thoughtful. It was all very embarrassing, but we had sunk so far into the ground already we could not escape.

Around the hall hung pictures painted by the pupils. Scrawled underneath they had written comments about Chile owning Bolivia's coastline - statements declaring it was all the governments' fault and that one day they would get it back, at whatever the cost. No wonder the Bolivians had never got over the fact they had lost the land to Chile in 1879, and reading these comments it was unlikely they would ever be able to forgive their neighbours. It was a little bit disconcerting and we were glad to be British and not Chilean tourists.

Catherine and Charles ventured onto the dance floor to demonstrate 'how westerners dance'. As they did the Director stopped the music to announce over the microphone that non-residents, that is the five gringos in the room, had to pay to attend the festival. We were all wishing the ground would open up and suck us to safety.

Charles and Caius were feeling particularly intimidated and uncomfortable, so they headed outside in an attempt to avoid the glares. It was no better out in the playground, which was still full of blokes, all of whom were too scared to go inside the hall in case they had to dance. The house dog seemed to be having the most fun, working his way round all the bitches in turn and then running off with his tail in the air in search of the next shag.

To keep our host family happy we all danced to one song. It was difficult to try and dance as badly as the local couples, but we did not want to show them up by putting on a good performance. One dance was more than enough torture, so we just sat at the side of the hall trying to think of a polite excuse to leave.

Our excuse presented itself soon enough. After a few more beers, the village lads plucked up enough courage to venture inside the hall. Gathering in the corner like a herd of bulls ready to charge we decided it was definitely time to go before they stampeded. We feigned exhaustion after our long day on the saddle and made our departure, legging it across the playground as fast as we could.

Our backsides were feeling extremely tender and we were all glad to lie down to ease the pain. Charles informed us that he was going to, "cream his

268

arse" and we quickly turned out the light before we witnessed anymore. In the dark we all followed suit, plying our bruised bums with quantities of calendula and arnica in the hope that they would be fully recovered by the morning.

Getting back onto the saddle the following morning was particularly uncomfortable. The precautions we had made applying the cream had been to no avail, and we all had bruises down the inside of our legs and bums. As soon as the horses started trotting, the pain became almost unbearable, but we just had to grin and bear it. Tobacco had regained his energy and stormed on ahead, closely followed by the rest of the group.

We crossed the river and headed downstream along the side of the valley. The scenery looked very different from the previous days journey even though it was the same river. The horses plodded on, occasionally trotting, but generally they were a lot more subdued. We cut down through fields - the contrast between the brilliant blue sky, the red mountains and the green fields was blinding.

As soon as we rode back into the river valley the horses woke up again with the sound of the running water and started to gallop. Apache went flying off ahead and Tobacco could not catch up. Because he hated being behind he tried bucking again to get rid of his heavy load. Eventually the guide was able to control the horse, and even though Caius had lost his stirrups he was lucky to still be on the saddle.

At lunchtime we met up with Josh and Ali, who were on a day trip. They had decided that, due to Josh's 'condition', a two-day horse ride might not be the best remedy. We had obviously chosen the best horses on offer at the stables because the horse they had given Josh was far too short for him. He looked like he was perched on a sausage dog, the horses legs were so short. We all laughed, as its legs seemed to go about 10 times faster than any of the other horse to keep up with the rest of the group.

The new arrivals had upset the pecking order of the pack again and while the horses were trying to push their way to the front, Catherine's horse bucked and threw her off. Luckily she only grazed her arms, but she, and everyone else, was a bit shaken by the incident. The horses sensed our concern, making them even more jumpy. The guides also sensed our insecurity, helping to keep them under control as best they could.

The afternoon was torture. The horses kept taking off on their own accord, especially when there was an open road ahead of them. With speed came even more pain. Our backsides were so sore and tender that even plodding along felt uncomfortable. We were glad we had only opted for two days and not three. Our guides had told us the pain did not get any better until you had spent at least six days in the saddle. Our knees had seized up, our lower backs were stiff, our arms ached and our arses were in excruciating agony. We were all still a bit jittery after Catherine's fall, which took some of the pleasure out of the ride. Apart from those few minor issues, the countryside was fantastic and the company was great.

Although we had enjoyed the two days, everyone was pleased when we rode into Tupiza. It felt so good to stand back on solid ground, especially as we knew we would not have to get back on the horse again. No doubt, once the memory of the pain has faded we will climb back into the saddle. We tipped our guides, said our goodbyes and headed to the hotel for hot showers, a beer and a lie down. Luckily the toilet seats in our hotel were padded (something you only get in Bolivia), and it was the one place we could sit down without feeling too much discomfort.

Everywhere we went there seemed to be a festival of some sort, and Tupiza was no exception. We were all 'festivalled out', but we could not resist the lure of the music. We had become so blasé; there are millions of people in the world who travel continents to see these processions. Dragging ourselves away from our seat by the pool we headed into town to find out what all the noise was about. Our main thought was that if we didn't go and watch we might miss something really special.

The festival was in full swing and it turned out that some kind of competition was taking place. We stood and watched a few groups go by, who

270

were dancing around the square in colourful costumes. We thanked our lucky stars that it was not being held in a school hall. Because it was a competition we had to wait for each group to finish completely before the next lot set off. Interesting – but tedious. It was one of those events that are only really enjoyable if you are taking part. Needless to say we didn't hang around for too long, sneaking back to the poolside to catch the last few rays of sunshine.

Two bus services a week operated from Tupiza to Uyuni and the train was even more infrequent. For a couple of quid extra we treated ourselves, opting to catch the daily 'mas rapido' jeep. We thought this would be good value - anything to avoid having to sit in an uncomfortable bus all day.

Josh and Ali came along to the Terminal Terreste to wave us off. They stood laughing at us as our bags were piled on the roof, along with the belongings of about 10 other passengers. This must be a mistake, we thought - they must just be transporting the goods and not actually travelling themselves. Josh and Ali laughed even louder when everyone all started to squeeze into the jeep. Behind the three seats at the front (us and the driver), there were four adults in the middle, with four adults and their four children in the very back. The Toyota Landcruiser had 15 passengers crammed in. By the time we messed around filling up with fuel, stopping at security checkpoints and picking up another passenger (who somehow managed to squeeze into the middle row), we were thinking "mas rapido, my arse".

With 16 people on board we finally crawled our way up through the valley towards Uyuni. It was not long before the driver decided it was time to stop for lunch in a tiny village. It was only just past 11.00am.

An hour later, we were off again, climbing up through the red cliffs and over big rolling hills. The dirt road ahead was potholed, bumpy and very dusty. A few hours later we arrived in the sleepy mining town of Atocha where we had to change jeeps. Having to hang around for an hour was not our idea of fun, especially as we did not have a clue what was happening. And, just to make matters worse, everyone was staring at us.

Vicky Brewis & Caius Simmons

All the jeep drivers were drinking beer and we started to get a bit nervous. Eventually our 'chauffeur' turned up, and luckily appeared to be sober. Our 'mas rapido' trip continued. This time we squeezed into the back seat, but luckily there were only 11 in this jeep, including a bloke who was totally pissed and drinking quantities of beer. Maybe this was the way to make the journey more enjoyable. He kept trying to pass a tinny to the driver, who luckily declined it. We picked up a couple more passengers on the way, who decided to spread themselves out in the back and take up all our space. There was no way we wanted to start a conversation, especially as the drunk was becoming more obnoxious, so we pretended to be asleep to avoid eye contact.

The scenery along the way was spectacularly barren. A huge flat expanse of nothing spread out ahead of us, behind us, and to each side. In the far distance, right on the horizon we could make out the peaks of a mountain chain. They never seemed to get any closer. Its bleakness made it all the more beautiful. Our driver was thoughtful enough to point out a lone *vicuna* to us – the only sign of life we could see for miles.

Much to the amusement of the rest of the passengers, the drunk finally drank himself to sleep. He then began to snore loudly.

The men next to us spread themselves out even more, squashing us further into the corner. Still, we managed to avoid eye contact.

The journey seemed to take forever.

Finally we arrived in the dusty town of Uyuni, with its long wide roads. It was 5pm and our 200km journey had taken about 7 hours. It had been anything but 'mas rapido' and we dreaded to think how long the bus would have taken. We had passed the bus going the other way, the engine hood propped open with a broom pole to keep it cool.

# Train Cemetery

Whilst unpacking our rucksacks it dawned on us that 25 BOB for a nice comfortable double bed, en-suite including breakfast was a bit cheap. We were soon packing up again when the receptionist told us it was US$25 not 25 BOB. The owner thought we were totally stupid, as if we should have known. We told him that this was actually Bolivia and not America.

The town of Uyuni has one tourist highlight - a train cemetery. A short walk out of town through a rubbish dump took us to a pile of scrap metal. In an attempt to stop the rabid dogs from following us we employed the usual tactic – throwing stones. It didn't really have the effect we were hoping because the mangy dogs just chased after the stones, before returning with bared teeth.

If a pile of rusty metal was the best Uyuni could offer, then we were not impressed. The shell of old railway trucks wasn't even enough to inspire us to get the camera out. Where were the engines, the impressive locomotives? Loads of kids were playing, yelling and screaming in amongst the trucks, so we decided to turn back. It was just the kind of place where we could have easily been mugged again.

The real, and only, reason why people flock to Uyuni is because it is where jeep tours across the Uyuni Salt Flats begin. For three days you travel by jeep across the Salar de Uyuni, the largest and highest salt desert in the world, until you finally reach Chile, 1000km later.

The next day was spent trying to arrange the trip. Scores of little agencies lined the streets, all of them trying to sell a Salar trip. Which one do we choose? There were far too many to choose from for people as indecisive as ourselves. Our first stop was the tourist information office to read a comments book to see what others had to say about the agencies. We were horrified by the stories: drivers falling asleep at the wheel or too pissed to even stand up, terrible food or no food at all, jeeps breaking down, guides driving off and abandoning the tourists in the middle of nowhere. The list was endless. Eventually we bit the bullet and went with Tonito Tours, a well-established agency that someone had recommended to us. We paid just that little bit extra in the hope that nothing would go wrong.

We had a 'New Years Eve' feeling about the trip, a mixture of excitement and apprehension. Was it going to live up to the hype that surrounded it? We hoped it would not be a flop, like many New Year's Eves end up being. Our optimism lay with the many travellers who had recommended it as one of the highlights of their trip to South America.

That evening we went to the bus station to meet Josh and Ali off their bus. It was already dark and the bus pulled in an hour later than expected. We were relieved we had taken the 'mas rapido' jeep the day before. It was our turn to laugh as they stepped off the bus. It had been a very long and dusty ride. They were pleased we had sorted out a room, food and transport already for them. To be honest there hadn't been much else to do all day.

# Uyuni Salt Flats

The only thing we had to do before leaving Uyuni was to get an exit stamp from immigration. The official charged us 15 BOBS, that's £1.50 in real money, just to get out of the country. Vicky argued with the official for 10 minutes. After all, we had not had to pay to leave Ecuador or Peru. It was all a bit sceptical, but begrudgingly we paid the £1.50. We were also becoming really tight with our money, questioning the cost of everything. It was not that we didn't have enough funds, it was just that we were fed up with the feeling of being continually ripped off.

Back at the hostel we realised that the passports had been stamped with the wrong date, with August instead of September. The official was not pleased to see us again as we were disturbing his afternoon nap. He took our passports and tippexed out the date and wrote over the top.

Luckily we had taken Charlie's advice, ensuring we got a 90-day instead of a 30-day visa when we entered Bolivia in Copacobana. Nick, a tall French chap, also on our Uyuni tour, had not been so fortunate. Not realising that his passport was stamped for 30 days, Nick was surprised to learn he would have to pay $300 before he could leave Bolivia. He had been in the country for over three months and the Immigration official was charging him for his unofficial extended stay.

Nick had not intended to stay so long in Bolivia but when his boat trip, which should have taken three days, ended up being almost three weeks long he had little choice but to stay. He had found a boat and captain who was prepared to take him for a small price down a tributary of the Amazon to a town called Trinidad. The boat consisted of two barges tied together, which was transporting rice, vegetables and fruit. Because the weather had been so dry, the river was very low, and Nick spent many hours in the water trying to push the boat back afloat. After the first day they had only travelled one kilometre. On day two the boat hit a rock and one of the barges sank. The boat was carrying $3000 worth of food so it had to be salvaged, dried out on the bank, reloaded onto a new boat and then transported slowly and very cautiously down river. They were not allowed to eat the cargo, instead hunting in the jungle and drinking the river water. 17 days later, he arrived in Trinidad.

The Immigration Official must have taken pity on Nick, eventually settling for a payment of about $5. The paper work was probably going to be too much effort for him.


The riots in Northern Bolivia had been escalating over the previous few weeks. Road blockades were still in place on the routes out of La Paz, and Christie, the other passenger on our jeep, had been caught in a few riots. Locals had started stoning her bus, which eventually forced its way through with the help of a police escort. Unfortunately the situation had got to a stage where all border crossings with Peru and Chile had been closed. Our tour agency assured us we would not have any problems getting over the border. The crossing would be unmanned and was the only route open in the whole country.

Along with Bernado (the driver), his wife (the cook), Ali, Josh, Nick and Christie we piled in the jeep, with all our bags secured on top. Before we had even got comfortable, we reached our first stop: the train cemetery. Luckily, this time it was the other end, at the furthest point from the town, the part where we had not been to the day before. We couldn't believe our eyes, there were loads of clapped out steam trains, just sat in this dry wasteland, slowly being eroded away. There was plenty of graffiti, with the now familiar, 'Bush and Blair are terrorists' comments.

Following on from the train graveyard, our driver headed across a flat plain to a small village, Colchani, on the edge of the salt lake, where salt is processed. Iodine is added to the salt, (collected from the nearby salt flats), in

276

an attempt to reduce the levels of goitre and cretinism, which was once extremely rife in the area. It was our last chance to buy any presents before we left Bolivia, but we couldn't think of anyone who would appreciate the tacky carvings, ashtrays and paperweights made from blocks of salt.

From here we drove onto the Salar de Uyuni. Spread out before us, as far as we could see was a huge, flat expanse of white. Covering an area of $12,121km^2$, about half the size of Wales, the lake used to be part of a much larger lake, called Lago Tauca that encompassed most of southwest Bolivia. The salt was washed down from the mountains, slowly collecting in the lake. The concentrations of salt increased as the lake started to dry up until it started to form a crust on the top, just like a thick layer of ice.

The upper salt layer on the lake is about 6m thick, the top 10 to 25cms of which dries and hardens in winter to form an almost impenetrable crust. The surface of the lake was totally solid. Below about 6m the lake consists of either very cold water, or further layers of sediment and salt. Some areas of the lake are as much as 120m deep.

Situated in a semi-arid climate, the Salar has an average annual rainfall of about 25 cm per year. During the rainy season, from December to March, the Salar is covered with water, making it particularly freaky to drive through, as it makes the surface look like a mirror. During the dry season, as when we visited, the salt water evaporates and produces a flat surface covered with hexagonal cracks, cemented with salt crystals.

Small mounds of salt, about a metre high dotted the horizon. Our guide explained that it takes a day for a local *campesino* to scrape up a mound of salt crystals, which is then transported to Colchani for processing. There is a never-ending supply of salt, with an estimated 10 billion tons of it. New crystals are constantly been formed, especially around the edges of 'salt eyes'. Filled with bubbling waters, these holes are formed when warmer water rises to the surface of the lake. Our guide drove tantalisingly close to the edge of them, but we were keen to get away from them as quickly as possible.

The lake also contains the largest deposit of lithium in the world, a mineral commonly used in the computer chip industry. Extracting it has not really taken off, which is fortunate as it would create a horrendous ecological disaster. However, it would also probably solve all of Bolivians economic problems as lithium is very valuable.

The Salar is an astounding and utterly surreal place, where you feel like you are surrounded by snow. A pair of ice skates would not have gone amiss. We had to keep touching the surface to remind ourselves that it wasn't slippery. Like virtually every tourist who had been there, we couldn't resist running around with our eyes shut. With nothing to trip us up, we could have run and run. Being at an elevation of 3,650m was the only thing that stopped us going too far. Taking the obligatory perspective photos kept us amused for a while, but we drew the line at streaking.

Our guide drove in a straight line for about an hour across the lake, heading towards one of the many mirages that appeared on the horizon. It was a strange sensation, all white around us and with nothing to gauge how fast we were travelling or where we were going.

A small building appeared out of nowhere, and we pulled up to the Hotel Playa Blanca, a building made entirely of blocks of salt. It was not the cosiest looking hotels, or the cheapest. The rooms had beds and furniture made of salt blocks and the carpets were soft salt crystals. You are provided with proper blankets, but it was all a bit of a gimmick aimed at rich Americans.

We arrived at Isla Pescado, or 'Fish Island', just in time for lunch. The only thing missing was the vinegar and chips. This is probably the largest, and the most visited island within the lake. Nick told us he had hired a bike and cycled out here a few days before. The bike rental company told him that Fish Island was about 50km from Uyuni, it was actually 105km. Luckily Nick was fit, but still hadn't arrived until 8pm, in the pitch black, with temperatures plummeting well below zero. This area has some of the world's biggest variations in temperature range. Daytime temperatures can rise to 30°C and at night can drop as low as -30°C. Believing what the bike rental company was

278

saying, another couple had not arrived until 11pm and had been in a terrible state from the effects of sun and falling temperatures. There were plenty of stories about jeeps breaking down and entire families freezing to death while trying to find help, so it looked like the cyclists had been lucky.

Fish Island is famous for its giant cacti, which is the only thing that really grows in this inhospitable place. The cacti grow at 1cm per year, the largest being 12m high, making it 1200 years old. All the buildings, furniture, rubbish bins, signposts and seats are made out of the holey cacti, the only source of wood in the area. The cacti would probably disappear completely if they were not a protected species.

After a few more hours of what felt like treadmill driving, we drove off the lake, back onto the lumpy dirt tracks which we were so familiar with now. Heading through the mountains we eventually arrived at our hostel in the middle of nowhere. After hearing horror stories about the accommodation we had prepared ourselves for the worse. We were, however, all pleasantly surprised and it was better than many hostels we had stayed in. The dormitory was warm with good comfy beds and an adjoining toilet and hot shower.

In the morning Caius, Ali and Christie were desperate to use the toilet first. At some stage during our travels all three of them had been suffering from the 'shits'. Even though they had all thought they had got rid of the problem, unfortunately it had taken this moment to 'rear its ugly head', shall we say. *Diocalm* and iodine tablets were taken as quickly as possible in an attempt to block themselves up.

Every 10 or 15 minutes our driver had to stop while they ran off in different directions, clutching a bog roll, to try and find some sort of cover in the flat desolate landscape. "Baños Naturale", the driver would laugh. His metabolism was obviously a bit slower, and by mid afternoon, he was doing the same.

We drove past Volcán Ollagüe, Bolivia's only active volcano. Its peak is 5865m asl, making it 32 metres shorter than Cotopaxi in Ecuador, and unknown to most people. The summit technically belongs to Bolivia, although the magma chamber, which feeds the volcano, resides under Chilean soil. Thin plumes of Chilean smoke rose from the Bolivian peak.

At the base of Volcán Ollagüe, weird rock formations had been created in the lava field. Black volcanic rocks from past eruptions were strewn all over the place, with fine grey dust piling up around them, forming small dunes. Ancient lava flows were slowly becoming camouflaged by the Altiplano. Suspended in mid-air, erosion has shaped the red lava into wave like formations. A few surfers would not have gone amiss.

We crossed a couple of smaller salt lakes, and a railway track. If it weren't for the fact that the trains only ran at night his would surely be one of the most impressive train journeys in the world.

A remote checkpoint and military fort was comical rather than intimidating. There are some 'roads' that cross the Salar, but it would have been possible to avoid the checkpoint if anyone wanted to. After a passport check we were allowed to continue on our way.

Laguna Hediona, is home of hundreds of flamingos, obviously immune to the sulphurous stench. Their long elegant necks swayed back and forward as they filtered the lake waters for algae. In the Andes there are three species of flamingo (Andean, James and Chilean), we had no idea what these were. A group of Israelis from another tour were determined to spoil it for everyone else and kept chasing the birds until they flew away.

Even though the birds were only about ten metres away from us, Josh insisted he needed to get closer for a better photograph. When he came to jump back onto the edge of the lake, the solid ground that he thought he had been standing on, sucked one of his shoes off. We all fell about laughing, much to his annoyance, as he had to wade back through the soft smelly mud to retrieve the lost shoe. His shoes and socks were carefully wrapped up in bags, but the jeep hummed of flamingo shit for the remainder of the journey.

One of the other highlights of the tour is the Reserva de Fauna Andina Eduardo Avaroa, the Bolivian National Park. Covering over 7000km$^2$ of wildlife reserve and Altiplano lakes, it is home to some unique wildlife and over 80 bird species.

The landscape was particularly desolate; the only vegetation consisted of a few clumps of windswept grass. Sat in the middle of this desert is Arbol de Piedra (Stone Tree), an eight metre high *zeuge*. This is a tabular mass of rock perched on a pinnacle of softer rock which has been abraded and shaped by wind-blown sediment over thousands of years. The same group of Israelis who had scared away the flamingoes hogged the rock. Intent on trying to climb it they just got in the way, much to the annoyance of everyone else who wanted to take a decent photo.

Hidden in amongst the nearby rocky outcrops, we could see a peculiar animal that looks like a rabbit with a big bushy squirrel-like tail - a *viscacha*. Again the Israelis appeared from nowhere and the photo opportunities rapidly disappeared as they insisted on getting as close to them as possible. Not surprisingly, the *viscacha* didn't hang around for long.

Our next camp was on the shores of the Laguna Colorada, a 60km$^2$, 80 metre deep lake. The striking red waters are fringed by white borax and salt and, as we pointed out to Josh, quicksand. The red colouration is due to natural pigments of the algae that live in its shallow, mineral-laden water. Like the other lakes, it was inhabited by hundreds of flamingos and other wading birds.

Countless other travellers told us that we would not get any sleep here – it would be freezing cold and being at an altitude of nearly 5000m asl would keep us awake all night. A bottle of singani and a few red wines seemed to do the trick. Having spent at least a couple of months at relatively high levels, all of the group were totally accustomed to the altitude and had no problems breathing. We decided that it was people travelling north along the Chilean coast who would have suffered most, as they would not have had any real opportunity to acclimatise properly.

The sky was a clear black canvas with millions of stars when we departed the following morning. Although we did not recognise many, we spotted the Southern Cross and the Milky Way was particularly bright. Much as we wanted to stand and gaze at this huge expanse of universe, it was 5am and bloody freezing, so we quickly piled into the truck.

Frost had formed on the inside of the windows and we huddled together until the jeep warmed up, which seemed to take forever. We arrived at the highest geysers in the world, Sol de Mañana, (5200m asl) just as the sun rose above the mountains. The air temperature was about -15°C, and our faces, feet and hands were numb from the cold. The first geyser was hot enough to put your hands into, but others reached temperatures of about 5000°C. As usual there were stupid idiots, trying to get as close as possible to get a good photo. There were stinking fumaroles belching out cement grey and sludge brown mud, and boiling pools of mud and sulphur. The geysers are most powerful first thing in the morning and diminish in force as the air temperature rises through the day. We forgave our guides for getting us up so early.

At Laguna Salada we were given the opportunity to wallow in a rather murky looking thermal pool. It was not warm enough to justify stripping, and we sat warming our toes in the warm waters instead.

Whilst sitting by the hot pool we got chatting to a group of students who were working on a project in association with Edinburgh University. Their assignment was measuring the effects of altitude at 6000m. Most research so far has been carried out by the likes of Dr Mark Stroud, who is mega fit and used to exercising in extreme conditions. This was the first real study undertaken with 'normal people'. One student who had flown directly to La Paz had been whisked off to hospital on arrival because his oxygen levels were critically low.

The students were also the dumbest bunch of people we had met so far. They were due to fly out of La Paz the next day, but they still had a full days drive back to Uyuni. They were hoping to catch the overnight bus from Uyuni to La Paz in time to catch their flight the following evening. There was no chance of them getting there, especially as all the roads into La Paz had been blockaded. Just to make their chances of catching their flight even slimmer, one of the jeeps they were travelling in had lost a wheel across the desert. Luckily they were part of a three-jeep convoy, so had all piled into the remaining two vehicles. Not so lucky was the fact that one of these two jeeps was such a wreck that they could not even get it re-started. They had got a 'good deal' with the tour agency and we were glad we had paid a little extra. Like the Inca trail, it did not cost much more to get a hugely better service. Eighteen of them were going to have to pile into one jeep if they were going to try to get to La Paz on time. After our 'mas rapido' journey from Tupiza to Uyuni, we knew 16 was feasible, but 18 was pushing it.

Near to where all the tour jeeps were parked was the 'toilet block'. Facing directly towards where everyone was having breakfast, the loos were drop toilets with no doors. No one really wanted to go in full view of everyone so sneaked behind the back for a bit of dignity. Every tour before us must have done the same and the piles outside the back were almost as big as the surrounding mountains, the toilet paper sticking on the top acting as the snow.

Our last main stop on the tour was Laguna Verde, yet another isolated marvel. It is called the 'green lake' because a cocktail of minerals in the water turns it an incandescent emerald-green as the day progresses and the water heats up in the sun. The lake reflects the image of Volcán Licancabur (5868m), a perfectly coned mountain, in its waters. Chile, our next and final country, was just on the other side of the mountain.

Vicky Brewis & Caius Simmons

# The Border Crossing to Chile

On the shores of Laguna Blanca was a collapsing sign saying, "Esta es mi Tierra... Bolivia. Bienvenidos!". Unfortunately for us we were heading the other way and this was our last, rather than our first, view of Bolivia. After nearly five weeks travelling around Bolivia we had only managed to cover a third of the beautiful country and wished we had the time to see more. Apart from being robbed, the long uncomfortable night bus journeys and the salty beer we couldn't really think of anything bad to say about this country.

Bolivian immigration consisted of a small hut and a barrier. We were relieved to see there were no road blockades either, like those that were closing the borders in the North. There were no other fences marking the boundary between Bolivia and Chile, and if anyone really wanted to get past the barrier all they need to do was drive around the hut. The Bolivian official didn't even notice the tippexed mess his Uyuni colleague had made on our passports, stamping them without question. We had left Bolivia.

Soon we reached a tarmac road. As the lumpy road gave way to a quiet, smooth surface, a small cheer could be heard from the back of the bus. This was the first bit of paved road we had travelled on for any distance since our journey from Sucre to Potosí, almost three weeks previously. These first impressions made us think that Chile was a bit more civilised compared to Bolivia, Peru or Ecuador and we hadn't even officially arrived. This was 'No-Mans-Land' with 40km to go before we arrived at the Chilean border control.

From the Bolivian border we drove down (and down) towards the village of San Pedro de Atacama, dropping almost 2500m in altitude.

284

All our other border crossings had just involved getting an exit stamp from the country we were leaving and then another visa stamp from the country we were going to.  Not in Chile.  On arrival in San Pedro we had to go through immigration and customs.  All we could think about were accidental bags of coca leaves and alpaca toenail rattles.

The Chilean government were obviously concerned about travellers smuggling coca leaves into Chile in case they intended processing it into cocaine.  How much cocaine they thought we could make out of a handful of leaves we were unsure of.  Seeing as it was illegal to bring the coca into the country we had used the last of our leaves at breakfast time in a cup of Mate de Coca.  The leaves had been in our rucksack since Potosí and it would have been quite easy to forget that we even had any.  A chap we had met in Arequipa had told us the story of how, when he arrived in San Pedro it wasn't until the customs officer stuck his hand into the side pocket of his rucksack did he remember that he had a few coca leaves in there.  Luckily for him the leaves must have got mixed up with his dirty socks and the official didn't find them.  The first litter bin he found he disposed of the leaves and didn't buy any more.

The first thing we had to do when we stepped into the customs building was to disinfect our boots.  The customs officials were on the lookout for more shoes and boots to clean because they were concerned about Foot and Mouth being brought into Chile.  There were about 20 travellers preparing themselves to have the contents of their rucksacks tipped onto the floor so that their spare sandals, boots and trainers could be washed.  Josh's flamingo shit covered trainers were attracting quite a lot of attention, but the officials didn't seem bothered about disinfecting any others.  Judging by the number of shoes they had missed we reckoned the foot and mouth story was just a ploy to check the bags for drugs.

Our main concern was the Alpaca toenail rattle we had bought in Tarabuco.  It was fairly obvious we shouldn't be taking them through customs, but should we declare them, or keep quiet.  Before we could make a decision whether or not to tell them, the customs man had his hand down the inside of

Vicky's rucksack. We could hear the toenails rattling around in the bag, which was right at the top of the rucksack. They had a good feel of the contents and then waved us pass.

Locked within the dry sands of the Atacama Desert is a small green oasis where the village of San Pedro de Atacama is sited. Nestled in a small cluster of trees, the compact settlement sits on the edge of a small river on the northern fringes of the huge saline lake, Salar de Atacama. Looming two kilometres above the town is the Andean Cordillera, the majestic and mystic volcano Licancabur making a spectacular backdrop. Last time we had seen this mountain was from the other side, on the shores of Lake Verde in Bolivia.

The difference between the two countries, Bolivia and Chile, was far more apparent then we had experienced between Ecuador and Peru, and Peru and Bolivia. It was not just the obvious things, like the paved roads, but things like the quality of the food and wine. Our usual menu options of soup, omelette, chicken and rice, and beer were replaced with salads, sandwiches, fish, pasta, Crème Brulee and a choice of wines. Perhaps it was because we were in a very popular tourist area that the food was so great and we took delight in eating some decent food. The food hadn't been that bad in Bolivia, but the food in Chile was just what we needed after eating scrambled eggs, unleavened bread, soup, dodgy pizzas and rice for three months.

Overall, Chile appeared so much more affluent than Bolivia. The people walking down the streets were smart and clean and many appeared to own cars. Away from the harsh environment of the Altiplano, people looked healthy rather than weathered and battered. The inhabitants of Chile are very much Mediterranean in their appearance and there was very little sign of an indigenous population in San Pedro. There were also people who were over 5ft 6in and even though we didn't 'blend in', we were certainly didn't stand out quite as much as usual.

# Gringos in the Driest Desert in the World

Any kind of precipitation is virtually non-existent in the Atacama Desert, and even the surrounding mountains are devoid of any snow. San Pedro only manages to grow trees and few crops because it is located right next to the river and the water table is close to the surface. A couple of kilometres out of the centre of the town, and away from the shade from trees, the conditions are harsh, with searing hot days and freezing temperatures at night.

The couple of days we had planned to spend relaxing in the warm sunshine didn't last very long because there was too much to see and do. There were plenty of tours and activities to do nearby: sand boarding, flamingo watching, geyser spotting or mountain biking. Along with our fellow Uyuni companions, Josh, Ali and Nick we decided to hire some bikes and head out to the Valle de la Luna (Valley of the Moon) to see some eroded rocks. To avoid the intense heat of the midday sun we waited until mid-afternoon before we set off on our adventure.

Considering the bikes were hired, they were pretty smart, with front fork suspension, decent brakes, good gears and even the tyres were pumped up. The first part of the journey along the paved road was easy going and we all whizzed along at a fair speed. As soon as we turned off the main road it was a different story.

The nice tarmac soon disappeared, to be replaced by a bumpy dirt road. Travelling at high speed in a jeep you probably wouldn't have noticed the bumps, but sitting on a hard narrow saddle on two skinny wheels, even with front fork suspension, every single stone and dip quickly became annoying and painful. The look on Ali's face told us she was not particularly enjoying herself, and didn't seem to share our view that it was good fun and a bit of an adventure. To add to the 'enjoyment', we could see a big hill ahead of us. Just as we had gathered some speed up on the bikes we kept hitting patches of sand. The sand, blown across the road, made cycling almost impossible and if the bike didn't just stop dead as the wheels got stuck in the sand, then the wheels would skid all over the place making it particularly difficult to pedal. Three months at high altitude was paying off and even though we were at about 2500m asl we all managed it to the top of the hills without getting out of breath too much. It was just hot, very hot. The temperature was well over 30°C and without anything to shade under there was no escaping the heat.

On the plus side was the scenery with views across to the Chilean-Bolivian Andes and by the side of the road there were some classic textbook dune formations. Shaped by the wind, the sand had been sculpted against the eroded cliffs into huge banks and crescents. The temptation to jump down them was almost irresistible. Almost irresistible if it wasn't for the fact we would have to walk back up again.

We were heading further and further into the desert and there was still no sign of the eroded rocks we had been promised. Eventually we came to the top of a hill – should we cycle down in the knowledge that we would just have to come back up again, or should we turn around and head back along the same road, or should we continue and cycle a complete circuit back to San Pedro. Our badly sketched map implied that if we cycled on we would join onto another road that would take us back to the town. After convincing Ali, (who by now had resigned herself to the fact that it couldn't get any worse), that we were more than half way around we decided the best and quickest option would be to carry on. At least we would get to see the Vallee de Luna, which still hadn't materialised.

Two other cyclists coming the other way informed us that the rock formations were still quite a way to go at the bottom of the hill, but they didn't

288

know anything about another road back to San Pedro. As we set off again Caius noticed that his pedal was feeling a bit wobbly. He managed to cycle a couple of hundred metres before it fell off, much to the amusement of Josh, who hadn't really forgiven him for laughing at him when he lost his shoe in the flamingo shit. After a couple of attempts to secure it back on we decided that a penknife just wasn't up the job and without the proper tools we were never going to be able to fix it. We stopped a couple of jeeps, but the drivers were either really miserable or just didn't have the right size spanner. To make matters worse they all told us different stories about the road to San Pedro, all of which were totally unhelpful – "What road", "You're better off going back the way you came", or "You are best off heading straight on". At least if we went straight on it was down hill and Caius could coast.

Finally we arrived at the Valley of the Moon which, after the eroded 'Stone Tree' we had seen during the Uyuni tour, was a bit of a let down. They only warranted one photograph just to prove we had been there. It was starting to get late and the sun was getting low in the sky, so we didn't hang around for long.

The downhill didn't last for much longer and Nick had to act as Caius' tow, supporting him as he pushed his way along the road on one leg. At a steady pace we pedalled and pushed our way towards a road junction that we could see ahead of us. Once we got to this point we would be on the main road and from then on it would be straightforward. Just as we thought we were making some progress, Josh's chain snapped. Our laughter was at the ridiculousness of it all, rather than at Josh. We think the heat may have got to Ali, because even she was laughing, but only just.

A passing jeep stopped to try and help, but with two knackered bikes there was little they could do. He hadn't driven very far, when they turned around and came back towards us. It was to warn us that we were cycling through the middle of an old mine field and we shouldn't try any short cuts to the main road. The Chilean Army once used the area for training and had left many unexploded and forgotten mines lying about. It was probably some excuse to deter the Bolivians from claiming back their 'lost lands'. We asked if we could borrow his mobile phone so we could call the bike hire people to come and collect us. There was no signal. To top it all we had just finished our water. The only thing we had on our side was the fact the sun hadn't set – yet.

With Nick towing Josh and Caius pushing himself along on one leg we finally made it to the main road. There was no way we were all going to make it back to San Pedro before it got dark. Luckily, Nick spoke pretty good Spanish so we had flagged down a car and asked the driver if they could phone the bike hire place as soon as they could get a signal. The driver promised to drive to San Pedro and would raise an alarm with the bike hire people, but we couldn't guarantee the message would get through, or trust the bike hire people to come and rescue us so decided it would be best for Vicky and Nick to cycle back to San Pedro. We had seen the road when we had been for a walk the previous evening and reckoned they only had to get to the top of the next hill and it would be down hill from then on.

With Caius, Josh and Ali walking, and Vicky and Nick cycling we made our way back to San Pedro. Walking wasn't too bad, but after about half an hour we could still see Vicky and Nick pedalling madly up the hill. It quickly dawned on us that the road was actually longer than we had first realised. As the sun went behind the mountains we watched the light rapidly disappear. Racing across the land, the last bit of sun was being chased by a line of darkness. Within a matter of seconds, night had overtaken day and won the race, leaving us to walk along in the dusky light.

The cyclists were probably having the least fun. Their relief of making it to the top of the hill was shattered when they were faced with another hill ahead of them, longer and steeper than the first. They battled on; convinced they would be able to see San Pedro once they reached the top. Luckily for them, we had managed to hail a Jeep, being driven by two French tourists who were returning from a romantic day out. We loaded the bikes onto the back and squeezed in. Nick and Vicky were half way up the second hill when we stopped to pick them up. They were completely exhausted and were more than grateful that they had been rescued from their torture, their bikes were piled on the top. The road back to San Pedro was a lot longer than we thought and there were at least four more hills up before it descended into the town. It would have taken ages to cycle back, at least another hour or more.

Back at the bike hire agency we plonked the broken pedal and chain onto the counter. They were extremely embarrassed, gave us a full refund and let us help ourselves to bottles of water. They had got our SOS message, but had gone along the wrong road to collect us.

Safely back in San Pedro, with a beer in hand, even Ali had to admit it had been an adventure, but there was no way she was getting on a bike again.

Vicky Brewis & Caius Simmons

# **Santiago**

Leaving San Pedro de Atacama was just another reminder that we were heading home.  Our 'travel companions' were all going separate ways, Nick to Northern Chile, and Josh and Ali were heading into Argentina.  It was sad to see them go, especially Josh and Ali, who, over the previous three weeks we had seen quite a lot of.  Even though we visited different places, ever since Cochabamba we had been crossing each other's paths and now it was time to continue our journeys alone.  Within 24 hours we were going to be in Santiago, the last stop on our trip.

The Nobel Prize-winning Chilean poet Pablo Neruda called his birthplace "the thin country".  Every school kid in the world who has ever looked at a map of South America could have told him he was stating the obvious.  Hemmed in by the Pacific Ocean and the Andes, Chile is only 180km across at its widest point.  To get to Santiago we needed to travel almost 1000 miles, and we would only cover about one third of the length of the country.

The first part of the journey to Calama was a bit of a blur, which probably had something to do with too many Pisco Sours the night before.  It was unlike any bus journey we had been on so far – it left exactly on time, it was comfortable, it didn't jolt around, there were no vendors and we arrived on time.

Apart from the largest open cast copper mine in the world, Calama doesn't have a lot going for it.  Apparently this one mine, called Chuquicamata, exports so much copper, it accounts for about 17% of Chiles annual export income.  We could see why Bolivia was a bit pissed off when Chile took control of the region.  All Bolivia ended up with was a vast expanse of uninhabitable,

292

uncultivable, cold, windswept mountain plains and a load of salt flats. No wonder they are desperate to get it back again. Calama is also one of the driest places in the world, proudly boasting that it has never seen a drop of rain in living memory. It is estimated the last time it rained here was about 3000 years ago, long before any settlements existed.

The bus terminal was right in the middle of an Industrial Estate and from what we had read about Calama, it wasn't worth the effort to go into town. While we waited for our connecting bus, we laughed at what Charlie had written about Calama, "Hotel Splendid – don't bother – the worst place we have ever stayed in".

If we had thought the bus from San Pedro had been comfortable, then the bus for Santiago was pure luxury. Ever since Peru, when people had told us about *"bus camas"* we had been desperate to travel on one. We had been subjected to some particularly small and uncomfortable buses and had come to the conclusion that they didn't exist.

We hadn't managed to book the seats on the bottom deck, which reclined fully to make single beds, settling for the seats on the top deck instead. They had been described as *semi-cama*, and after being told this story on numerous other occasions throughout our trip we were fully expecting to be cramped up with a knee stuck in our backs. Across the width of the bus there were only three seats, with nine seats along the entire length. When fully reclined the seats were a good distance from the person sitting behind and there was no chance that we were going to end up with spinal damage. The seats were comfortable and just to make sure we were nice and cosy we were given pillows and blankets. Individual headphones for the TV and radio were fitted to the seats and at meal times we were supplied with food and drink. The bus 'hostess' seemed to spend the entire time opening and closing curtains to make sure the sun didn't shine in our eyes. It was better then being on a plane. Just as well really, because the journey to Santiago from Calama took about 17 hours.

It wasn't the passing countryside we remember most about this journey, but the joy of finally catching a *bus cama*. There wasn't a lot to see out of the window and the landscape was even more desolate than the rich landscape features we had become accustomed to. There was no greenery for miles, not even a cactus, just expanses of grey sand and the occasional rocky outcrop. The only highlight was in Antofagasta, where we saw the sea for the first time in about two months. Huge rollers crashed against the coast, and after breathing dust and llama shit for so long, the smell of the damp salty air was lovely and refreshing.

To pass the time of day we compiled a top 10 list of things we were really looking forward to when we got home.


1. Home cooking.
It was fun eating out every night, but we had not cooked a proper meal for months and there were certain things that the South Americans didn't cook or get quite right like tuna lasagnes, bread, sausage casserole, apple pie and custard.

2. Drinking water straight from the tap.
Something we take so much for granted. We will still moan about the high water rates and the fact it smells of chlorine and is full of other chemicals, but at least we can go to the tap and quench our thirst whenever we want.

3. Not having to put used bog roll in the bin.
This had become second nature to us and it was going to take us weeks to forget the habit. We became totally paranoid we would forget.

4. Going to the cinema
Sitting in comfy seats, looking up at the big screen, with surround sound and a mountain of popcorn.

5. English fried breakfast
None of this dried bread, rubbery scrambled eggs and rank coffee. What we wanted was eggs, beans, toast, tomatoes, mushrooms, sausages, bacon, ketchup and fresh coffee - Yum

6. Long beds with duvets

The thought of not having our feet hanging over the edge, or not being crushed by the weight of blankets on top, put a smile on our faces.

7. A bath

Where we could soak in a bubble bath for hours, engrossed in a good book

8. Listening to the radio

Just before leaving we forked out and bought a brand new short wave radio, so we could maybe pick up the BBC World Service en route. This had been totally pointless, trying in vain to pick up a frequency. These occasional sound bites we had managed to find would be cut off on the hour because they changed the frequencies. We managed to listen to two programmes, one of which was a repeat of something we heard before.

9. Driving where and when we wanted

To be able to get in the car and drive off to see a friend or go for a walk, without having to think about booking a bus or go on a tour.

10. Glass of cold milk (Vicky), a pint of Guinness (Caius)

Just the simple things we take for granted back at home

We then got depressed when we turned it around to ten things we weren't looking forward to when we got home, like finding a house, getting a job, motorways, paying a fortune for everything. This list didn't get completed, and we sat in silence watching the view. We were quite sad about the thought of reaching the end of our trip, and it was unlikely we were going to have any more mini adventures, but at the same time we were tired of travelling for now and looking forward to getting home to share all our adventures with friends and family.

We fell asleep to the sounds of the Scorpion King (again) and woke up fully refreshed after a great nights sleep, with our destination only a couple of hours away. The scenery from our window had transformed. We were looking at rolling green fields filled with grazing sheep and cattle, trees covered in blossom blowing in the wind (it was Spring) and rows and rows of budding vineyards.

The Chilean capital is a big city with nearly six million inhabitants (about a third of Chiles population). Santiago has a provincial, cosmopolitan feel to it and it was easy to blend in. Apart from all the traffic and the stress of crossing the road we found it quite relaxing. The centre is very compact, covering most of it on foot. Looming over the smog on the horizon are dramatic jagged Andean peaks, which surround the city.

These mountains are home to Chiles (and South Americas) main ski resort, but unfortunately for us it was the end of the season and even though there was still snow draped over the higher peaks the resorts were closed.

Caius was lying on the bed while Vicky took a shower, when the bed started to shake, slowly at first, and then quite rapidly. He looked around the bed to see if he had turned on the 'vibrate' button by accident, but seeing as the bed was at least 50 years old this was not really possible. It became apparent that Caius had just experienced his first earthquake. Santiago's proximity to the Andes means this region is also susceptible to earth tremors. As the mountains are still being forced upwards, the stresses and strains of the land being pushed around results in (sometimes large) earthquakes. Vicky had said the shower had stopped momentarily, but apart from that she was totally oblivious to what had just happened. After checking it out on the Internet we found out it had definitely been an earthquake and not just someone digging the street up outside the hostel. The centre of the earthquake was located a few kilometres outside of Sanitago and registered 5.6 on the Richter scale. Not the biggest, but enough to make the earth move for me.

We had grand plans for visiting the area around Santiago, but when it came down to it we really couldn't be bothered, or have the energy. For a start we didn't have a guidebook so didn't have any idea of where to go or what to see. Our good intentions for visiting the town of Valapariso on the coast were shelved in favour of spending three days 'westernising' ourselves.

296

Getting used to paying more than a couple of quid for accommodation and food was a good start to make us feel like we were at home. It wasn't as if it was that costly in Chile, it was just that in comparison to Ecuador, Peru and Bolivia, things seemed quite a bit more expensive. It took us ages to get used to the Chilean currency and we were a bit shocked to find out our accommodation was going to cost us $16,000 for the night (luckily the dollar sign is the symbol they use for the peso).

The rest of our time was spent visiting museums, art galleries, and gardens and buying presents to take home (nothing like leaving it to the last minute). Santiago was hosting the outdoor photographic exhibition by Yann Arthus-Bertrand. This was the third time we had seen the photos, having viewed the show in both London and Oslo, within the last year. Looking at the photos we felt we could have quite easily been back in England, strolling around outside the Natural History Museum. We made the most of being in a city and all the facilities it has to offer, namely a cinema. Okay, the films were crap, but at least it wasn't the Scorpion King, and they were in English.

Away from the tourist hotspot of San Pedro it dawned on us that Chileans speak a completely different Spanish to the one we had learned. By the time we left Bolivia, we felt quite pleased with our ability to 'converse' in Spanish. It was still limited to accommodation, food and transport, and was pretty basic but we could easily get by, even on the telephone. We met quite a few people, who had done a couple of weeks language course in Quito at the beginning of their trip and we thought their Spanish was amazing. It turned out ours was just as good; it was just that we all had different set phrases, that after three months we had become expert at saying. Arriving in Santiago felt like we were complete beginners again. The accent was totally different and we understood how foreign travellers must feel when they leave London and then go to Glasgow or Liverpool. We didn't have a clue what anyone was saying to us and making ourselves understood was just as difficult. Even asking for the menu became a chore, resorting back to the universally acceptable method of conversing – pointing.

As if we hadn't seen enough fiestas to last us a couple of years, on our last day the city centre was closed off for a parade. Compared to the festivals we had seen in Peru and Bolivia it wasn't as nearly as colourful or exuberant. Most of it seemed to consist of youth bands or military groups, and the dancing troupes were pretty tame. Looking at the passing youths we remembered the posters hung up in the school near Tupiza saying, "We will have our coastline back one day, whatever the consequences". Against these cadets, who were all togged up in uniform with guns slung over their shoulders, the Bolivian military forces paled into insignificance. It is very unlikely that Bolivia will see their coastline in the near future.

Before we knew it, three days passed by and we were sitting on a bus heading towards the airport. Our last remaining challenge was getting ourselves, and an Alpaca toenail rattle, through American customs.

# Bibliography

Darwin, C. R. 1839. *Narrative of the surveying voyages of His Majesty's Ships Adventure and Beagle between the years 1826 and 1836, describing their examination of the southern shores of South America, and the Beagle's circumnavigation of the globe. Journal and remarks. 1832-1836.* London: Henry Colburn.

Guevara, E. 2003. *The Motorcycle Diaries: A Latin American Journey.* Consortium Book Sales & Dist.

Jenkins, D. 2000. *The Rough Guide to Peru.* Rough Guides Ltd.

Kunstaetter R. & D. 2003. *Ecuador & Galapagos Handbook.* Footprint Handbooks.

Menzie, G. 2003. *1421: The Year China Discovered the World.* Bantam Dell Pub Group.

Read, J. 2002. *The Rough Guide to Bolivia.* Rough Guides Ltd.

Printed in the United Kingdom by
Lightning Source UK Ltd., Milton Keynes
139305UK00001B/164/P